Contributions to Finance and Accounting

The book series 'Contributions to Finance and Accounting' features the latest research from research areas like financial management, investment, capital markets, financial institutions, FinTech and financial innovation, accounting methods and standards, reporting, and corporate governance, among others. Books published in this series are primarily monographs and edited volumes that present new research results, both theoretical and empirical, on a clearly defined topic. All books are published in print and digital formats and disseminated globally. This book series is indexed in Scopus.

Peng Zhou • Dong Guo

Climate Finance in the Net-Zero Transition

From Conception to Implementation

Springer

Peng Zhou
Cardiff Business School
Cardiff University
Cardiff, UK

Dong Guo
Treasury & Financial Markets
China Development Bank
Beijing, China

ISSN 2730-6038 ISSN 2730-6046 (electronic)
Contributions to Finance and Accounting
ISBN 978-981-92-0826-5 ISBN 978-981-92-0827-2 (eBook)
https://doi.org/10.1007/978-981-92-0827-2

This Springer imprint is published by the registered company Springer Nature Singapore Pte Ltd.
The registered company address is: 152 Beach Road, #21-01/04 Gateway East, Singapore 189721, Singapore

Preface

"The best time to plant a tree was twenty years ago. The second-best time is now."
—Chinese proverb

Across civilizations and centuries, humanity has been reminded of a simple truth: prosperity and responsibility must go hand in hand. Ancient wisdom from East and West alike teaches that long-term well-being depends on how we steward the resources entrusted to us. Yet the modern world has entered an era in which this balance is increasingly fragile. Climate change has transformed from a distant scientific concern into one of the defining challenges of our time. The question is no longer whether the global economy must transform, but how—and how quickly.

At the center of this transformation lies finance.

Climate change is fundamentally an economic problem as much as it is an environmental one. The transition toward a low-carbon and climate-resilient economy requires a massive reallocation of capital: away from high-carbon activities that intensify environmental risks and toward investments that support clean energy, resilient infrastructure, and sustainable production systems. Estimates from international organizations suggest that trillions of dollars of new investment will be required each year to achieve global climate targets. Without finance, the technologies, policies, and innovations needed for the transition cannot scale. In this sense, climate finance is not simply a niche area of financial markets—it is the bloodstream of the global transition toward a net-zero future.

This book was written to understand how that financial transformation actually works.

In recent years, climate finance has moved from an abstract aspiration to a rapidly evolving ecosystem of financial instruments, regulatory frameworks, and market institutions. Corporate green bonds finance renewable energy projects; sovereign green bonds embed climate priorities into national fiscal systems; blue finance addresses the sustainability of oceans and water systems; and carbon markets attempt to place a price on emissions and reshape economic incentives. These developments demonstrate both the creativity and the complexity of modern financial systems as they confront the climate challenge.

Nevertheless, the literature and policy debate often remain fragmented. Some discussions focus on high-level concepts, while others emphasize technical market details. Some analyses examine developed financial markets, while others consider the unique challenges faced by developing economies. Still others speak primarily to investors or policymakers, rarely bridging the two perspectives. This fragmentation makes it difficult to see the full picture of how climate finance evolves from idea to implementation.

This book seeks to bridge these divides with three intended features.

First, the book follows climate finance from conception to implementation. Rather than treating climate finance as a collection of isolated instruments, the analysis traces how climate objectives are translated into financial reality. It begins with the conceptual foundations and institutional frameworks that shape climate finance, then examines specific financial instruments such as green bonds and blue finance, and finally explores system-level mechanisms such as carbon trading and carbon finance. The aim is to show how ideas become institutions, how institutions shape markets, and how markets ultimately influence real economic outcomes. Climate finance, after all, succeeds only when financial innovation translates into measurable environmental and economic impact.

Second, the book looks at climate finance across both developed and developing economies. Climate change is a global problem, but financial systems, institutional capacities, and development priorities vary widely across regions. Advanced economies often pioneer financial innovation and regulatory standards, while developing economies face the urgent need to mobilize capital for infrastructure, adaptation, and sustainable development. Understanding climate finance therefore requires a global perspective that recognizes both the opportunities and constraints faced by different economies. By examining examples and institutional frameworks across jurisdictions, this book highlights how climate finance can evolve in diverse economic contexts.

Third, the book speaks to both practitioners and policymakers. Climate finance operates at the intersection of financial markets and public governance. Investors and financial institutions develop innovative instruments and allocate capital, while governments and regulators design the rules, incentives, and institutional structures that make these markets credible and effective. A meaningful understanding of climate finance must therefore integrate both perspectives. Throughout the book, attention is given not only to financial performance and market behavior, but also to governance, policy design, and institutional credibility.

Underlying these themes is a broader conviction: climate finance represents one of the most ambitious experiments in economic transformation in modern history. It asks financial systems—traditionally oriented toward **short-term** returns and private incentives—to help solve a **long-term** global public challenge. This is not a simple task. It requires credible institutions, transparent markets, innovative financial instruments, and cooperation across countries and sectors.

Yet, there are reasons for optimism. Financial history shows that markets can adapt remarkably quickly when incentives, institutions, and innovation align. Just as finance once helped build railways, electrification, and the digital economy, it can also play a decisive role in enabling the transition to a net-zero world. The emergence of green bonds, climate disclosure standards, carbon markets, and other instruments suggests that the foundations of a new financial architecture are already taking shape.

The journey is far from complete. Climate finance remains an evolving field, characterized by experimentation, debate, and continuous improvement. Some initiatives will succeed; others will fall short. But taken together, they represent humanity's effort to align the mechanisms of modern finance with the long-term stability of the planet.

This book is written with the hope that understanding these mechanisms—their logic, their limitations, and their possibilities—can contribute, in some small way, to that broader endeavor. After all, if the challenge of our century is to build a sustainable future, then finance must become not merely a tool of economic growth, but a vehicle of planetary stewardship.

Cardiff, UK Peng Zhou
Beijing, China Dong Guo

Competing Interests The authors have no competing interests to declare that are relevant to the content of this manuscript.

Contents

Part II Green Bonds and the Net-Zero Transition

Abbreviations

\$	US Dollar or USD
£	Great Britain Pound
€	Euro or EUR
¥	Chinese Yuan or RMB
CBI	Climate Bonds Initiative
ESG	Environment, Society, Governance
EU	European Union
Forex	Foreign Exchange
GBP	Green Bond Principles
GVA	Gross Value Added
ICMA	International Capital Market Association
IMF	International Monetary Fund
ISSB	International Sustainability Standards Board
OECD	Organization for Economic Cooperation and Development
SDG	Sustainable Development Goal
SEC	Securities and Exchange Commission
TCFD	Task Force on Climate-related Financial Disclosures
UK	United Kingdom
UN	United Nations
US	United States

About the Authors

Peng Zhou is Professor of Economics, University Dean of International, and Director of the Cardiff Confucius Institute at Cardiff University (UK). He is a Principal Fellow of the Higher Education Academy, recognized for his nonlinear-teaching pedagogy, and a Fellow of the Learned Society of Wales, recognized for his global-civic research. His academic footprint spans economic growth, economic inequality, financial economics, and innovation economics, with a strong track record of publications in leading journals across these fields. Beyond academia, he provides consultancy and expert opinions to media, charities, governments, and companies in the UK and China.

Dong Guo is a senior economist and senior manager at the China Development Bank, and a research fellow certified by the People's Bank of China. He is also a visiting professor at Shandong University of Finance and Economics and the University of International Business and Economics. His research focuses on sovereign bonds, exchange rates, fiscal and monetary policy, and financial sanctions. He has extensive experience in green finance and fintech, having led RMB green bond issuance projects worth billions and contributed to the development of standards for blockchain-based financial infrastructure.

List of Figures

List of Tables

Part I
Foundations

Chapter 1
Conception

Introduction

"Climate finance is not charity. It's an investment." This famous pronouncement by UN Secretary-General António Guterres in late 2024 highlighted a pivotal truth: the fight against climate change hinges on self-interested investment and how it is used (UN, 2024). In the same breath, he warned that "the world must pay up, or humanity will pay the price", stressing the grand challenge we face.

The numbers put this challenge in perspective. As of 2019–2020, total global climate finance flows were on the order of $650 billion per year, which sounds enormous—until one realizes this was far below the $4–6 trillion per year that experts estimate is needed by 2030 to limit warming to agreed targets (Climate Policy Initiative, 2022; NDC Partnership, 2023). Even with recent progress—annual climate finance reached a record $1.9 trillion in 2023—we are still less than halfway to the lower end of required investment levels (Climate Policy Initiative, 2025). This stark gap forms one of the central puzzles of climate finance: how can the world rapidly mobilize trillions of dollars for climate action in time to prevent catastrophic climate change? The urgency is further magnified by inequities—only a fraction of climate investment reaches the developing countries most vulnerable to climate impacts (Climate Policy Initiative, 2022). Clearly, scaling up climate finance is not just a technical necessity but a matter of global solidarity and enlightened self-interest.

In this opening chapter, we explore what "climate finance" really means, why it matters, and how it fits into the broader concept of sustainable finance. We also lay out a roadmap for the rest of the book, which will journey from high-level concepts to on-the-ground implementation of climate finance in the push for net zero.

P. Zhou, D. Guo, *Climate Finance in the Net-Zero Transition*, Contributions to Finance and Accounting, https://doi.org/10.1007/978-981-92-0827-2_1

What: A Taxonomy

At the outset, it is important to clarify a distinction that underpins this book. *Net zero* and *carbon neutrality* are often used interchangeably in public discourse, but they are not identical concepts. Carbon neutrality typically refers to balancing carbon dioxide (CO_2) emissions with removals or offsets, often at the level of individual projects, firms, or products. This focus reflects the fact that CO_2 is the most significant and long-lived component of anthropogenic greenhouse gas (GHG) emissions, and thus the primary driver of cumulative warming. Net zero, by contrast, is broader and more demanding. It refers to achieving a balance between emissions and removals across all GHGs at the economy-wide level, consistent with temperature stabilization goals under the Paris Agreement. As such, net zero is the dominant framing in contemporary climate policy, financial regulation, and investment practice. This book therefore adopts net zero as its organizing concept. The net-zero transition is a long, uncertain, and capital-intensive process of transforming economic systems, financial markets, and institutions so that aggregate GHG emissions decline to (and are sustained at) net zero over time.

At the same time, discussions on funding climate solutions also involve overlapping terms: green finance, climate finance, sustainable finance, even blue finance and carbon finance. What do all these terms mean, and how do they relate? It is helpful to establish a simple taxonomy.

Climate finance generally refers to financing tools dedicated to addressing climate change—primarily by reducing GHG emissions (mitigation) and by helping society adapt to climate impacts (adaptation). In practice, climate finance can include public climate-related development aid, private investments in renewable energy or energy efficiency, funds for climate-resilient infrastructure, and market mechanisms like carbon credit purchases. The term gained prominence through UN climate negotiations, often denoting the financial transfers or investments needed to implement the Paris Agreement and other climate policies.

Green finance has a broader connotation. According to the European Parliament's research service, climate finance is a subset of green finance (Spinaci, 2021). Green finance encompasses all environmentally beneficial financial flows—not only those for climate mitigation and adaptation, but also investments in other environmental objectives such as biodiversity conservation, pollution prevention, sustainable water management, and so on. In other words, green finance covers climate change and other "green" issues. A corporate loan to install pollution control technology, a bond to fund reforestation or habitat restoration, or a private equity fund for clean water projects would all fall under green finance, even if they are not strictly about climate change.

Green finance includes a range of instruments and markets: for example, *green bonds*—bonds whose proceeds are earmarked for environmental projects—have become a flagship product of green finance as well as climate finance. We will explore green bonds in depth in Part II of this book. Since the first green bonds appeared in the late 2000s, the market has grown exponentially. By the end of 2020, cumulative green bond issuance worldwide had surpassed \$1 trillion (Climate Bonds Initiative, 2020), and annual green bond issuance broke over \$500 billion in 2021 alone (Climate Bonds Initiative, 2022). Other examples of green finance instruments include *green loans* (bank lending for green projects, often at preferential rates), *green funds* (which channel investors' capital into sustainable assets), and even innovative instruments like *blue finance*. Blue finance is a special category of green finance designed to fund marine and ocean-based projects—for instance, protecting oceans, sustainable fisheries, and coastal resilience. The world's first sovereign blue bond, issued by the Republic of Seychelles in 2018, raised \$15 million to support sustainable marine fisheries, demonstrating how capital markets can be harnessed for ocean conservation (World Bank, 2018). In short, green finance is an umbrella encompassing climate finance but not limited to it, since not all environmental issues are climate related.

Broader still is *sustainable finance*, the most inclusive term. Sustainable finance extends beyond environmental projects to incorporate ESG criteria—Environmental, Social and Governance factors—in financial decision-making. In sustainable finance, the goal is to support overall sustainable development, balancing environmental protection, social development, and economic growth. Thus, sustainable finance includes green/climate finance and also covers social objectives (such as poverty reduction, gender equality, health and education financing, etc.) and governance considerations. One can think of these terms as nested subsets as illustrated in Fig. 1.1: climate finance $\subset$ green finance $\subset$ sustainable finance (Spinaci, 2021). A sustainable finance initiative might, for example, involve issuing social bonds to fund affordable housing or healthcare (addressing social goals), or requiring corporations to disclose governance and environmental risks to inform investors. Sustainable finance is about reorienting the entire financial system to account for long-term ESG outcomes. In recent years, many banks, asset managers, and

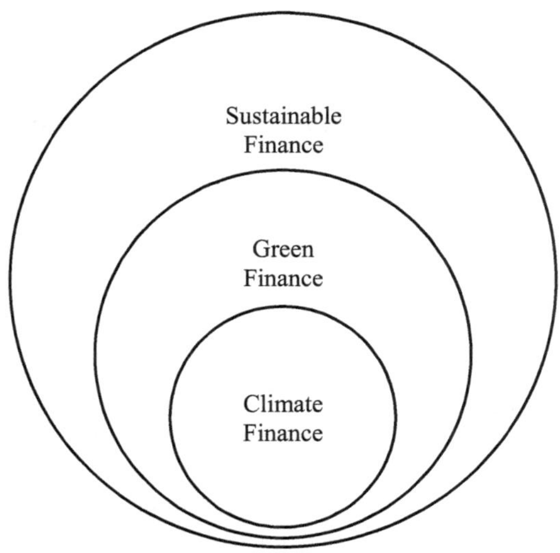

Fig. 1.1 Taxonomy of climate finance

regulators have adopted sustainable finance principles, recognizing that issues like climate change and social inequality pose material risks to the economy. Green finance can be seen as an early evolutionary stage—initially focusing on environmental projects—that has broadened into today's sustainable finance movement integrating social and governance aspects (International Capital Market Association, 2020).

It is worth noting a couple of specialized terms often encountered alongside climate/green finance. One is *carbon finance*, which typically refers to the financing of projects that reduce or avoid carbon emissions through the generation of carbon credits. Carbon finance is closely tied to carbon markets and carbon trading—mechanisms where carbon emission allowances or credits are bought and sold. In carbon finance, an investor might fund a wind farm or a forest conservation project in exchange for carbon credits (each credit representing a tonne of CO_2 reduced or removed), which can then be sold to companies or countries needing to offset their emissions. Essentially, carbon finance puts a monetary value on emissions reductions, creating financial incentives to cut greenhouse gases. We will investigate carbon trading systems and markets in Part IV of this book.

In summary, while these terms overlap, they can be distinguished as follows: climate finance targets climate change mitigation and adaptation; green finance targets environmental sustainability more broadly; sustainable finance encompasses environmental and social goals, aligning finance with sustainable development. All are crucial pieces of the puzzle. In practice, the lines are sometimes blurry—for example, a renewable energy project could be called green finance or climate finance (both would be correct). What matters is that, taken together, these emerging branches of finance represent a shift in how capital is allocated, aiming to channel funds toward solving the grand challenges of our age. Financial instruments such as green and blue bonds, green loans, sustainability-linked loans, carbon credits, and impact investments are the tools by which the abstract concept of climate/green/sustainable finance is being turned into concrete action.

Why: A Must-Have or a Nice-to-Have

Why has climate finance become such a focal point in recent years? The simple answer is that stabilizing the climate will require a wholesale transformation of our economies—and finance is the enabling fuel of economic activity. It is a must-have rather than a nice-to-have. The concept of climate finance arises from the recognition that huge investments are needed to transition to a low-carbon, climate-resilient future.

The International Energy Agency and other bodies have calculated that to reach net-zero carbon emissions by 2050 (in line with the Paris Agreement goals), energy infrastructure investments on the order of trillions per year are required this decade. These funds must finance everything from renewable energy scale-up, electrification of transport, and energy-efficient buildings to climate-resilient agriculture, flood defenses, and new technologies like green hydrogen and carbon capture. The Paris Agreement itself, in Article 2.1(c), enshrined a goal of "making finance flows consistent with a pathway toward low greenhouse gas emissions and climate-resilient development"—effectively elevating climate finance to one of the treaty's three overarching objectives alongside mitigation and adaptation (UN, 2015). In other words, the world's nations agreed that aligning financial flows with climate goals is indispensable to solving climate change. Climate finance, in conception, is about unleashing a tidal wave of capital reallocation: away from high-carbon activities that drive global warming and toward climate solutions that can halt it.

Crucially, climate finance is not only about the quantity of investment but also its direction and impact. It is about bridging what the IPCC calls the "climate financing gap"—the shortfall between current investment levels and those needed to achieve climate targets (IPCC, 2023). The latest IPCC assessment emphasized that while climate finance is rising, it remains far below what's required for a 1.5 °C or 2 °C pathway, and that all sectors and regions are experiencing this shortfall. Tracked financial flows are only a fraction of the necessary levels; closing this gap is one of the greatest challenges in mitigating climate change.

Yet climate finance is more than a dollar figure—it embodies a strategy for transformation. By investing in clean energy, energy efficiency, public transit, sustainable agriculture, and other low-carbon solutions, we address the root causes of climate change (cutting emissions). By funding seawalls, drought-resistant crops, early warning systems, and climate insurance, we bolster adaptation to the impacts that are already unavoidable. Every dollar devoted to climate action is, in theory, an investment in a safer, more stable climate future—and often yields co-benefits like cleaner air, energy security, and jobs in green industries. This is why Guterres and others stress that climate finance should be seen as an investment, not charity. The returns may not always be monetary in the narrow sense, but they are overwhelmingly positive for society and for the planet's habitability.

However, the conception of climate finance also encompasses a keen awareness of fairness and political feasibility. Climate change is a global problem, but those who bear the greatest costs of transition (or of inaction) are unevenly distributed. Developing countries, which historically contributed least to greenhouse gas emissions, often face the gravest climate impacts and have the least financial capacity to respond. Thus, climate finance carries a justice dimension: significant funds need to flow from wealthier, high-emitting nations to poorer, vulnerable nations to support their mitigation and adaptation efforts. This was formally recognized in the pledge by developed countries to mobilize $100 billion per year in climate finance for developing countries, a target initially set for 2020. Although that specific $100 billion goal has been repeatedly delayed and critiqued for being inadequate relative to needs, it highlights the ethical premise that climate finance is part of a global bargain—building trust that all countries will be supported in the transition. The notion of a "just transition" is relevant here: climate action (SDG13) should also address social outcomes, for example by retraining workers from fossil fuel industries and ensuring energy access for the poor. Climate finance, if deployed wisely, can help ensure that moving to a green economy also reduces inequality and alleviates poverty, rather than exacerbating them.

Another reason climate finance matters is its role in engaging the private sector and shifting broader financial flows. Public finance (government budgets, development banks, etc.) alone cannot foot the multi-trillion-dollar price tag—it must be used strategically to leverage much larger private investment. This insight has led to creative financing structures like blended finance (combining public and philanthropic funds to de-risk projects and attract private investors) and green investment frameworks to entice institutional investors (pension funds, sovereign wealth funds) into climate-friendly investments. There is also a rapidly growing awareness of climate-related financial risk in the mainstream financial system. Central banks and financial regulators, from the Bank of England to the European Central Bank, have warned that climate change poses systemic risks to the economy—through both physical risks (like disasters destroying assets) and transition risks (like sudden losses in fossil fuel asset values). This has prompted moves to incorporate climate scenarios into financial stability monitoring and to improve corporate climate risk disclosure (e.g., Task Force on Climate-related Financial Disclosures). In sum, what began as a niche idea—financing green projects—has evolved into a comprehensive agenda to reshape finance itself. Aligning trillions of dollars with climate goals is now seen as not only desirable but necessary to safeguard the global economy. The IPCC (2023) notes encouragingly that the costs of many low-carbon technologies have fallen dramatically, making the investment case easier; yet it also flags that overall, global capital is still misallocated, with more money often still flowing into fossil fuels than into climate solutions. Redressing this imbalance is a core motivation behind the climate finance push.

To illustrate, consider a few salient comparisons: governments worldwide still spend hundreds of billions of dollars each year on fossil fuel subsidies—$7 trillion in 2022 by one IMF estimate (Black et al., 2023)—effectively subsidizing the drivers of climate change. Meanwhile, climate finance flows, as noted, are only a fraction of that. Redirecting even a portion of these subsidies or private capital from high-carbon to low-carbon activities could make a decisive difference. Climate finance, therefore, is about redirecting the river of global finance. It asks: how can policy, public pressure, and financial innovation funnel the vast pools of capital in global markets away from activities that imperil our future and into those that secure it?

Finally, climate finance matters because it represents hope and opportunity. The massive investments needed can spur innovation, create jobs, and foster sustainable development. We often speak of the climate crisis, but there is also a "climate opportunity"—an opportunity to modernize infrastructure, develop clean technologies, and build more equitable societies. Mobilizing climate finance is how we seize that opportunity. It is inspiring that, despite the challenges, momentum is building. Green bond markets are booming, major financial institutions are committing to net-zero portfolios, and new mechanisms (like the Green Climate Fund and various climate investment funds) are being deployed to support climate action around the world. Each solar farm financed, each electric bus fleet deployed, each coastal mangrove restoration funded—these are tangible victories made possible by climate finance. In the chapters ahead, we will see many concrete examples of how climate finance is being conceived and implemented in different contexts. But first, let us outline how this book is structured to navigate the diverse facets of climate finance in the journey toward a net-zero transition.

How: A Roadmap from Conception to Implementation

This book is structured to reflect how climate finance moves from an idea into practice—how abstract climate objectives are translated into financial standards, instruments, market behavior, and ultimately measurable economic and sustainability outcomes. The ten chapters are organized into four parts that follow this progression from conception to implementation and system-level impact.

Part I (Chaps. 1 and 2) establishes the conceptual and institutional foundations of climate finance.

Chapter 1 introduces climate finance as a distinct yet interconnected domain within sustainable finance, clarifying its scope, rationale, and economic function in the net-zero transition. It frames climate finance not merely as a collection of labeled instruments, but as a response to climate-related market failures, public-good provision, and long-term risk reallocation. Chapter 2 then moves from conceptual grounding to institutional design, examining how standards, disclosure frameworks, and regulatory initiatives shape the credibility and effectiveness of climate finance across jurisdictions. Together, these chapters define the "rules of the game" within which climate-aligned capital is mobilized.

Part II (Chaps. 3–5) focuses on green bonds as a core implementation channel for climate finance.

These chapters follow green bonds at different levels. Chapter 3 analyzes corporate green bonds, emphasizing how firms conceptualize green projects, structure use-of-proceeds frameworks, and integrate environmental objectives into conventional debt finance. Chapter 4 shifts to sovereign green bonds, highlighting the role of public issuers in signaling national climate commitments, financing public goods, and embedding green bonds within fiscal and regulatory systems. Chapter 5 completes the green bond analysis from the investor perspective, evaluating how green bonds function within portfolios, how they perform under different market conditions, and whether they contribute to risk management and hedging objectives. Together, these chapters connect issuance, governance, and performance.

Part III (Chaps. 6 and 7) extends the analysis to blue finance and the ocean economy.

Chapter 6 introduces blue finance, clarifying how ocean-related climate challenges generate distinct financing needs and governance requirements compared to terrestrial green finance. It develops a typology of blue finance instruments and examines early blue bond initiatives. Chapter 7 then focuses on implementation at scale, analyzing how blue finance supports the sustainable development of the ocean economy through governance structures, blended finance arrangements, and case-based evidence. This part shows how climate finance principles are adapted to sectors characterized by common-pool resources, cross-border externalities, and demanding monitoring requirements.

Part IV (Chaps. 8–10) turns to carbon finance and carbon trading as system-level market mechanisms.

Chapter 8 provides an overview of prevailing carbon finance systems, emphasizing governance structures and theoretical perspectives that underpin carbon pricing and market design. Chapter 9 examines carbon trading more directly, synthesizing empirical evidence and theoretical insights on emissions trading systems and their economic and sustainability impacts. Chapter 10 concludes the part by linking carbon finance to broader sustainable development outcomes, using empirical analysis to assess how carbon markets interact with SDGs and long-term transition pathways.

Across these four parts, the book advances a unified argument: climate finance is most effective when conception, institutional design, financial functionality, and market outcomes are aligned. By moving systematically from foundational concepts to concrete instruments and finally to economy-wide mechanisms, the book provides an integrated roadmap for understanding how climate finance operates—and how it can be improved to support a credible and durable net-zero transition.

The journey from conception to implementation is complex and still ongoing, but it is also inspiring. Climate finance, as we have seen in this chapter, sits at the intersection of urgent need and innovative response. It represents the financial ingenuity and collective willpower that will either enable the net-zero transition or, if we fall short, mark a costly missed opportunity. The chapters ahead aim to equip the reader with a deep understanding of this field—one that is as critical for policymakers and investors as it is for every global citizen concerned about a livable future. By comprehending the mechanisms and debates in climate finance, we become better positioned to contribute to, and advocate for, the solutions that will shape a sustainable, thriving world. The conception is clear: climate finance is foundational to climate action. Now, we turn to the practical structures and examples that bring this concept to life.

References

Black, S., Parry, I., & Vernon, N. (2023). *Fossil fuel subsidies surged to record $7 trillion.* International Monetary Fund.

Climate Bonds Initiative. (2020). *$1 trillion mark reached in global cumulative green issuance.* Climate Bonds Initiative.

Climate Bonds Initiative. (2022). *Sustainable debt global state of the market 2021.* Climate Bonds Initiative.

Climate Policy Initiative. (2022). *Global landscape of climate finance 2021.* Climate Policy Initiative Press.

Climate Policy Initiative. (2025). *Global climate finance hits $1.9 trillion—Bridging the climate investment gap remains within reach.* Climate Policy Initiative Press.

International Capital Market Association. (2020). *Sustainable finance—High-level definitions*. International Capital Market Association.

IPCC. (2023). *Climate change 2022—Mitigation of climate change*. Cambridge University Press.

NDC Partnership. (2023). *Closing the climate finance gap*. NDC Partnership.

Spinaci, S. (2021). *Green and sustainable finance*. European Parliament.

UN. (2015). *Paris agreement: United Nations framework convention on climate change*. United Nations.

UN. (2024). *Secretary-general's remarks at world leaders climate action summit (COP29)*. United Nations.

World Bank. (2018). *Seychelles launches world's first sovereign blue bond*. World Bank.

Chapter 2
Institutions

Introduction

A central challenge in climate finance is *greenwashing*—the practice of portraying financial products, issuers, or strategies as climate-aligned without substantive action or impact (Lyon & Maxwell, 2011; Lyon & Montgomery, 2015; UN, 2026). In financial markets, greenwashing often arises from information asymmetry: issuers and asset managers know more about how capital is used and what risks they face than investors do. When verification is costly and definitions are ambiguous, "green" labels can become marketing devices rather than credible signals (Montiel et al., 2019).

Greenwashing has several distinctive features in climate finance. First, it can be taxonomy-based: an activity is labeled "green" under a permissive definition even when its climate contribution is questionable. Second, it can be process-based: products advertise ESG integration while relying on weak screens or inconsistent metrics. Third, it can be disclosure-based: selectively reporting favorable indicators while omitting material exposures, especially transition risks and emissions in value chains (ISSB, 2023). Fourth, it can be ratings-based: firms exploit the divergence across ESG ratings providers to justify claims that are not robust across methodologies (Berg et al., 2022). These mechanisms matter because they distort price signals, misallocate capital, and ultimately delay decarbonization by crowding out genuinely climate-aligned investments.

Several market characteristics amplify this problem. Climate outcomes are often long-horizon and multi-dimensional, while many market incentives are short-horizon and benchmark-driven. Investors may accept "good enough" climate narratives if the verification costs of challenging claims are high, especially when disclosure is heterogeneous (Financial Stability Board, 2017). At the same time, the rapid growth of labeled products increases the payoff from opportunistic labeling,

P. Zhou, D. Guo, *Climate Finance in the Net-Zero Transition*, Contributions to Finance and Accounting, https://doi.org/10.1007/978-981-92-0827-2_2

particularly when enforcement is weak or standards are fragmented (File, 2023). This is not only a reputational issue; it can also become a financial stability issue if climate risks are systematically under-disclosed and therefore mispriced (Financial Stability Board, 2023; Ilhan et al., 2020; Bolton & Kacperczyk, 2021).

Recent enforcement actions have reinforced the point that greenwashing can carry material legal and financial consequences. For example, Germany's DWS (Deutsche Bank's asset management arm) was fined €25 million after investigators concluded it had exaggerated aspects of its ESG credentials (Reuters., 2025). In the US, the SEC has proposed rules to enhance and standardize climate-related disclosures, reflecting concerns about inconsistent reporting and misleading claims (SEC, 2022). These developments mirror a broader global pattern: regulators are increasingly treating greenwashing as a market integrity problem rather than a niche reputational risk (Financial Stability Board, 2023).

In climate finance, standards and regulations are the primary institutional response. They aim to (1) clarify what qualifies as climate-aligned (taxonomies and eligible-use rules), (2) require consistent reporting of climate risks and impacts (disclosure standards), and (3) raise the cost of misrepresentation through supervision, assurance, and legal liability (ISSB, 2023). In short, tackling greenwashing is not a peripheral concern; it is a precondition for mobilizing climate finance at scale.

International Frameworks

Over the past few years, a suite of international standards and regulatory frameworks has emerged to govern climate finance. These initiatives—spanning disclosure rules, taxonomies, and voluntary principles—collectively aim to create common rules of the game for climate-focused investing (Financial Stability Board, 2023). Below we review the most prominent frameworks, emphasizing those specific to climate finance (rather than broad ESG), and how they work to improve transparency and integrity.

EU Sustainable Finance Disclosure Regulation

One cornerstone is the EU's Sustainable Finance Disclosure Regulation (SFDR), which took effect in 2021. SFDR requires asset managers, banks, and other financial institutions to disclose how they integrate sustainability (including climate) factors into their services and products, with the explicit aim of increasing transparency and reducing greenwashing risk in investment products (European Parliament, 2019).

SFDR effectively creates categories for financial products: those simply integrating sustainability risks, those promoting environmental or social characteristics, and those with a dedicated sustainable investment objective. Products in the latter categories face additional disclosure requirements as proof of their sustainability claims.

Empirical evidence suggests that the stricter "sustainable investment" designation is valued by investors and can influence fund flows, consistent with the notion that credible labels act as market signals (Scherer & Hasaj, 2023). The SFDR experience also highlights a practical governance challenge: as regulators clarify definitions and supervisory expectations, funds may revise classifications to avoid non-compliance, which can itself become a discipline mechanism against aggressive labeling.

Despite various challenges, SFDR has become a reference point for climate-finance transparency at the product level, illustrating both the power of disclosure and the need for ongoing supervision to enforce the spirit of the rules.

EU Taxonomy for Sustainable Activities

Complementing SFDR's entity and product disclosures is the EU Taxonomy, a legally grounded classification system defining which economic activities can be considered environmentally sustainable (European Parliament, 2020). The Taxonomy establishes technical screening criteria for activities contributing to six environmental objectives, with climate change mitigation and adaptation at the core of climate finance relevance. Its primary role is to create a "common language" for what counts as a climate-aligned investment, reducing definitional ambiguity that enables greenwashing (Financial Stability Board, 2023).

The Taxonomy's regulatory logic is operational: firms and financial institutions subject to reporting requirements must disclose how much of their activity aligns with Taxonomy criteria, shifting sustainability claims from narrative statements to measurable alignment metrics (European Parliament, 2022). Although implementation is complex, the Taxonomy has become an anchor for climate finance governance in Europe, and an influential template in global discussions on classification convergence.

Climate-Related Financial Disclosure

Disclosure of climate-related financial risks is another pillar of climate finance regulation. The influential precursor is the Task Force on Climate-related Financial Disclosures (TCFD) framework, which provides recommendations for reporting climate governance, strategy, risk management, and metrics & targets (Financial Stability Board, 2017). The rationale is straightforward: to mobilize climate finance, investors need consistent, decision-useful information on climate risks and opportunities, including emissions and scenario-based transition risks (Ilhan et al., 2020).

Building on the TCFD architecture, the International Sustainability Standards Board (ISSB) issued its inaugural standards in 2023: IFRS S1 (general requirements for sustainability disclosure) and IFRS S2 (climate-related disclosure). IFRS S2 is explicitly designed to create a comparable, investor-focused baseline for climate reporting, closely aligned with TCFD's four-pillar structure. IOSCO's endorsement is important for diffusion because it supports the integration of ISSB standards into securities regulation across jurisdictions (IOSCO, 2023). Collectively, these disclosure frameworks aim to reduce information asymmetry and improve pricing of climate risks in capital markets (Salvi et al., 2025).

Voluntary Market Standards

Long before formal regulations took shape, market actors developed voluntary standards to guide climate finance instruments—most notably in the green bond market. Two leading frameworks are the ICMA Green Bond Principles (GBP) and the CBI Standard (ICMA, 2021; CBI, 2021). The GBP provides principles-based guidance around use of proceeds, project selection, proceeds management, and reporting, while the CBI Standard provides more prescriptive sector criteria and a certification process.

Evidence indicates substantial convergence between these standards. Using machine-learning textual comparison, Zhou et al. (2025) report a similarity metric of 85.3% between ICMA and CBI documentation, consistent with qualitative content analysis of the two standards. Both frameworks emphasize post-issuance transparency—green bond frameworks, allocation reporting, and impact reporting—often supported by third-party verification (ICMA, 2021; CBI, 2021). Table 2.1 compares the ICMA and CBI in terms of pre-issuance and post issuance requirements.

This credibility dimension matters for pricing and demand. A broad literature documents a "greenium" in many settings, with greener labels sometimes associated with lower yields, although estimates vary and depend on verification and market structure (Zerbib, 2019; Bachelet et al., 2019; Larcker & Watts, 2020; Flammer, 2021). For the EU bond market, Zhou et al. (2025) show that green labels reduce required yields in the long run, with stronger effects when labels are externally certified rather than self-labeled, consistent with a credibility and signaling interpretation. This evidence supports the view that voluntary standards can function as quasi-regulatory devices by increasing comparability and raising the reputational and informational costs of greenwashing (Lyon & Montgomery, 2015).

National Regulatory Initiatives

While international standards set the overall direction, implementation occurs at the national or regional level. Different jurisdictions tailor climate finance governance to local institutional contexts, even as they interact with global frameworks. Table 2.2 compares key facets of climate finance standards across major jurisdictions, illustrating the differences in disclosures, taxonomies, and bond standards.

Table 2.1 ICMA and CBI requirements on green bonds

Panel A: Prior-issuance requirement of ICMA and CBI

Stage	Documents		ICMA	CBI
Pre-issuance	Green bond framework	Use of proceeds	In the event that all or a proportion of the proceeds are or may be used for refinancing, it is recommended that issuers provide an estimate of the share of financing vs. re-financing, and where appropriate, also clarify which investments or project portfolios may be refinanced, and, to the extent relevant, the expected look-back period for refinanced eligible green projects	The issuer shall document the nominated projects and assets which are proposed to be associated with the bond, and which have been assessed as likely to be eligible projects and assets. The issuer shall establish a list of nominated projects and assets that can be kept up to date during the term of the bond The expected net proceeds of the Bond shall be no greater than the issuer's total investment exposure to the proposed nominated projects and assets, or the relevant proportion of the total market value of the proposed nominated projects and assets that are owned or funded by the issuer
		Process for project evaluation and selection	The issuer of a green bond should clearly communicate to investors: 1. The environmental sustainability objectives of the eligible green projects 2. The process by which the issuer determines how the projects fit within the eligible green projects categories (examples are identified above) 3. Complementary information on processes by which the issuer identifies and manages perceived social and environmental risks associated with the relevant project(s)	The issuer shall establish, document, and maintain a decision-making process that it uses to determine the eligibility of the nominated projects and assets. The decision-making process shall include, without limitation: 1. A statement on the climate-related objectives of the bond 2. How the climate-related objectives of the Bond are positioned within the context of the issuer's overarching objectives, strategy, policy, and/or processes relating to environmental sustainability 3. The Issuer's rationale for issuing the bond 4. A process to determine whether the nominated projects and assets meet the eligibility requirements specified in the climate bonds standard
		Management of proceeds	The net proceeds of the green bond, or an amount equal to these net proceeds, should be credited to a sub-account, moved to a sub-portfolio or otherwise tracked by the issuer in an appropriate manner, and attested to by the issuer in a formal internal process linked to the issuer's lending and investment operations for eligible green projects So long as the green bond is outstanding, the balance of the tracked net proceeds should be periodically adjusted to match allocations to eligible green projects made during that period. The issuer should make known to investors the intended types of temporary placement for the balance of unallocated net proceeds The principle encourages a high level of transparency and recommends that an issuer's management of proceeds be supplemented by the use of an external auditor, or other third parties, to verify the internal tracking method and the allocation of funds from the green bond proceeds	The systems, policies, and processes to be used for management of the net proceeds shall be documented by the Issuer and disclosed to the verifier, and shall include arrangements for the following activities: 1. Tracking of proceeds: The net proceeds of the bond can be credited to a sub-account, moved to a sub-portfolio, or otherwise tracked by the issuer in an appropriate manner and documented 2. Managing unallocated proceeds: The balance of unallocated net proceeds can be managed as per the requirements in Clause 7.3 3. Earmarking funds to nominated projects and assets: An earmarking process can be used to manage and account for funding to the nominated projects and assets and enables estimation of the share of the net proceeds being used for
		Reporting	Issuers should make, and keep, readily available up-to-date information on the use of proceeds to be renewed annually until full allocation, and on a timely basis in case of material developments	The issuer shall prepare a green bond framework and make it publicly available prior to issuance or at the time of issuance The issuer shall prepare an updated report at least annually while the bond remains outstanding

Panel B: Post-issuance requirement from ICMA and CBI

Stage	Documents	ICMA	CBI
Post-issuance	Asset allocation report	The annual report should include a list of the projects to which green bond proceeds have been allocated, as well as a brief description of the projects, the amounts allocated, and their expected impact. Where confidentiality agreements, competitive considerations, or a large number of underlying projects limit the amount of detail that can be made available, the principle recommends that information be presented in generic terms or on an aggregated portfolio basis	The allocation reporting shall include, without limitation: 1. Confirmation that the bonds issued under the framework are aligned with the Climate Bonds Standard. This may include statements of alignment with other applicable standards 2. A statement on the climate-related objectives of the bond 3. The list of nominated projects and assets to which net proceeds have been allocated (or re-allocated) 4. The amounts allocated to the nominated projects and assets 5. An estimate of the share of the Net Proceeds used for financing and refinancing, and which nominated projects and assets have been refinanced 6. The geographical distribution of the nominated projects and assets
	Impact report	Transparency is of particular value in communicating the expected and/or achieved impact of projects. The principle recommends the use of qualitative performance indicators and, where feasible, quantitative performance measures and disclosure of the key underlying methodology and/or assumptions used in quantitative determination. Issuers should refer to and adopt, where possible, the guidance and impact reporting templates provided in the harmonized framework for impact reporting	The impact reporting shall, without limitation: 1. Provide the expected or actual outcomes or impacts of the nominated projects and assets with respect to the climate-related objectives of the bond 2. Use qualitative performance indicators and, where feasible, quantitative performance measures of the outcomes or impacts of the nominated projects and assets with respect to the climate-related objectives of the bond 3. Provide the methods and the key underlying assumptions used in the preparation of the performance indicators and metrics
	Eligibility report	NA	The eligibility reporting shall include, without limitation: 1. Confirmation that the nominated projects and assets continue to meet the relevant eligibility requirements specified in Part C of the Climate Bonds Standard 2. Information on the environmental characteristics or performance of nominated projects and assets which are prescribed by the relevant sector's eligibility criteria
Others	Additional costs related to the label/certification	ICMA has varied membership fees for tier 1, 2A, 2B, and 3 members. The membership fee for tier 3 is CHF 17,500 per year for full and associate membership. (Tier 3 is basic membership: Subsidiaries of all international/regional/domestic firms, all public institutions, associate members (non-full members), and firms similar to domestic firms but with a smaller revenue base)	A minimum fee of $2000 for issuers in developed countries and $1000 for issuers in developing countries will be charged by the CBI upon awarding the certification label. Following the issuance of any certified bond (or a series of bonds in a programmatic certification process) a variable fee of 1/10th of a basis point (i.e., × 0.00001) of the bond issuance amount will be calculated. For example, on a $500 million bond, the certification fee is $5000 For programmatic issuers, the minimum fee will only apply to the first bond issued under the program; the variable fee for each subsequent programmatic issuance will be calculated based on the aggregate issuance amounts under the program and any fees previously billed (including the minimum fee) will be deducted from the cumulative variable fee

Table 2.2 Influential climate finance standards across jurisdictions

Aspect	US	EU	China
Climate risk disclosure	Proposed SEC climate disclosure rule (as of 2025) would require listed companies to disclose climate-related risks, governance and GHG emissions (Scope 1, 2, and certain Scope 3) in SEC filings (Finalization pending amid legal scrutiny.) Many companies currently report voluntarily (TCFD or CDP), but no federal mandate yet	Mandatory TCFD-aligned reporting for large companies under the CSRD (from 2024); financial institutions must report climate metrics under SFDR. EU to incorporate ISSB standards for a unified approach	Regulators are moving toward compulsory climate disclosure: the CSRC issued guidelines for listed firms to disclose environmental and climate information by 2025. Several pilot programs and the PBoC's climate stress tests for banks are introducing TCFD-like disclosures, but a nationwide mandatory climate reporting regime is still emerging (largely on a "comply or explain" basis for now)
Green taxonomy & standards	No official taxonomy or national green standards. Climate finance relies on market-led norms (e.g. many US green bonds follow ICMA's GBP). The SEC and FTC, however, have signaled stricter oversight of ESG claims—e.g. proposed "Names Rule" enhancements to ensure funds labeled "green" or "sustainable" adhere to stated criteria. Any green bond misrepresentation could fall under general antifraud provisions, but the US lacks a dedicated taxonomy	EU Taxonomy Regulation defines technical screening criteria for climate-mitigating activities. Companies and investors must disclose Taxonomy-alignment (percentage of revenues/ investments meeting climate criteria). Also, the EU Green Bond Standard (voluntary) was created in 2023: bonds labeled as "European Green Bonds (EuGB)" must allocate 100% of proceeds to Taxonomy-aligned projects and obtain external verification	China's Green Taxonomy: the PBoC, NDRC, and CSRC unified guidelines in the Green Bond Endorsed Project Catalogue (2021), which lists eligible green projects (notably excluding clean coal from 2021 onward to better align with global norms). This acts similarly to a taxonomy, guiding banks and issuers on what qualifies as green. China and the EU have also collaborated on a Common Ground Taxonomy for mapping

(continued)

Table 2.2 (continued)

Aspect	US	EU	China
Green bond regulations	The US has no dedicated green bond regulation. Green municipal bonds benefit from certain tax incentives (e.g. Qualified Energy Conservation Bonds in the past), but corporate green bonds are self-labeled following market principles. The SEC has started to punish egregious cases of greenwashing—e.g. in 2022, the SEC fined an asset manager for mischaracterizing its ESG fund criteria—signaling that misleading green bond marketing could trigger enforcement. Additionally, the SEC's climate risk rule (if enacted) would indirectly enforce disclosure of use-of-proceeds for climate-focused debt	No mandatory green bond law (issuers can choose whether to label a bond green), but the voluntary EU Green Bond Standard provides an official benchmark. In the interim, European issuers overwhelmingly follow ICMA's GBP. Enforcement of green bond claims comes via market scrutiny and, if misrepresentation occurs, general EU securities laws. Notably, EU regulators (ESMA and national authorities) are preparing to supervise external reviewers of green bonds to ensure quality and avoid "label shopping"	Regulators tightly guide the green bond market. The PBoC and NDRC require that issuers of labeled green bonds allocate at least 70% (formerly 100% for some categories) of funds to green projects, with unambiguous categories defined in the Catalogue. Pre-issuance approval is often needed (especially for state-owned entities), and post-issuance reports on use of proceeds are mandatory. While external reviews are encouraged (and many Chinese issuers obtain them), some bonds are self-labeled; regulators have recently increased oversight to harmonize standards with international norms

Source: Made by the authors

In the following, we survey representative national initiatives focusing on how each is enforcing climate finance standards and coordinating internationally.

China: Green Finance Taxonomy and Guidelines

China has emerged as a major player in green finance, with a regulatory approach that emphasizes taxonomy clarity, quota-guided lending, and gradual disclosure mandates. A linchpin of China's strategy is the Green Bond Endorsed Project Catalogue, first issued by the People's Bank of China (PBoC) in 2015 and updated in 2021. This Catalogue serves as China's official list of projects eligible for green bond financing, effectively functioning as a taxonomy. It covers projects in renewable energy, clean transport, sustainable water, etc., and significantly, the 2021 update removed "clean coal" and other fossil fuel projects to more closely align with international definitions of green. Chinese regulators—including the PBoC, China Securities Regulatory Commission (CSRC), and National Development and Reform Commission—have coordinated so that all types of domestic green bonds adhere to a unified classification standard, reducing greenwashing risk from inconsistent definitions. Green bond issuers in China are required to allocate the majority of proceeds (typically at least 70%) to projects listed in the Catalogue and to report on the use of proceeds in annual reports. Many issuers also obtain third-party verification through agencies approved by the PBoC, though this is not yet mandatory for all issues.

Beyond bonds, China has integrated climate priorities into banking regulation. Through its Green Credit Guidelines and subsequent policies, bank lending is steered toward greener projects (e.g. banks must report their green loan balances, and the PBoC offers incentives such as relending facilities for climate-friendly loans). In terms of disclosure, China is moving from voluntary to mandatory. The CSRC has issued guidelines urging listed companies to disclose environmental information, and announced that by the end of 2025 environmental (including climate) disclosure will be compulsory for all listed firms. This push has been accelerated in part by international pressure—China is a member of the G20 and co-chaired the G20 Sustainable Finance Working Group, signaling support for TCFD principles. Indeed, pilot initiatives are underway: for example, the Shanghai and Shenzhen stock exchanges have encouraged TCFD-aligned reporting for certain large companies, and a handful of Chinese financial institutions participate in the Network for Greening the Financial System climate risk stress tests. In the financial sector, the PBoC conducted climate stress test exercises on major banks in 2021–2022 to assess vulnerabilities under carbon transition scenarios, effectively nudging those banks to improve climate risk management.

Enforcement in China relies on a top-down yet progressively tightening approach. Initially, green finance standards were mostly incentive based (e.g. providing reputational benefits or cheaper funding for green projects). But over time, regulators introduced hard requirements: e.g. banks must meet green lending quotas, and issuers of green bonds on certain exchanges must follow mandatory rules on proceeds and reporting. The government also uses moral suasion—public rankings of banks by their green finance performance—to encourage compliance. While China's disclosure regime is not as comprehensive or transparent as the EU's yet, its taxonomy is very detailed and leaves less room for greenwashing in what qualifies as a "green" project. Furthermore, China has worked with the EU on the Common Ground Taxonomy, mapping intersections between their standards to facilitate cross-border green capital flows. This cooperative stance indicates that China seeks international credibility for its climate finance efforts.

In summary, China's climate finance regulation is characterized by clear definitions, guided flows (via bonds and loans), and a transition toward mandatory disclosure, all enforced through a mix of regulatory mandates and incentives. As the world's largest developing economy and carbon emitter, China's stringent green finance guidelines (especially the exclusion of coal in green bonds) send a powerful signal and help raise global standards (Montiel et al., 2019; Financial Stability Board, 2023).

US: Climate Disclosure Rules and Market Enforcement

In the US, climate finance regulation has, until recently, lagged Europe in formal rules, relying more on market-driven initiatives and general anti-fraud statutes. However, this is rapidly changing. The SEC in March 2022 proposed a landmark climate disclosure rule that would mandate all publicly listed companies to include extensive climate-related information in their annual 10-K filings. This rule (expected to be finalized in 2024) draws heavily on TCFD: companies would have to disclose their climate governance and strategy, material climate risks (physical and transition), metrics like Scope 1 and 2 GHG emissions (and Scope 3 emissions if material or if the company has set emissions targets covering Scope 3), as well as climate-related financial statement impacts. Such disclosures, once in force, will be subject to the same legal liability as financial disclosures—a strong enforcement mechanism to ensure accuracy. The proposed rule has generated considerable debate, but if implemented, it will put the US on a similar footing to the EU and the UK regarding corporate climate transparency. In anticipation, many large US companies have already started voluntary climate reporting, consistent with TCFD to prepare for compliance.

Parallel to the corporate disclosure rule, the SEC has also turned its attention to investment funds and greenwashing. In 2022, the SEC proposed changes to its "Names Rule" to prevent funds from using misleading ESG labels. Under the proposal, a fund calling itself "Climate Friendly" or "Sustainable" would need to invest at least 80% of its assets in ways consistent with that strategy and provide clarity on what criteria it uses. The SEC also proposed enhanced ESG disclosure requirements for asset managers, forcing them to reveal the criteria and data underlying any ESG claims. Even before these rules are finalized, enforcement has begun: the SEC's Climate and ESG Task Force brought one of its first cases in 2022 against BNY Mellon Investment Management, fining it for misrepresenting how it applied ESG screens in some funds. Another high-profile investigation involved DWS (linked to the global case mentioned earlier) and Goldman Sachs Asset Management, indicating US regulators are willing to penalize exaggerated sustainability claims. Moreover, the US Department of Justice and state attorneys general have shown interest in climate and ESG disclosures, raising the stakes for companies—false or misleading climate statements could trigger not just SEC action but also consumer protection lawsuits (as seen in cases where NGOs challenged banks' climate pledges, accusing them of deception).

Apart from disclosures, the US does not have a national green taxonomy or specific green bond regulation, but it employs other tools to influence climate finance. For instance, federal procurement and subsidies have climate strings attached (the Inflation Reduction Act of 2022 provides massive funding for clean energy which indirectly steers private finance). Bank regulators (e.g., Federal Reserve) have started incorporating climate risk into supervisory frameworks: the Fed ran a pilot climate risk analysis with big banks in 2023, and the Office of the Comptroller of the Currency has issued principles for climate risk management at banks. These are not binding capital rules yet, but they signal that banks should monitor and disclose climate-related risks in their portfolios.

Internationally, the US has engaged in harmonization efforts through bodies like IOSCO and the G20. The SEC's proposed climate rule, while domestically oriented, is quite aligned with global norms (TCFD and ISSB), meaning US companies would be reporting similar information as European or Asian companies—a boon for investors making cross-country comparisons. And while the US has not embraced a taxonomy, it participates in dialogues on sustainable finance taxonomy (through the IPSF as an observer) to ensure any future developments (perhaps at state levels or industry-led standards) consider global standards.

In summary, the US is moving from a largely laissez-faire approach (where climate finance was driven by investor demand and voluntary action) to a more regulatory approach focusing on transparency and truthfulness. The combination of the SEC's climate disclosure mandate and anti-greenwashing enforcement means that market discipline is being backed by the force of law. Companies and financial institutions will have to back up climate pledges and product labels with data—or face legal consequences. Given the US's global financial influence, these steps are highly significant in pushing climate finance standards forward (Financial Stability Board, 2017; ISSB, 2023; Salvi et al., 2025).

EU: Comprehensive and Enforced Climate Finance Rules

The EU is widely seen as the frontrunner in climate finance regulation, with a multipronged framework that spans disclosures, taxonomies, product standards, and prudential rules. We have already discussed two key pillars—the SFDR and EU Taxonomy—which together create a comprehensive system for defining and reporting sustainable (including climate-aligned) activities. Here we highlight implementation and enforcement aspects, as well as additional EU initiatives, to illustrate how the EU's approach functions in practice and interacts internationally (European Parliament, 2019).

Disclosure and Reporting: The EU's Corporate Sustainability Reporting Directive (CSRD), effective 2024, will dramatically expand climate and sustainability reporting to ~50,000 companies (up from ~11,000 under the old Non-Financial Reporting Directive). Companies will report in line with detailed European Sustainability Reporting Standards (ESRS) that cover climate change in depth (largely mirroring TCFD requirements, but with even more granular metrics). These reports will be subject to mandatory external assurance by auditors by 2025, meaning a company's climate data (GHG emissions, targets, etc.) must be verified—a strong quality control measure. Non-compliance could lead to regulatory sanctions in each member state. Additionally, the SFDR and the forthcoming EU "MiFID ESG" rules compel financial advisors and asset managers to consider clients' climate preferences and to disclose how products align with climate objectives. This regulatory ecosystem is enforced by European Supervisory Authorities (ESMA, EBA, EIOPA) in conjunction with national regulators. For example, funds that misclassify themselves under SFDR can be forced to reclassify or face penalties; indeed, in late 2022 and 2023 many funds downgraded themselves from Article 9 to 8 amid stricter guidance, showing the regulator's bite in policing labels.

EU Green Bond Standard (EuGB): In 2023, EU legislators approved the creation of an official Green Bond Standard. Participation is voluntary—an issuer may choose to label a bond as "European Green Bond (EU GB)"—but if they do, they must meet stringent requirements. These include 100% Taxonomy-aligned use of proceeds (with limited flexibility for temporary holdings), pre-issuance review by an accredited External Reviewer, and detailed allocation and impact reporting, all under supervision of ESMA. The EuGB is intended to set a high bar and spur best practices: even if many issuers continue issuing green bonds under ICMA's more flexible regime, the existence of EuGB provides a benchmark for excellence (and perhaps, over time, a price advantage if investors prefer officially labeled bonds). The standard also has an international cooperation angle: non-EU issuers can use it, and the hope is to inspire similar robust standards elsewhere or even work toward mutual recognition (e.g. if another jurisdiction creates an official standard, the EU might seek harmonization). By legislating a green bond standard, the EU moves voluntary market norms into a regulatory domain—a response to concerns that voluntary adherence alone did not eliminate greenwashing in some cases.

Prudential and Other Measures: The EU is also exploring climate finance through bank and insurance regulation. The European Central Bank (ECB) now explicitly integrates climate risks into its supervisory reviews and ran its first climate stress test for banks in 2022. While EU banks are not yet required to hold extra capital for climate-risky assets, discussions (including at the Basel Committee level) continue on whether a "green supporting" or "brown penalizing" factor is justified. Additionally, the EU's Benchmark Regulation introduced Climate Transition Benchmarks and Paris-aligned Benchmarks to guide investors—index providers must follow certain decarbonization criteria to label indices as such, ensuring passive investments also align with climate goals.

Enforcement and International Alignment: Enforcement of EU climate finance rules can be seen in actions like the European Securities and Markets Authority (ESMA) clamping down on fund greenwashing and national regulators (e.g. BaFin in Germany, AMF in France) issuing guidance and conducting examinations of ESG claims. As noted, one of the largest greenwashing fines to date involved DWS in Germany (though prosecuted under existing laws), exemplifying Europe's willingness to penalize misrepresentation. Moreover, the European Banking Authority (EBA) in 2023 explicitly warned banks of rising greenwashing risk and is working on guidelines for ESG risk management. On the international front, the EU actively pushes for convergence: it co-founded the International Platform on Sustainable Finance (IPSF) to share taxonomy approaches, and it coordinated with the IFRS/

ISSB such that the EU's own climate reporting standards (ESRS E1) have mappings to IFRS S2 (to ensure companies can comply with both with minimal friction). There is ongoing work between the ISSB and EU to reconcile any differences in climate disclosure requirements. The EU's leadership has effectively set a benchmark—jurisdictions like the UK have emulated parts of SFDR and taxonomy, and many emerging markets look to the EU model when crafting their policies.

In sum, the EU's climate finance regulatory regime is holistic and institutionalized. It addresses the problem of greenwashing and climate transparency from multiple angles—corporate disclosures, investor disclosures, product standards, and definitions of sustainability—all backed by legal force. This comprehensive approach, enforced by regulators and aligned with international standards, aims to ensure that climate finance in Europe is not just abundant but also credible and impactful. Real-world examples from the EU (e.g., French institutional investors disclosing portfolio alignment with 1.5 °C goals under national law, or German companies adjusting business models to meet Taxonomy criteria) illustrate that these rules are influencing behavior and accelerating the climate transition. The EU's experience also highlights challenges: implementing detailed standards can be complex and costly, and regulators must continuously update criteria (e.g., debates over whether gas and nuclear power belong in the Taxonomy). Nonetheless, the EU's strong stance has indisputably raised the global bar for climate finance governance.

UK: TCFD Mandates and the Road to SDR

The UK, while no longer part of the EU after Brexit, has crafted its own robust climate finance framework, often complementary to or building on global standards. In 2019, the UK became one of the first countries to signpost that TCFD-aligned disclosures would become mandatory. This was phased in: starting with premium-listed companies on the London Stock Exchange (from 2021) and large financial institutions (asset managers, insurers, pension schemes in 2022) and extending to nearly all large companies by 2023. The UK Financial Conduct Authority (FCA) and Prudential Regulation Authority (PRA) supervise these requirements, reviewing company reports for compliance. As a result, many British companies have been disclosing board oversight of climate risks, conducting scenario analyses, and reporting their emissions and climate targets in line with TCFD. This early adoption of TCFD by the UK set an example internationally and also gave UK financial institutions a headstart in adjusting to climate transparency expectations.

Beyond disclosures, the UK government is developing a broader framework called Sustainability Disclosure Requirements (SDR). Announced in 2021 and refined in 2023, SDR will encompass corporate disclosures (likely incorporating the ISSB standards into UK company law), asset manager and product disclosures, and even a requirement for firms to publish net-zero transition plans. A new Transition Plan Taskforce in the UK has outlined guidelines for what a credible corporate climate transition plan should include, and the government has indicated that such plans could become mandatory for large companies and financial institutions on a comply-or-explain basis. The FCA has also proposed a sustainable investment labeling regime as part of SDR: under this, investment products (including funds) could carry labels such as "Sustainable Focus" or "Sustainable Improver" if they meet certain criteria, helping retail investors distinguish truly climate-conscious products from others. This is effectively the UK's answer to SFDR, aiming to prevent greenwashing in how funds are marketed to consumers.

On the taxonomy front, the UK initially planned to copy over the EU Taxonomy (since much technical work was done) and adapt it to UK-specific goals (such as including nuclear energy, which the EU taxonomy eventually did as well, or excluding certain technologies based on UK climate strategy). A UK Green Taxonomy was expected in 2022, but as of end-2025 its implementation has been delayed amid reviews to simplify the approach. The current expectation is that the UK will still introduce a taxonomy but perhaps take a more principle-based, less granular approach than the EU's. In the interim, UK green bond issuers typically adhere to ICMA principles and often get CBI certification; similarly, UK companies raising sustainability-linked loans or bonds follow market standards with input from the FCA's greenwashing guidance. The Green Finance Institute in London and other industry groups have been active in promoting best practices and could help shape the forthcoming taxonomy.

The UK has also integrated climate considerations into prudential regulation and central banking. The Bank of England was one of the first central banks to integrate climate change into its mandate and conducted a comprehensive climate stress test of major banks and insurers in 2021. The results (published in 2022) highlighted substantial exposures in certain portfolios under disorderly transition scenarios, reinforcing the need for firms to manage these risks. While the Bank of England did not (yet) adjust capital requirements, it set expectations for firms to include climate in risk management and indicated that if banks do not adequately address climate risks, capital add-ons could be considered. Moreover, the UK has altered its corporate bond purchase scheme (during quantitative easing) to tilt toward greener issuers—a form of climate-tilted monetary policy, albeit modest.

Enforcement in the UK has teeth, especially on disclosure. The FCA can issue fines or public censure for misstatements in financial reports, and the UK's Financial Reporting Council (FRC) can review company reports for TCFD compliance. Additionally, the UK's Advertising Standards Authority has cracked down on misleading environmental claims in financial advertising. For instance, in 2021 the ASA banned two bank advertisements for overstating their green credentials—sending a message that even marketing needs to be truthful. Combined with the possibility of legal action (UK law now allows climate-focused litigation, such as claims under directors' duties or pensions law if climate risks are ignored), these enforcement channels make the UK's climate finance framework fairly robust.

Internationally, the UK positions itself as a convener on climate finance. It used its presidency of COP26 in 2021 to launch the Glasgow Financial Alliance for Net Zero (GFANZ), a coalition of financial institutions committing to net-zero portfolios by 2050, which works in tandem with official regulation. The UK also was early to endorse ISSB's efforts and has signaled it will adopt the ISSB standards in its SDR framework. By aligning with global norms (TCFD/ISSB) and also innovating (e.g. mandatory transition plans), the UK contributes to setting high international benchmarks.

In summary, the UK's climate finance regulatory initiative is characterized by mandatory risk disclosure, forthcoming holistic sustainability reporting, and a focus on transition planning. Real-world examples include large British banks like HSBC and Barclays publishing detailed TCFD reports and announcing plans to phase out coal financing—a response not only to stakeholder pressure but also to the scrutiny of regulators on whether their strategies are Paris-aligned. The UK's pragmatic yet progressive approach shows how a country can leverage both hard rules and soft power (industry alliances, global forums) to advance climate finance objectives.

Academic Perspectives

The expansion of climate finance governance has generated a growing academic literature on whether standards and regulation improve transparency, deter greenwashing, influence pricing, and shift capital allocation. Several themes are particularly influential.

Signaling Effects and the "Greenium"

One well-documented phenomenon is the pricing differential (often called the "greenium") observed for green financial instruments. A number of studies have found that, on average, green bonds tend to have slightly lower yields (higher prices) than comparable conventional bonds. This suggests investors are willing to accept a lower return in exchange for the green label—either due to preferences for sustainable investments or expectations of lower risks. Crucially, the magnitude of this greenium appears to depend on the credibility of the label.

Zhou et al. (2025) show that in the European bond market, green labels significantly reduce required yields in the long run, and the effect is more pronounced when the green label is externally certified. In their study, self-labeled green bonds (where issuers just declare a bond is green) did exhibit a yield benefit, but it was smaller and mainly attributed to a weak signaling effect. By contrast, bonds adhering to rigorous standards (like those aligned with ICMA/CBI and reviewed by third parties) enjoyed a larger greenium driven by both signaling and investors' pro-environmental preferences. These findings reinforce a central argument of climate finance: standards serve as signals of quality. When an issuer follows recognized principles or obtains certification, it sends a credible signal to the market about the bond's environmental integrity, which investors reward. Conversely, without standards, green claims might be discounted by investors.

Another study by Baker et al. (2022) finds that US municipal green bonds saw yield reductions particularly when there was third-party verification, indicating the market's sensitivity to credibility. In equity markets, research on stock price reactions (e.g. Flammer, 2021) found that companies announcing a certified green bond issuance experienced a positive stock jump, whereas uncertified green bond announcements did not—again underscoring the value of external standards as a signal of genuine commitment.

Market Discipline and Transparency

A key rationale for climate disclosure mandates (like TCFD or ISSB) is that "sunlight is the best disinfectant". By forcing firms to reveal their climate risks and strategies, investors and stakeholders can better assess who is a climate leader or laggard, and capital can reprice accordingly. Emerging evidence supports this disciplining function.

Salvi et al. (2025) examine firms' market performance and find that greater transparency on climate issues enhances investor confidence and reduces perceived risk, leading to a lower cost of capital for firms with better climate disclosure. In practical terms, as companies publish more complete and credible climate data (such as emissions or scenario analyses), investors incorporate this information—for example, firms with lower carbon footprints or robust transition plans may see their stock volatility decrease and valuations improve relative to high-carbon peers.

Another study focusing on TCFD compliance in the financial sector (Hasan et al., 2025) found that banks in jurisdictions with mandatory TCFD reports tend to reduce high-carbon lending faster than those without, suggesting that disclosure coupled with stakeholder scrutiny can prompt real decarbonization actions. In Taiwan, where regulators mandated TCFD reports for financial institutions, researchers attributed improvements in banks' decarbonization efforts to the heightened stakeholder scrutiny enabled by those disclosures. This aligns with broader observations: when climate data is out in the open, activist investors, NGOs, and even customers can exert pressure, whereas previously climate risks were opaque and often ignored in decision-making.

However, transparency alone is not a panacea; the data must be reliable and comparable. This is where standardization (ISSB, taxonomy metrics) plays a vital role—ensuring that what one company calls "emissions avoided" or "green revenue" is measured similarly by another. Without such standardization, disclosures could confuse rather than clarify. Hence, academics have been supportive of efforts like the ISSB's global baseline as likely to improve market efficiency by making climate performance easier to compare and reward.

Credibility, Labels, and Greenwashing

Scholars have also scrutinized the credibility of various climate finance labels and whether some amount to "greenwashing lite". For instance, not all green bonds are created equal—some might finance clearly impactful projects like wind farms, while others might fund projects of more debatable greenness. Zhou et al. (2025), in their analysis of green bond labels, concluded that externally certified bonds derive their pricing benefit from both a signaling effect and genuine investor preference, whereas self-labeled bonds reflect mostly signaling and potentially skepticism. They highlight that investors "value the reassurance that third-party certifications provide about the ethical use of bond proceeds", and thus stricter oversight (e.g. verification of how proceeds are spent) enhances the integrity of the market.

Another study by Cheng et al. (2022) looked at various green bond frameworks and suggested that those under more stringent standards showed better post-issuance reporting and environmental impact, lending credence to the idea that strong standards correlate with better environmental performance. On the fund side, research by Ceccarelli et al. (2023) found that many ESG-labeled funds before SFDR did not significantly differ from conventional funds in holdings—essentially label arbitrage. However, after SFDR's implementation, there is evidence that Article 9 funds started aligning portfolios more closely with sustainable objectives, as fund managers adjusted to meet the higher bar. This indicates regulation pushed labels to be more meaningful. Yet, challenges remain: academics caution about "impact washing"—funds claiming to have real-world impact without evidence—and emphasize the need for ongoing monitoring and potentially refining standards (e.g. SFDR's criteria for Article 9 were tightened to require 100% sustainable investments, prompting downgrades of funds that could not comply).

Overall, the literature finds that credible standards can mitigate greenwashing by reducing information asymmetry. However, if standards are too lenient or allow excessive flexibility, firms might technically comply while still engaging in greenwashing. For example, some companies might set distant net-zero targets without interim goals—ticking the disclosure box but not fundamentally changing. This has led researchers to argue for enforcement of not just disclosure but performance: proposals include linking executive compensation to climate metrics or requiring evidence of progress for continued use of green labels. The theme of verification is also prominent: independent audits or third-party reviews (for bonds, for sustainability reports) are seen as critical to uphold trust, which is why moves by regulators to regulate ESG ratings or verifiers are welcomed in academic circles.

Enforcement and Regulatory Effectiveness

Finally, studies have begun evaluating how effective these regulations are on the ground. One approach is to look at outcomes like emissions or capital flows. For instance, Schreiner and Beyer (2024) found banks subject to climate-related supervisory expectations in Europe shifted lending away from fossil fuels faster than those that were not—a sign that even soft regulation can bite. More data-driven analyses show that after the EU's mandatory disclosure of portfolio climate alignment (under Article 173 in France and now SFDR/Taxonomy), portfolios started to slowly decarbonize, as asset managers did not want to be seen lagging peers. Research on green bond impact (e.g. Flammer, 2021) found that companies issuing green bonds tend to increase their environmental investments and cut more CO_2 than similar non-issuers, implying that committing to the green bond standard had a real impact on corporate behavior. However, a strain of literature also warns of potential unintended consequences: if standards are too stringent, some issuers/investors might exit the "green" label space altogether (a few studies note a slight drop in new Article 9 funds right after SFDR's stricter rules, though this might be temporary). Moreover, if only a subset of firms adopts voluntary standards, there could be a selection effect—companies with better climate performance are more likely to disclose (making themselves look good) while poor performers stay silent (hiding their risk), which suggests mandates are needed to bring laggards in.

Enforcement is repeatedly flagged as the differentiator between well-intentioned policy and actual change. The DWS case in 2025 (discussed earlier) is a real-world example analyzed in commentary: it showed that substantial fines and public enforcement can jolt the industry into rigor. The academic consensus is forming that consistent enforcement (and litigation where needed) is essential to give "teeth" to climate finance rules. Some researchers have started examining climate-related litigation risk as a form of enforcement: as more countries put climate duties on companies and fiduciaries, lawsuits by investors or NGOs might become an enforcement mechanism of last resort, especially in the US and the EU.

In summary, recent academic research largely validates the direction of current climate finance standards—they are found to improve transparency, create valuable signaling mechanisms, and channel capital modestly but measurably toward greener projects. Yet, research also highlights the need for continual improvement of standards (to close loopholes and keep up with evolving science) and robust enforcement or assurance to maintain credibility. Themes like the importance of third-party certification, the benefit of harmonization (to avoid "forum shopping" for weaker standards), and the empowerment of stakeholders via information are recurrent. In essence, the literature suggests that when done right, climate finance regulations can leverage market forces (investor preferences, reputational concerns) to reward genuine sustainability efforts—thereby making market discipline an ally of climate action. Conversely, weak or fragmented standards could dilute this power. Thus, the push for international convergence (e.g. ISSB global baseline, taxonomy alignment efforts) seen in policy circles is strongly supported by academics as a way to enhance effectiveness and minimize arbitrage.

Conclusion

Standards and regulations in climate finance have swiftly evolved from niche considerations to core components of the financial system's response to climate change. Motivated by the pressing problem of greenwashing and the imperative to align finance with the Paris Agreement, policymakers worldwide have introduced a mosaic of disclosure rules, taxonomies, and product standards. This chapter has traced that evolution: from international frameworks like the EU Taxonomy, SFDR, TCFD, and ISSB that set common guidelines, to national implementations in China, the US, the EU, and the UK that illustrate different paths toward the same goal—a transparent, credible, and accountable climate finance market. A clear thread through all these efforts is the balancing act between flexibility and rigor: the need to mobilize innovation and capital at scale, while ensuring integrity and preventing "green" from becoming a mere marketing slogan. Early evidence and academic research are encouraging, indicating that well-designed standards do make a difference—they bring tangible signaling benefits, sharpen market discipline, and reduce information asymmetries, all of which help drive capital toward genuinely sustainable activities.

Yet, the journey is far from complete. As climate science and technologies advance, standards will need to be updated; as markets globalize, regulations will need to harmonize. The interaction of various frameworks—say, how a Chinese bank using the national catalogue reports to a European investor under SFDR, or how a US company's ISSB-aligned report satisfies UK regulators—will require ongoing cooperation and mutual recognition. Ultimately, climate finance standards are tools to build trust: trust that a green label has real impact, trust that disclosed risks are not hidden, trust that finance is playing its part in the climate transition. Maintaining that trust will require vigilance by regulators (enforcing rules), responsibility by market participants (avoiding the temptation to game definitions), and continued research to inform policy adjustments. For the graduate student or professional reading this, the landscape of climate finance standards is not just a set of rules to memorize—it is a living, adapting framework that will shape where and how trillions of dollars are invested in the coming decades. By understanding its current architecture and the evidence of what works, one is better equipped to contribute to its future refinement and to ensure that the promise of climate finance—mobilizing capital for a sustainable, net-zero world—is fulfilled with integrity and impact.

References

Bachelet, M. J., Becchetti, L., & Manfredonia, S. (2019). The green bonds premium puzzle: The role of issuer characteristics and third-party verification. *Sustainability, 11*(4), 1098.

Baker, M., Bergstresser, D., Serafeim, G., & Wurgler, J. (2022). The pricing and ownership of US green bonds. *Annual Review of Financial Economics, 14*, 415–437.

Berg, F., Kölbel, J. F., & Rigobon, R. (2022). Aggregate confusion: The divergence of ESG ratings. *Review of Finance, 26*(6), 1315–1344.

Bolton, P., & Kacperczyk, M. (2021). Do investors care about carbon risk? *Journal of Financial Economics, 142*(2), 517–549.

CBI. (2021). *Climate bonds standard: Version 4.0*. Climate Bonds Initiative.

Ceccarelli, M., Ramelli, S., & Wagner, A. F. (2023). Low carbon mutual funds. *Review of Finance, 28*(1), 45–74.

Cheng, G., Ehlers, T., & Packer, F. (2022). Sovereigns and sustainable bonds: Challenges and new options. *BIS Quarterly Review*.

European Parliament. (2019). *Regulation (EU) 2019/2088 of 27 November 2019 on sustainability-related disclosures in the financial services sector (SFDR)*. European Parliament.

European Parliament. (2020). *Regulation (EU) 2020/852 of 18 June 2020 on the establishment of a framework to facilitate sustainable investment (EU Taxonomy Regulation)*. European Parliament.

European Parliament. (2022). *Directive (EU) 2022/2464 of 14 December 2022 as regards corporate sustainability reporting (CSRD)*. European Parliament.

File, C. (2023). *Global greenwashing regulations: How the world is cracking down on misleading sustainability claims*. Sustainalytics.

Financial Stability Board. (2017). *Final report: Recommendations of the task force on climate-related financial disclosures*. Financial Stability Board.

Financial Stability Board. (2023). *Progress report on climate-related disclosures*. Financial Stability Board.

Flammer, C. (2021). Corporate green bonds. *Journal of Financial Economics, 142*(2), 499–516.

Hasan, I., Lee, H., Qiu, B., & Saunders, A. (2025). Climate-related disclosure commitment of the lenders, credit rationing, and borrower environmental performance. *Review of Accounting Studies, 31*, 74–117.

ICMA. (2021). *Green bond principles: Voluntary process guidelines for issuing green bonds*. International Capital Market Association.

Ilhan, E., Sautner, Z., & Vilkov, G. (2020). Carbon tail risk. *The Review of Financial Studies, 34*(3), 1540–1571.

IOSCO. (2023). *IOSCO endorsement of ISSB standards IFRS S1 and IFRS S2*. International Organization of Securities Commissions.

ISSB. (2023). *IFRS S1: General requirements for disclosure of sustainability-related financial information; IFRS S2: Climate-related disclosures*. IFRS Foundation.

Larcker, D. F., & Watts, E. M. (2020). Where's the greenium? *Journal of Accounting and Economics, 69*(2), 101312.

Lyon, T. P., & Maxwell, J. W. (2011). Greenwash: Corporate environmental disclosure under threat of audit. *Journal of Economics & Management Strategy, 20*(1), 3–41.

Lyon, T. P., & Montgomery, W. (2015). The means and end of greenwash. *Organization & Environment, 28*(2), 223–249.

Montiel, I., Christmann, P., & Zink, T. (2019). The effect of sustainability standard uncertainty on certification decisions of firms in emerging economies. *Journal of Business Ethics, 154*(3), 667–681.

Reuters. (2025). *Deutsche Bank-owned asset manager DWS fined $27 million for greenwashing*. Reuters.

Salvi, A., L'Abate, V., Petruzzella, F., Vitolla, F., & Raimo, N. (2025). Rising temperatures, rising transparency: Revealing the financial benefits of climate change disclosure. *International Review of Economics & Finance, 101*, 104208.
Scherer, B., & Hasaj, M. (2023). Greenlabelling: How valuable is the SFDR Art 9 label? *Journal of Asset Management, 24*(7), 541–546.
Schreiner, L., & Beyer, A. (2024). The impact of ECB Banking Supervision on climate risk and sustainable finance. In *ECB Working Paper Series*, 2952.
SEC. (2022). *The enhancement and standardization of climate-related disclosures for investors (proposed rule)*. Securities and Exchange Commission.
UN. (2026). *Greenwashing: Deceptive environmental claims and tactics*. United Nations.
Zerbib, O. D. (2019). The effect of pro-environmental preferences on bond prices: Evidence from green bonds. *Journal of Banking & Finance, 98*, 39–60.
Zhou, P., Jin, S., Mazouz, K., & Ding, W. (2025). Choices and effects of different green labels in the EU bond market. *Journal of Business Ethics, 200*(1), 207–229.

Part II
Green Bonds and the Net-Zero Transition

Chapter 3
Corporate Green Bonds

Introduction

In late 2007, a group of Swedish pension funds approached the World Bank with a novel request: to invest in projects that help the climate. Less than a year later, in November 2008, the World Bank issued the first-ever green bond, transforming development finance and sparking a sustainability revolution in capital markets. This pioneering issuance—bonds dedicated exclusively to financing climate-focused projects—created a blueprint for linking investor capital with climate solutions. It demonstrated that capital markets could be mobilized at scale for environmental good without sacrificing financial rigor. In the years since, the green bond market has evolved from a niche experiment by multilateral institutions into a mainstream financing mechanism embraced by corporations, governments, and investors worldwide. This chapter focuses on corporate green bonds—bonds issued by private companies to fund environmentally beneficial activities—and their role in the net-zero transition. From the concept's emergence and early market formation to its development in major economies, we explore how corporate green bonds have grown into a cornerstone of climate finance. We also review academic research on their financial and environmental performance, and analyze implications for policy, corporate strategy, and investment practices. The story of corporate green bonds is one of innovations at the intersection of finance and sustainability: a story that begins with visionary first movers and continues today with a global push to align capital flows with the Paris Agreement and net-zero goals.

Corporate green bonds are debt securities issued by private-sector firms in which proceeds are earmarked for eligible green expenditures and governed by a disclosure and reporting regime. In the net-zero transition, their practical role is straightforward: deep decarbonization requires large, front-loaded capital expenditures in power, buildings, transport, and industrial processes, and corporate balance sheets and capital markets must finance a substantial share of that investment. The green

P. Zhou, D. Guo, *Climate Finance in the Net-Zero Transition*, Contributions to Finance and Accounting, https://doi.org/10.1007/978-981-92-0827-2_3

bond format can reduce information frictions by linking funding to a defined green asset or expenditure base, often supported by external review.

We begin with green bonds because they are the most established and widely used instrument through which climate finance has been implemented in mainstream capital markets. Among labeled instruments, green bonds have moved furthest toward institutionalization: they are issued by corporates, sovereigns, and development institutions, and are purchased by a broad investor base that includes both dedicated sustainable funds and conventional fixed-income managers. Their scale and market depth make them an especially informative starting point for understanding how climate objectives are translated into standard financial contracts, disclosure practices, and secondary-market behavior. Green bonds are also analytically valuable because they concentrate a central challenge of climate finance—credibility. A green bond is typically a conventional debt instrument distinguished mainly by its use-of-proceeds commitment and associated reporting. As a result, the instrument's climate value depends less on contractual cash flows than on governance: eligibility definitions, proceeds management, impact reporting, and verification. The rise of green bonds has therefore accelerated the development of standards, external reviews, and regulatory attention designed to reduce greenwashing and improve comparability. Studying green bonds early in the book thus provides a concrete way to link the conceptual foundations of climate finance to the institutional "rules of the game" that make climate-aligned capital allocation credible.

For these reasons, this part uses green bonds as an entry point to climate finance implementation. The objective is not to treat green bonds as the entirety of climate finance, but to use the most mature and observable instrument to establish a consistent evaluative lens—one that distinguishes labels from substance and connects standards to incentives. This foundation prepares the reader for the later parts of the book, which extend the analysis to blue finance and carbon markets, where governance challenges and economy-wide mechanisms become even more consequential.

Conception of Corporate Green Bonds

Green bonds are typically structured as use-of-proceeds instruments: proceeds are allocated to eligible green projects, tracked internally, and reported to investors. The ICMA's Green Bond Principles (GBP), first published in 2014 and updated regularly, formalize expectations along four components: (1) use of proceeds, (2) process for project evaluation and selection, (3) management of proceeds, and (4) reporting (ICMA, 2025). The GBP are voluntary, but they operate as a coordination device across issuers, underwriters, investors, and external reviewers.

For corporates, the implementation burden is not primarily financial engineering, but internal governance. A credible Green Bond Framework requires a defensible definition of eligible categories, clear exclusions, an internal process to select projects, an auditable tracking system for proceeds, and a commitment to post-issuance reporting. In practice, implementation quality varies substantially, and that heterogeneity is a key driver of market outcomes.

The sustainable bond market includes multiple instrument types with distinct incentive properties. OECD (2025) classifies sustainable bonds into two broad categories: use-of-proceeds bonds (green, social, sustainability) and Sustainability-Linked Bonds (SLBs), in which financial characteristics can vary with the issuer's achievement of sustainability performance targets, without requiring earmarking of proceeds (Table 3.1). For corporate finance strategy, the distinction matters because it changes what investors can verify: use-of-proceeds bonds are tied to assets and expenditures, while SLBs are tied to firm-level performance metrics.

As the market expanded, external review became a cornerstone of credibility. External review can take several forms, including second-party opinions, verification, and certification against science-based criteria. The academic literature repeatedly finds that credibility mechanisms are economically meaningful. For example, evidence on pricing differentials suggests that externally reviewed or certified issues are more likely to obtain favorable pricing, and that credibility is central to whether a greenium exists at all (Kapraun et al., 2021; Fatica et al., 2021). For corporates, external review reduces the perceived risk that the green label is used strategically without substantive environmental commitment.

Post-issuance reporting is equally central. Allocation reporting describes where proceeds were used; impact reporting seeks to quantify environmental outcomes (for example, renewable capacity installed, emissions avoided, or energy saved). While impact measurement is technically challenging and often model-based, consistent reporting is a practical discipline that reduces information asymmetry over time. In many jurisdictions, market expectations have converged toward annual reporting until full allocation, and then periodic updates thereafter.

Voluntary guidance supports market formation, but it does not guarantee comparability across jurisdictions. The EU's sustainable finance architecture illustrates a

Table 3.1 Sustainable debt instruments used by corporates

Instrument	What is contractually linked	Typical verification focus	Implementation risk
Green bond	Eligible projects/ expenditures	Eligibility criteria, allocation reporting, and (where possible) impact reporting	Greenwashing via weak definitions or poor reporting
Social bond	Eligible social projects	Project eligibility and reporting	Impact measurement and beneficiary definition
Sustainability bond	Mix of green and social projects	Eligibility and reporting across both domains	Dilution if categories are too broad
SLB	Issuer-level targets	KPI selection, ambition, calibration, and verification of performance	Weak KPIs, target gaming, and limited additionality
Transition bond	Transition investments in hard-to-abate sectors	Credibility of transition plan and asset-level alignment	Reputational risk if transition narrative is contested

shift toward taxonomy-linked regulation. The EU Taxonomy Regulation provides a classification system for environmentally sustainable activities (European Parliament, 2020). The European Green Bond Regulation (EU) 2023/2631 creates the European Green Bond (EuGB) label and specifies disclosure templates, taxonomy-alignment expectations, and the role of external reviewers (European Parliament, 2023). The regulation entered into application on December 21, 2024.

A distinctive implementation feature of the EuGB label is the requirement that at least 85% of net proceeds be allocated to activities aligned with the EU Taxonomy, while allowing a 15% flexibility pocket for specific cases where technical screening criteria are not yet available (European Parliament, 2023). This design aims to balance stringency with usability for sectors and activities that are relevant to the transition but not fully covered by taxonomy criteria.

China's approach has relied on catalog-based definitions and coordinated guidance among regulators. The Green Bond Endorsed Projects Catalogue (2021 Edition), issued jointly by the People's Bank of China, the National Development and Reform Commission, and the China Securities Regulatory Commission, is widely recognized as a major step toward standardization and international alignment (People's Bank of China et al., 2021; Ng, 2022). In parallel, taxonomy convergence efforts under the International Platform on Sustainable Finance, including the Common Ground Taxonomy, reduce cross-border due diligence costs and facilitate international participation (IPSF, 2021).

Implementation of Corporate Green Bonds

Market-level data highlight both the scale and the cyclicality of green bond issuance. CBI estimates that by the end of 2024, cumulative aligned GSS+ volume reached $5.7 trillion, with $1.05 trillion of aligned deals priced in 2024; the green theme accounted for $671.7 billion (CBI, 2025). Within aligned green bonds, private-sector issuers in the financial and non-financial corporate sectors together accounted for 51% of 2024 green volume ($344 billion). Non-financial corporates alone contributed 30% of the 2024 market share, issuing $202 billion across 763 aligned green instruments from 418 issuers.

OECD (2025) provides a complementary perspective using an issuer-sector lens. It reports that in 2024 green bonds were the most important type of sustainable bonds issued by the corporate sector, with $382 billion, and emphasizes that European corporate issuance accounts for roughly half of global corporate sustainable bond issuance (Fig. 3.1). These estimates reinforce a simple point: corporate green bonds have become a mainstream financing channel in the EU-centered fixed-income ecosystem, and corporate issuance is increasingly material in China.

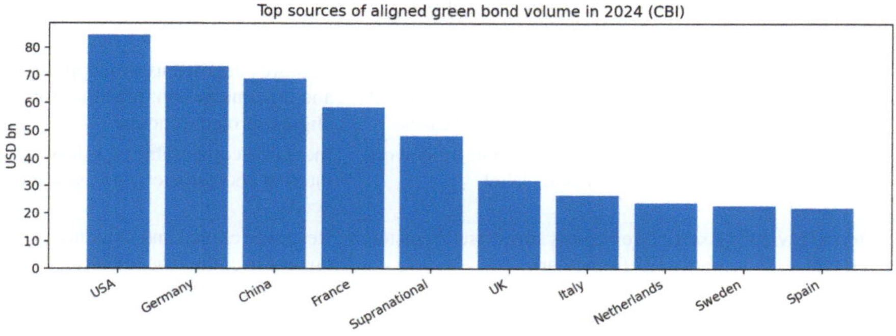

Fig. 3.1 Top sources of aligned green bond volume in 2024

EU: Market Leadership, Standardization, and Implementation Practice

Europe has been the global center of gravity for labeled green bonds, and corporate issuance is particularly important in the euro-denominated credit market. The EU's leadership reflects a combination of deep capital markets, strong institutional investor demand, a substantial pipeline of decarbonization investment, and a regulatory environment that increasingly penalizes ambiguous sustainability claims.

Implementation in the EU is shaped by the interaction between market standards (the GBP) and regulatory architecture (the EU Taxonomy and the EuGB Regulation). For corporates, this interaction matters in day-to-day execution. Taxonomy alignment requires granular asset-level mapping and documentation - especially in sectors such as real estate, transport, and manufacturing where technical screening criteria can be detailed. At the same time, the EuGB label is voluntary; firms may choose to issue under GBP-aligned frameworks without adopting the EuGB label, but investor expectations are shifting toward greater transparency about taxonomy alignment where feasible.

ESMA has been designated as the supervisor of external reviewers for European Green Bonds, an institutional choice intended to reduce variation in review quality and strengthen market integrity (ESMA, 2025). From an issuer's perspective, this implies that external review will not be a simple marketing add-on: reviewer selection, documentation quality, and the ability to provide evidence for taxonomy mapping will become more consequential. For investors, it lowers some due diligence costs, but it does not eliminate the need to assess materiality and additionality.

Real-life implementation examples illustrate how corporate and quasi-corporate issuers use the format (Table 3.2). In France, energy and transport issuers have repeatedly tapped green bond markets to finance renewable generation, grid upgrades, and low-carbon transport infrastructure. In Germany, corporate issuance has been used to fund electric mobility platforms, energy efficiency, and clean manufacturing investments. While issuer strategies differ, a common pattern is the use

Table 3.2 EU corporate green bond implementation

Feature	Requirement (high-level)	Practical implication
Taxonomy allocation threshold	At least 85% of net proceeds to EU Taxonomy-aligned activities; up to 15% flexibility pocket in specified cases	Requires detailed asset mapping and documentation; planning for eligible project pipeline
Pre-issuance disclosure	Standardized templates and framework disclosure for EuGB label	Increases comparability; raises internal coordination and assurance needs
External review oversight	External reviewers supervised/registered under EU framework	Reviewer choice and evidence quality become strategically important
Post-issuance reporting	Allocation reporting and, where feasible, impact reporting using standardized templates	Creates ongoing reporting obligations; can support investor engagement

of green bonds to finance multi-year capital expenditure programs, often with annual allocation reporting that aligns with investor stewardship expectations.

China: Rapid Scaling, Taxonomy Refinement, and Increasing Corporate Participation

China's green bond market expanded rapidly after 2015, supported by coordinated policy initiatives, a substantial domestic investor base, and a large pipeline of eligible investments in energy, transport, and environmental infrastructure. CBI reports that China issued $68.9 billion in aligned green bonds in 2024, making it the third largest source of aligned volume after the US and Germany; China's cumulative aligned issuance reached $442.4 billion by end-2024 (CBI, 2025).

China's regulatory model has prioritized definitional clarity through catalog-based guidance. The Green Bond Endorsed Projects Catalogue (2021 Edition) is widely viewed as a decisive step toward standardization and greater international compatibility, including the removal of certain fossil-fuel related categories (People's Bank of China et al., 2021; Ng, 2022). The policy logic is implementation-oriented: by narrowing eligible categories and improving disclosure expectations, regulators aim to sustain market confidence while maintaining issuance capacity for large-scale investment needs.

A notable feature of China's recent data is the shift in issuer composition. Aligned volumes from financial corporates declined sharply in 2024, while non-financial corporates increased, consistent with a market that is becoming more directly linked to corporate capital expenditure and transition investment rather than primarily reflecting bank issuance to fund green lending (Fig. 3.2).

Implementation practice in China also reflects the coexistence of onshore and offshore issuance. Offshore RMB and foreign-currency green bonds are used by some corporates to diversify funding sources and reach international investor

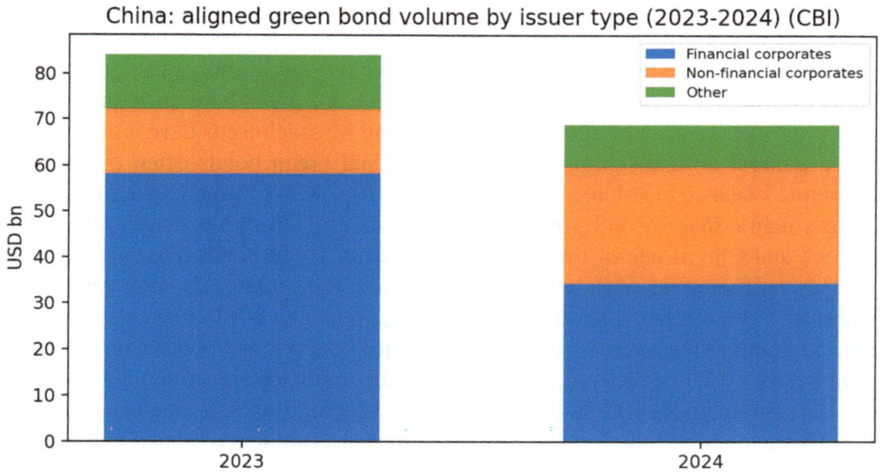

Fig. 3.2 Aligned green bond volume by issuer type of China

segments, while onshore issuance benefits from deep domestic liquidity and policy support. Taxonomy convergence through the Common Ground Taxonomy lowers friction in cross-border participation, particularly for investors who rely on mapped definitions to compare Chinese and European eligible categories (IPSF, 2021).

US: A Significant Market with a Unique Profile

The US has also developed a sizable green bond market, though its structure differs from the EU and China. US green bond issuance began around 2013–2014, initially led by supranationals and municipalities rather than corporates. One early corporate-related green bond was issued by Bank of America Merrill Lynch in 2013 (one of the first corporate green bonds globally, as noted). Subsequently, Apple Inc.'s landmark $1.5 billion green bond in 2016 signaled the entry of blue-chip American corporates; Apple's issue, aimed at financing renewable energy for its facilities and supply chain improvements, was at the time the largest green bond from a US corporation and was heavily oversubscribed, reflecting strong investor interest in corporate sustainability efforts. Since then, several prominent US companies have issued green bonds: Google/Alphabet (to fund clean energy for data centers), Verizon (multiple green bonds to expand its fiber and renewable energy use), PepsiCo and Walmart (to fund sustainable packaging, water-saving, and clean energy in their operations), among others. The US corporate green bond market is broadening beyond tech and consumer brands—utility companies (e.g. Duke Energy, Southern Power) have issued green bonds for renewable projects, and some real estate investment trusts (REITs) issue green bonds for green buildings.

However, the US stands out for the prominence of the municipal green bond segment. Many US cities, states, and public authorities issue green municipal bonds (munis) to finance infrastructure like clean water systems, public transit, and school energy retrofits. For example, New York's MTA has a green bond program for subway improvements, and states like California and Massachusetts have issued sizable green general obligation bonds. These municipal green bonds often overshadow corporate issuance in volume year to year. In 2020–2022, US municipal green bonds were a major share of US green debt. By 2025, the US had become (along with Europe and China) one of the top three sources of green bonds annually, but with roughly half or more of its volume coming from the municipal sector rather than corporates. In the first half of 2025, US corporate green bond issuance actually slowed (amid rising interest rates, US corporates issued fewer bonds overall), dropping nearly 60% year-on-year; interestingly, the municipal green bond issuance in the US rose by about 30% in the same period, keeping total US green issuance stable. This underscores how policy (tax incentives for municipal bonds) and investor appetite for stable, tax-exempt green investments drive the US market in a unique way.

In terms of regulatory frameworks, the US does not have a federal green taxonomy or an official green bond standard. The market has been largely market-led, with US issuers voluntarily aligning with ICMA's GBP (many US corporates obtain second-party opinions for credibility). There is growing scrutiny from regulators on ESG claims—e.g. the SEC has proposed rules to prevent misleading fund names ("green" funds) and is looking at climate risk disclosure rules for companies—but nothing as prescriptive as the EU taxonomy yet. Some US states, like California and New York, are considering their own green bond guidelines, but these are nascent. Thus, US corporate issuers enjoy more flexibility in defining green projects, which can lead to variation in quality. Nonetheless, investor expectations (especially among large institutional investors who are often PRI signatories) push US issuers toward best practices. As a result, many US corporate green bonds also feature robust reporting and external reviews, akin to European issues. For example, Apple has published detailed Green Bond Impact Reports annually, outlining the CO_2 emissions avoided and renewable energy capacity installed via its bond-funded projects.

Looking at issuance volumes: US corporates cumulatively have issued tens of billions in green bonds (e.g., Apple alone at $4.7 billion over 2016–2019, Verizon $3+ billion). The financial sector is increasingly represented—major US banks like Goldman Sachs and Morgan Stanley have issued green bonds (often to finance green loans and mortgages), and even asset-backed green bonds (e.g. mortgage-backed securities for green buildings) have appeared, supported by entities like Fannie Mae (which incidentally has been the world's largest green bond issuer by number of deals, through green mortgage-backed securities). However, outside of a few leaders, many US corporates have been slower to issue green bonds compared to Europeans. Reasons include the absence of regulatory push, and the fact that US companies have alternative financing routes (some prefer sustainability-linked loans or use internal cash for projects). Nevertheless, as investor demand for ESG investments continues to rise and as US federal policy potentially shifts (for instance, with the Inflation Reduction Act of 2022 incentivizing climate investments, companies may issue green bonds to capitalize on those opportunities), we can expect US corporate green bond issuance to grow further. Already by 2025, the US green bond market (corporate + municipal) had surpassed $300 billion outstanding and was growing, albeit at a moderate pace.

In summary, across these major economies: Europe provides the template of a policy-supported, high-standards market with diverse corporate participation; China illustrates rapid scaling under government guidance and the importance of taxonomy alignment; and the US shows a market-driven approach with significant subnational issuance. Together, they account for the bulk of the world's green bond issuance. We now turn to what academic research tells us about these markets—particularly regarding the pricing of green bonds (do they enjoy a "greenium"?), their credibility and transparency, the quality of projects financed, and their environmental impact.

Effects of Corporate Green Bonds

Pricing and the Greenium: What Is Known, and Why It Varies

A core question is whether green bonds reduce issuers' cost of debt. A large empirical literature estimates a yield differential between green and comparable conventional bonds, often termed the greenium. Evidence generally points to a modest average effect and substantial heterogeneity by issuer type, currency, liquidity, and verification quality. Using matched bonds, Zerbib (2019) finds a small but statistically significant yield discount for green bonds, consistent with investors pricing pro-environmental preferences.

Issuer type is a repeated source of heterogeneity. Fatica et al. (2021) show that a yield benefit is more likely for supranational institutions and non-financial corporates than for financial institutions, a pattern consistent with investors finding it easier to map use of proceeds to real assets for corporates than to banks' balance-sheet intermediation. Credibility is similarly central. Kapraun et al. (2021) emphasize that perceived green credibility of the bond and issuer is a key determinant of whether a green premium exists. Bachelet et al. (2019) document that third-party verification is associated with differences in pricing outcomes, reinforcing the practical importance of external review.

Market Reactions and Corporate Behavior: Beyond Bond Yields

Researchers have examined whether issuance affects corporate value and investment behavior. Tang and Zhang (2020) document positive equity-market reactions to green bond announcements and report evidence consistent with increased institutional ownership and enhanced liquidity for green bonds, suggesting that the instrument can broaden the investor base. Flammer (2021) provides evidence that green bond issuance is associated with increases in environmental investments and improvements in emissions-related indicators, indicating that issuance can be linked to real corporate behavior changes rather than purely financial relabeling.

Evidence from China is particularly informative because policy-driven scaling created quasi-experimental variation. Zhang et al. (2021) study Chinese corporate issuances and report that green bond issuance is associated with reductions in corporate cost of capital, using matching approaches. While identification challenges remain, the emerging consensus is that well-designed green bond programs can be associated with measurable shifts in financing terms and corporate investment, especially where credibility mechanisms are strong.

Liquidity, Clientele Effects, and Secondary Market Dynamics

Green bonds are often held by buy-and-hold investors with sustainability mandates, which can tighten spreads but also shape liquidity conditions. Boutabba and Rannou (2022) analyze the term structure of liquidity premia in green bond markets and highlight that investors may demand compensation for liquidity risk across maturities. Liquidity considerations matter for corporate issuers because they influence the stability of pricing benefits and the feasibility of repeat issuance programs. Secondary market dynamics also interact with label credibility: if investors perceive dilution or greenwashing, any pricing advantage can disappear quickly.

Regulation, Verification, and the Shifting Boundary Between Market and Law

The literature increasingly treats the green bond market as an informational environment in which verification and regulation are complements. The EU's decision to regulate a high-standard label (EuGB) and to supervise external reviewers (ESMA, 2025) can be interpreted as an institutional response to a core market failure: investors cannot perfectly observe environmental quality, and weak verification can create adverse selection. For corporates, the implication is that disclosure systems and reviewer engagement are part of capital market access strategy, not simply compliance.

Conclusion

Corporate green bonds have moved decisively into the core of contemporary capital markets. What began as an experimental instrument pioneered by multilateral development banks has become a mainstream financing tool used by firms across sectors, currencies, and jurisdictions. This evolution reflects both necessity and opportunity. The scale of investment required for the net-zero transition is unprecedented, and corporate balance sheets—supported by public and private capital markets—must finance a substantial share of this transformation. Corporate green bonds respond directly to this challenge by linking long-term debt financing to defined environmental expenditures, embedded within disclosure and reporting regimes that reduce information asymmetry between issuers and investors. Several themes emerge clearly from the analysis in this chapter.

First, corporate green bonds are best understood as an institutional technology, not merely a labeled debt instrument. Their economic function lies in their capacity to structure credibility: earmarking proceeds, formalizing internal governance around project selection, and committing firms to post-issuance reporting. These features do not eliminate information problems, but they narrow the space for opportunistic behavior relative to unlabeled debt. The literature consistently shows that where these mechanisms are credible—supported by external review, clear taxonomies, and ongoing reporting—capital markets respond in economically meaningful ways. Yield differentials may be modest on average, but they are persistent, heterogeneous, and strongly conditioned by credibility.

Second, heterogeneity across jurisdictions matters, both for market outcomes and for policy design. The EU's approach emphasizes regulatory codification and standardization, culminating in the European Green Bond Regulation and the supervision of external reviewers. This model seeks to internalize environmental credibility into legal and supervisory structures, reducing reliance on purely reputational discipline. China's approach, by contrast, has prioritized definitional clarity and coordinated administrative guidance, using catalog-based eligibility and policy incentives to scale issuance rapidly while progressively tightening standards. The US and UK remain more market-led, relying heavily on disclosure enforcement and antifraud regulation rather than prescriptive taxonomies, but both are converging toward global baselines through TCFD- and ISSB-aligned reporting. For corporate issuers operating across borders, these differences translate into non-trivial strategic choices about framework design, disclosure depth, and investor targeting.

Third, academic evidence increasingly suggests that corporate green bonds influence real economic behavior, not only financial pricing. Studies linking issuance to subsequent increases in environmental investment, improvements in emissions intensity, and changes in ownership structure indicate that green bonds can operate as commitment devices. By tying financing to specific categories of expenditure and exposing firms to post-issuance scrutiny, green bonds raise the reputational and financial cost of deviation from stated environmental objectives. This effect appears strongest for non-financial corporates, where the mapping between proceeds and physical assets is most transparent, and weaker where proceeds are absorbed into balance-sheet intermediation. The implication is not that green bonds automatically deliver additionality, but that their design and governance conditions matter decisively.

Greenwashing remains the central constraint on further scaling, and it is here that the boundary between market practice and regulation becomes most salient. Voluntary standards such as the GBP have proven remarkably effective as coordination devices, but they were never designed to serve as enforcement mechanisms. As issuance volumes grow and issuer types diversify, reliance on voluntary discipline alone becomes insufficient. The move toward regulated labels, supervised reviewers, and taxonomy-linked disclosure should therefore be interpreted not as crowding out markets, but as stabilizing them. From this perspective, regulation and market standards are complements rather than substitutes: regulation raises the floor of credibility, while market competition continues to shape innovation above that floor.

For corporate strategy, the implications are increasingly concrete. Issuing a green bond is no longer a symbolic gesture; it entails durable commitments to internal data systems, cross-departmental coordination, and sustained transparency. Firms that treat green bonds as one-off marketing exercises risk reputational damage and the loss of any pricing or investor-base advantages. Conversely, firms that integrate green bond programs into long-term capital expenditure planning, transition strategies, and investor relations are better positioned to access deep pools of climate-aligned capital over time. In this sense, corporate green bonds are becoming part of the infrastructure of strategic finance rather than an add-on product.

For policymakers, the evidence suggests caution against over-promising and under-specifying. Corporate green bonds are not a substitute for carbon pricing, industrial policy, or public investment. They are a complementary mechanism that works best when embedded within a coherent policy environment that provides clear transition signals. Taxonomies, disclosure standards, and supervisory oversight should therefore be designed with usability and proportionality in mind, especially for sectors where transition pathways are complex or capital-intensive. Excessive rigidity risks discouraging issuance in precisely those sectors where transition finance is most urgently needed.

Finally, for investors, corporate green bonds illustrate the evolving nature of fiduciary responsibility in a net-zero world. Evaluating these instruments requires moving beyond binary judgments about labels toward a more granular assessment of credibility, alignment, and additionality. As climate risks become increasingly material to long-term asset values, the informational structures embedded in green bonds—frameworks, reviews, and reporting—become inputs into mainstream credit analysis rather than niche ESG overlays.

Taken together, the trajectory of corporate green bonds reflects a broader transformation in climate finance. Capital markets are being asked not only to price risk efficiently, but also to allocate capital in ways consistent with long-term climate objectives. Corporate green bonds do not resolve this tension, but they offer a pragmatic institutional response to it. Their continued evolution—shaped by regulation, academic scrutiny, and market discipline—will play a material role in determining whether private capital can be mobilized at the scale and speed required for the net-zero transition.

References

Bachelet, M. J., Becchetti, L., & Manfredonia, S. (2019). The green bonds premium puzzle: The role of issuer characteristics and third-party verification. *Sustainability, 11*(4), 1098.

Boutabba, M. A., & Rannou, Y. (2022). Investor strategies in the green bond market: The influence of liquidity risks, economic factors and clientele effects. *International Review of Financial Analysis, 81*, 102071.

CBI. (2025). *Sustainable debt: Global state of the market 2024*. Climate Bond Initiative.

ESMA. (2025). *External reviewers of European green bonds*. European Securities and Markets Authority.

European Parliament. (2020). *Regulation (EU) 2020/852 of 18 June 2020 on the establishment of a framework to facilitate sustainable investment (EU Taxonomy Regulation)*. European Parliament.

European Parliament. (2023). *Regulation (EU) 2023/2631 on European green bonds and optional disclosures for bonds marketed as environmentally sustainable and for sustainability-linked bonds*. European Parliament.

Fatica, S., Panzica, R., & Rancan, M. (2021). The pricing of green bonds: Are financial institutions special? *Journal of Financial Stability, 54*, 100873.

Flammer, C. (2021). Corporate green bonds. *Journal of Financial Economics, 142*(2), 499–516.

ICMA. (2025). *Green bond principles: Voluntary process guidelines for issuing green bonds*. International Capital Market Association.

IPSF. (2021). *Common ground taxonomy—Climate change mitigation*. International Platform on Sustainable Finance.

Kapraun, J., Latino, C., Scheins, C., & Schlag, C. (2021). *(In)-credibly green which bonds trade at a green bond premium*. MSCI Institute.

Ng, C. (2022). *China is building a more credible green finance market but state-owned enterprises' green bonds are in the way*. Institute for Energy Economics and Financial Analysis.

OECD. (2025). *Sustainable bonds: Trends and policy recommendations*. Organisation for Economic Co-operation and Development.

People's Bank of China, National Development and Reform Commission, & China Securities Regulatory Commission. (2021). *Green bond endorsed projects catalogue* (2021 edition).

Tang, D. Y., & Zhang, Y. (2020). Do shareholders benefit from green bonds? *Journal of Corporate Finance, 61*, 101427.

Zerbib, O. D. (2019). The effect of pro-environmental preferences on bond prices: Evidence from green bonds. *Journal of Banking & Finance, 98*, 39–60.

Zhang, R., Li, Y., & Liu, Y. (2021). Green bond issuance and corporate cost of capital. *Pacific-Basin Finance Journal, 69*, 101626.

Chapter 4
Sovereign Green Bonds

Introduction

In December 2016, Poland broke new ground by issuing the world's first sovereign green bond, marking the entrance of national governments into a market previously led by multilateral institutions and corporations. This milestone demonstrated that sovereign treasuries could directly raise capital for environmental projects and signaled a high-level commitment to financing the low-carbon transition (CBI, 2016). A month later, France followed with a record-setting €7 billion green bond in January 2017, which at the time was the largest and longest-maturity green bond ever issued (Ministry of Finance, 2017). These pioneering issuances showed that investor appetite for climate-friendly sovereign debt was substantial: France's inaugural issue attracted an order book exceeding €23 billion (over 3× oversubscription), evidencing remarkable demand from institutional investors for sovereign paper earmarked for green expenditures.

Since those early issuances, the sovereign green bond market has expanded rapidly from a novel concept into a mainstream component of public finance. By the end of 2024, 59 countries had issued some form of green, social, or sustainable sovereign bond, including 19 emerging markets and at least 4 African nations (Egypt, Nigeria, Seychelles, and Benin). Cumulative sovereign green bond issuance (aligned with rigorous definitions) reached on the order of $500–600 billion, comprising roughly one-fifth of annual green bond volumes (World Bank, 2025). What began with a few European frontrunners has spread across regions: large, advanced economies such as Germany, the UK, Italy, and Canada have established regular green bond programs, while emerging economies including Chile, Indonesia, and India have tapped international and domestic markets to fund climate investments. Notably, China debuted its first sovereign green bonds in 2023–2025, adding the world's second-largest economy to the sovereign green bond issuer club (London Stock Exchange, 2025).

P. Zhou, D. Guo, *Climate Finance in the Net-Zero Transition*, Contributions to Finance and Accounting, https://doi.org/10.1007/978-981-92-0827-2_4

Sovereign green bonds are now recognized as a key tool for governments to finance climate mitigation and adaptation initiatives, signal policy commitment, and catalyze private-sector market development. Their rise prompts important questions that this chapter explores. First, how do sovereign green bonds differ from corporate green bonds in their risk profile, credibility mechanisms, governance, and appeal to investors? Second, what have we learned from the evolution of the sovereign green bond market—from the experiences of early adopters like Poland and France to those of emerging-market innovators like Nigeria and Chile, and heavy issuers like Germany? Third, what do recent data and research show about the financial performance of sovereign green bonds, such as whether investors accept lower yields (a "greenium") and under what conditions? We also examine how sovereign green bonds maintain credibility through external reviews and reporting practices. Fourth, how has this market behaved during periods of crisis or stress—for example, during the COVID-19 pandemic and in sovereign debt restructurings? We discuss innovative applications like green bond swaps and debt-for-nature swaps that are being explored to reduce debt burdens while protecting the environment, including China's experience and potential role in such transactions. Finally, we compare the regulatory and standard-setting context across jurisdictions: the EU's Taxonomy and European Green Bond Standard for sovereign issuers, China's state-guided but evolving green definitions, and the more laissez-faire but investor-driven approach in the US, among others. Throughout, the chapter maintains an economic perspective, considering how sovereign green bonds balance the objectives of lowering financing costs, ensuring accountability for use of proceeds, and integrating climate priorities into public financial management.

Conception of Sovereign Green Bonds

Sovereign green bonds are use-of-proceeds debt securities issued by national governments in which the proceeds are earmarked for environmentally beneficial expenditures (Nevatia, 2026). In form, they closely resemble corporate green bonds—adhering to frameworks such as the ICMA Green Bond Principles for project selection, proceeds management, and reporting—but the sovereign context introduces distinct characteristics (Owusu-Mante et al., 2025). Several key dimensions differentiate sovereign green bonds from their corporate counterparts:

- **Credit Risk Profile:** Sovereign green bonds carry the credit risk of the issuing government and rank pari passu with the sovereign's conventional debt (Löffler et al., 2021). There is no project-level collateral; investors have full recourse to the government's general credit. For highly rated sovereigns, this typically means lower default risk and yields compared to corporate issues, and the bonds often serve as safe assets in domestic markets. Because green bonds do not change the debt's seniority or security, a country's green bonds should theoretically trade at the same credit spread as its normal bonds, barring any market premium or discount investors assign to the "green" label. Indeed, any sovereign's green bonds have identical creditworthiness to its conventional bonds, since payment of interest and principal is backed by the same full faith and credit. In practice, differences in issue size and liquidity can arise—sovereign green tranches are often smaller than benchmark government bonds—which can slightly affect yields. But fundamentally, unlike a corporate green bond which may carry idiosyncratic credit risk of a single firm or ring-fenced project, a sovereign green bond's risk reflects the broader fiscal and economic strength of the nation.

- **Issuer Credibility and Commitment:** When a government issues a green bond, it is making a sovereign commitment to deploy funds toward specified climate or environmental objectives (Lupo-Pasini, 2022). This can enhance credibility in two ways. First, it signals high-level policy commitment: the act of issuing a green bond often coincides with national climate strategies or budgetary greening efforts, lending weight to the country's environmental pledges. Second, sovereign issuers, by virtue of public accountability, may face greater reputational repercussions for "greenwashing" than a private company. There is strong incentive for governments to maintain credibility with investors and citizens by following through on promised green expenditures and transparently reporting outcomes. For example, France's program is overseen by an independent Green Obligations Assimilables du Trésor (OAT) Evaluation Council and subject to scrutiny by the national audit office, helping ensure that allocations remain aligned with stated objectives. On the other hand, sovereign credibility can be complicated by political risk—a new government might shift priorities or climate investments could become entangled in bureaucratic delays. Thus, the sovereign green bond framework often incorporates institutional checks (inter-ministerial committees, independent reviewers) to lock in the commitment across political cycles.
- **Governance and Use-of-Proceeds Management:** The governance processes for sovereign green bonds tend to be cross-cutting, as proceeds may finance a broad portfolio of public programs spanning energy, transport, water, agriculture, and more (Chavarría-Flores & Warren, 2024). In contrast to a corporate issuer (which might fund projects within its own operations), a sovereign must coordinate across multiple ministries and agencies to identify eligible green expenditures. Typically, the Ministry of Finance (or Debt Management Office) leads issuance, working closely with environment and sectoral ministries to define a Green Bond Framework and project selection criteria. For instance, France's government requires each ministry to flag budget line-items that qualify under the six environmental objectives of its Green OAT framework (climate mitigation, adaptation, biodiversity, pollution prevention, etc.); these are then vetted by an evaluation council of experts and approved by a committee under the Prime Minister's office. This interdepartmental process ensures that the use of proceeds is integrated into the regular budget (funds often go into the general treasury, but an equivalent amount is tracked and allocated to green projects). The need for such coordination means sovereign issuance can entail significant

administrative preparation—creating taxonomies of eligible expenditures, setting up monitoring systems—which is a governance challenge less acute for corporate issuers with narrower project scopes. However, once established, these governance structures can institutionalize climate considerations in public finance decisions.

- **Investor Base and Incentives:** Sovereign green bonds typically appeal to a wide range of fixed-income investors, including mainstream sovereign bondholders as well as specialized ESG-focused funds (Owusu-Mante et al., 2025). Many institutional investors (such as pension funds, insurers, and foreign reserve managers) have mandates to hold government bonds for liquidity and safety; sovereign green bonds allow them to fulfill those mandates while also meeting sustainability objectives. This can broaden the investor base or increase demand intensity. In France's January 2024 green OAT syndication, for example, fully 80% of the €8 billion issue was allocated to investors self-described as green or socially responsible, indicating that the green label attracted a differentiated pool of buyers. Investors are incentivized by the combination of high credit quality and positive environmental impact—a rare pairing historically. There is evidence that some investors will accept a slightly lower yield (pay a premium) for this benefit, as we discuss later. Moreover, certain central banks and official institutions have signaled preference for green assets; the European Central Bank, for instance, has included sovereign green bonds in its asset purchase programs and indicated that climate considerations will inform reinvestment, which may support demand. For emerging market sovereign issuers, tapping green bond buyers can diversify their funding sources and potentially reduce borrowing costs if a greenium is achieved. However, investor scrutiny of sovereign green bonds is intense—buyers expect sovereigns to lead by example on transparency and to align bond-funded expenditures with credible climate policies. If a government's climate actions are viewed as inconsistent with its green bond claims (for example, funding coal plants outside the bond while issuing a "green" bond), investors could penalize the sovereign through reputational damage or by demanding higher yields on future issues. In that sense, the green label imposes a form of market discipline on sovereign issuers.
- **Disclosure and Reporting Obligations:** Sovereign issuers generally adhere to robust reporting practices, similar to or exceeding those of corporates, given public sector transparency norms (Das et al., 2026). A sovereign green bond framework commits the government to publish allocation reports (detailing how proceeds have been distributed to eligible projects) and often impact reports (quantifying environmental results, like emissions avoided or renewable capacity added). Sovereigns usually report annually until all proceeds are allocated, and in many cases continue to provide updates on project performance thereafter. Because sovereign green bonds finance government budget items, reporting can leverage existing public finance systems (e.g. linking to the budget execution reports) but also requires methodologies to estimate climate impacts of budgetary expenditures. Many sovereigns engage external auditors or evaluators for

these reports. For example, the UK Treasury issues annual reports on its "Green Gilt" proceeds, including key performance indicators for each spending category, and engaged an external assurance provider to review the allocation of proceeds. France publishes an extensive Allocation and Performance Report each year audited by the Cour des Comptes (national audit office), and separate evaluation studies are conducted to assess longer-term impacts of the funded projects. Such rigorous reporting is critical to maintain investor confidence that funds are achieving their green purpose. In comparison, corporate green bond reporting, while often comprehensive, may be more variable in quality and is generally voluntary unless mandated by regulation; sovereigns, facing both market expectations and citizen accountability, tend to set a high bar. Indeed, studies have found that sovereign green bond issuance can help improve overall market standards for disclosure and verification, creating spillover benefits for private issuers in the same country.

In summary, sovereign green bonds share the fundamental concept of earmarking proceeds for green projects with other green bonds, but they operate at the scale of national budgets and carry the weight of government accountability. They are an "institutional technology" embedded in public finance that can enhance credibility and transparency around climate spending. By structuring debt issuance to support climate objectives, sovereigns effectively mainstream environmental considerations into debt management. This can reduce information asymmetry (investors gain visibility into a government's climate expenditures) and potentially mobilize capital at lower cost for green investments. However, the benefits depend on rigorous implementation—credible project selection, robust reporting, and consistency with broader climate policy. Without these, a green sovereign bond would be green in name only, undermining investor trust. The next sections explore how these principles have played out as the sovereign green bond market has developed across different countries and contexts.

Implementation of Sovereign Green Bonds

From First Movers to a Global Market

The sovereign green bond market's evolution can be viewed in phases. First movers in Europe established the blueprint, followed by a widening array of emerging markets and then larger advanced economies scaling up issuance. Table 4.1 provides a snapshot of the top sovereign issuers to date, illustrating how volumes are concentrated in a few countries, while many others have made smaller forays.

The early market (2016–2018) was dominated by European sovereigns, reflecting Europe's broader leadership in green finance. Poland's inaugural green bond in 2016 (PLN 750 million) proved the concept, and France's massive €7 billion issue

Table 4.1 Top sovereign green and sustainable bond issuers

Country	First issue	Cumulative vol.	Main bond themes
France	2017	$84.9 billion	Green (4 Green OATs)
Germany	2020	$81.5 billion	Green (twin bond program)
UK	2021	$73.5 billion	Green (Green Gilts)
Italy	2021	$53.7 billion	Green
Chile	2019	$48.8 billion	Green, Social, Sustainability, SLB
Hong Kong, China	2019	$28.2 billion	Green (multiple currencies)
Netherlands	2019	$27.2 billion	Green (Green DSL)
Belgium	2018	$22.0 billion	Green
Mexico	2020	$19.3 billion	Sustainability
Spain	2021	$16.9 billion	Green

Notes: amounts include green, social, sustainability and similar labeled bonds. *SLB* sustainability-linked bond, *OAT* Obligations Assimilables du Trésor, *DSL* Dutch State Loans. Source: CBI

in January 2017 proved the scale. France not only issued the largest deal but set a precedent with its approach: a long 22-year tenor (due 2039) and a comprehensive framework covering a wide span of environmental expenditures. The French green OAT was designed as a benchmark bond that could be tapped multiple times to build liquidity. Indeed, over subsequent years France reopened its 2017 green OAT and launched additional green bonds (including a 2044 maturity in 2021 and a 2049 maturity in 2024), accumulating a green debt stock of nearly $85 billion, the largest of any sovereign. Other European nations quickly followed suit: Belgium (2018) and Ireland (2018) each issued green bonds to finance climate-friendly infrastructure and energy projects, and Netherlands debuted in 2019 with a €6 billion green bond, which it framed around meeting domestic emissions targets. By 2019, virtually all major Western European economies had either issued a sovereign green bond or announced plans to do so—with the notable exception of those, like Germany and the UK, who were still in internal planning (they would join in the next phase).

Outside Europe, emerging market pioneers also embraced sovereign green bonds early on. Nigeria issued Africa's first sovereign green bond in 2017 (a ₦10.7 billion issue, approximately $30 million) to fund solar power and afforestation projects, followed by a second tranche in 2019. Fiji, vulnerable to climate change, became the first small island state to issue a sovereign green bond in 2017 (FJD 100 million) to support renewable energy and resilience in the Pacific. Indonesia made a landmark entry in March 2018 with a $1.25 billion 5-year green sukuk (Islamic green bond), integrating Islamic finance with climate objectives—the proceeds went to renewable energy, sustainable transport, and waste management projects aligned with Indonesia's climate action plans. Indonesia's successful issuance (which was oversubscribed and priced tighter than initial guidance) demonstrated that investor demand extended to emerging market credit when a credible green framework was in place. It also illustrated how sovereign green bonds can diversify funding: Indonesia tapped global shari'ah-compliant investor pools that appreciated the green label, and it has since issued multiple rounds of green sukuk domestically and internationally. Chile emerged as a standout case in Latin America: beginning in 2019, Chile issued a series of euro- and USD-denominated green bonds to finance its clean energy transition and resilient infrastructure, quickly amassing several billion in volume. By simultaneously issuing green, social, and sustainability bonds (often under a unified framework), Chile has raised about $50 billion equivalent, making over 40% of its central government debt "ESG-labeled"—the highest share globally. Chile's experience showed that sovereign labels can be integrated into overall debt strategy and used programmatically to support a comprehensive sustainable development agenda (covering not just climate but social goals as well). Other emerging economies that joined the market in this period include Brazil (via its state development bank BNDES in 2017, though Brazil's federal government has yet to issue a green bond as of 2025), Argentina (a small sustainable bond in 2020), and Egypt (the Middle East's first sovereign green bond in 2020, $750 million for clean transport and water projects).

The expansion phase (2019–2021) saw the entry of more advanced economies and larger deal sizes. Germany in particular had long debated green bonds, weighing the potential greenium against fragmentation of its bond market. In 2020, Germany opted for an innovative solution: it began issuing "twin bonds", pairing each new green federal bond with a conventional federal bond of the same maturity and coupon. For example, in September 2020 Germany issued a 10-year €6 billion green Bund alongside an existing 10-year conventional Bund, effectively creating two identical securities except for the green label. The twins trade in parallel, and investors have the option to swap the green for the conventional (maintaining fungibility of collateral), which preserves liquidity. The twin bond approach, pioneered by Germany, allows precise measurement of the greenium—any yield difference between the green and non-green twin reflects the market's pricing of the green label, controlling for other factors. By early 2025, Germany had issued green twins across four maturities (2025, 2030, 2031, 2050), accumulating over €80 billion outstanding. The German program has been very well received by investors and routinely oversubscribed. It has also established a secondary market benchmark: German green Bunds consistently trade a few basis points lower in yield than their twins (a greenium of about 2–5 bps under normal conditions). The transparent pricing differential validated the notion of a modest but real green investor preference in the sovereign market. Following Germany's lead, Denmark in 2022–2023 and Austria in 2022 also adopted twin structures for some issues, and the concept was incorporated into the EU's model for its forthcoming sovereign green bond standard.

The UK also joined in 2021, launching "Green Gilts". The UK's Debt Management Office issued two green gilts in September and October 2021 (raising a total of £16 billion) focused on funding renewable energy, clean transportation (like rail electrification), and adaptation measures (such as flood defenses). Investor demand was robust—the 12-year inaugural green gilt was heavily oversubscribed (orders over £100 billion for a £10 billion issue) and achieved a small greenium at issuance. The UK emphasized its intention to build a green yield curve over time, and it also created a retail Green Savings Bond via the National Savings scheme, allowing citizens to participate. Elsewhere in Europe, countries like Spain (which issued its first €5 billion green bond in 2021) and Italy (which debuted a €8.5 billion 2045 green BTP in 2021) added significant volume. Italy's deal, for instance, attracted over €80 billion of orders, reflecting that even higher-debt countries can obtain investor enthusiasm for well-structured green bonds. By 2024, 18 out of 27 EU member states had issued sovereign green or sustainable bonds, and Europe accounted for roughly 60% of sovereign sustainable bond volume that year. Within the EU, only a few (Finland, Portugal, Greece) had not yet come with a green bond by 2025—and some of those, like Greece, have signaled plans to do so as their financing needs allow.

In the post-2021 period, large-scale issuers and supranationals further propelled market growth. The EU itself, while not a "sovereign" country, became one of the largest green bond issuers when the European Commission began issuing green bonds in 2021 to finance the NextGeneration EU pandemic recovery fund. By 2024, the EU had issued over €35 billion in green bonds, and it topped the global issuer rankings in 2024 (at $20.9 billion issued that year). This EU program provided additional liquidity to euro sovereign green markets and a high-standard benchmark aligned with EU Taxonomy criteria. China, which had seen massive green bond growth in other segments, finally entered the sovereign green bond arena in 2023–2025: in April 2023, China's Ministry of Finance issued an inaugural sovereign green bond (RMB 6 billion, about $825 million) on the London Stock Exchange, and in 2025 it announced a Sovereign Green Bond Framework to guide further issuance. China's sovereign green bonds—issued as offshore yuan bonds—are notable as they align with both Chinese green standards and international norms, serving as a bridge for global investors to Chinese climate projects. Although the initial amounts are relatively small, China's entry is symbolic and could scale up, given its government's significant role in climate investment. Japan also began issuing sovereign green bonds (branded as "GX"—Green Transformation—bonds) in 2022, with the aim of raising funds for its energy transition and innovation programs; Japan plans to issue ¥20 trillion (around $150 billion) of these bonds in the coming decade, although its first issues in 2022–2023 were still modest in size. Outside of climate-specific bonds, new formats have emerged: for instance, SLBs at sovereign level—Thailand in 2023 issued a sovereign SLB (tied to greenhouse gas reduction targets), the first of its kind in Asia. While SLBs are structurally different (performance-based rather than use-of-proceeds), their appearance in sovereign funding underscores the innovation in sovereign sustainable finance.

The diversity of issuers has grown to encompass not only climate champions but also countries seeking financing innovation. By 2024, 37 emerging market governments had issued green, social, or sustainability bonds. The sovereign green bond has thus evolved from a niche experiment into a catalyst for sustainable debt markets around the world. One important observation is that sovereign issuance often has a demonstration effect: when a sovereign comes to market, it can pave the way for sub-sovereign and corporate issuers domestically. Research finds that after a sovereign's green bond debut, the number and volume of corporate green bonds in that country tend to increase, as the sovereign issue establishes a benchmark and raises awareness. For example, Poland's sovereign issue was followed by a surge in Polish corporate and municipal green bonds. Similarly, Chile's early and large issuances were accompanied by Chilean companies (like energy firm Colbún) and municipalities tapping green bonds. This "crowding-in" effect is supported by evidence that sovereign green bonds improve market liquidity and set standards that private issuers then emulate. In that sense, sovereign green bonds have not only grown as a segment but also served as a catalyst for the broader climate finance market development.

Financial Performance: Pricing, Greenium, and Investor Reception

Do investors accept lower yields for sovereign green bonds? The existence of a "greenium", defined as a yield discount (or price premium) for green bonds relative to otherwise equivalent conventional bonds, has been a central question in green finance (Zhou et al., 2025). For sovereign issuers, this question is particularly important: a greenium implies cheaper financing for the government (at taxpayer benefit) but also suggests excess demand or a scarcity of green assets among investors. Academic studies and market analyses indicate that sovereign greeniums have generally been positive but small. Using Germany's twin bonds as a natural experiment, researchers estimate a sovereign greenium of roughly 2–4 bps on average, with values at some maturities reaching about 5 bps (Ando et al., 2023). For instance, the German 10-year green "Bund" due 2030 traded around 2–3 bps lower in yield than its conventional twin on average. At times the greenium widened to ~5 bps, though in rare periods it even disappeared or turned slightly negative (e.g., during flights to liquidity where the larger conventional bond was preferred). Furthermore, the study found that greeniums tend to be larger for bonds from emerging markets and for bonds issued in foreign currencies.

One interpretation is that green bonds help emerging market sovereigns reach new investor segments, potentially improving demand and pricing—indeed, investors with ESG mandates might be more constrained in emerging market investments unless labeled debt is available, so they bid yields down more aggressively when an emerging market sovereign issues green. Another finding is that the greenium has increased over time as the market matures and more investors integrate climate considerations. Early on, some sovereign green bonds (like Poland's 2016 issue) saw no clear pricing benefit at launch. But by the early 2020s, it became more routine that sovereign green bonds would price a few basis points "inside" the yield of a regular bond. For example, India's debut sovereign green bonds in 2023 (10-year rupee bonds) achieved a greenium of about 5–6 bps—a notable result in a developing country context, attributed to very strong oversubscription by domestic investors keen to support the government's climate initiatives. Similarly, France's and Belgium's green OATs/BELs have been observed trading 2–4 bps richer than their curves. An IDB analysis of Latin American sovereign green bonds finds an average greenium of ~6 bps for advanced economies versus ~2 bps for LAC issuers, although statistically significant in both cases (the difference perhaps reflecting depth of markets and investor base composition). In summary, the pricing advantage ("greenium") for sovereign green bonds exists but is modest, on the order of only a few basis points. This implies that investors, while not forgoing return entirely, are willing to marginally prefer green bonds—likely due to portfolio mandates or positive screening—but the effect is constrained by arbitrage forces (e.g., non-ESG investors will sell the rich green bond and buy the cheap conventional until the gap narrows).

Even where a greenium is small, investor reception of sovereign green bonds has been overwhelmingly positive. Many sovereign green issues have been heavily oversubscribed, indicating ex ante demand above and beyond typical levels. As noted, France's €8 billion green OAT in 2024 garnered an extraordinary €98 billion order book (12× oversubscription), far higher than what conventional French bonds of similar size would normally attract. The long maturity and rarity value of a new green line likely amplified demand, but it underscores the depth of investor appetite. The French Treasury reported that a large majority of those orders came from investors with explicit sustainable mandates, reflecting a structural shift where a significant segment of bond investors now prioritize ESG characteristics. Germany's green twin bonds also saw order books multiple times the issue size in each auction/syndication. For emerging markets, oversubscription is similarly notable: Chile's initial green Eurobond in 2019 had orders several times the $1.4 billion offered and achieved a lower yield than Chile's conventional curve, suggesting investors were eager to participate in a high-quality green issuance. Investor roadshow feedback often highlights that certain funds (particularly in Europe) will invest only if the bond is green-labeled or if the issuer has a climate strategy, effectively making the green label a ticket to access deeper pockets of capital.

The investor base for sovereign green bonds tends to skew slightly toward "buy-and-hold" investors and ESG-oriented portfolios. Central banks and sovereign wealth funds have bought green bonds to align reserves with sustainability goals (e.g., some have announced green bond allocations as part of reserve management). Asset managers running dedicated green bond or climate-aligned funds will naturally gravitate to sovereign green issues for their liquidity and credit quality. In some cases, green bonds attract new investor types: for example, France noted increased participation from Scandinavian pension funds and responsible investment funds in its green OATs relative to conventional OATs. This broadened investor base can have ancillary benefits—potentially more stable demand and slightly lower volatility, as these investors may be less sensitive to short-term price fluctuations and more motivated by long-term climate objectives. On the other hand, concentration of buy-and-hold ESG investors could reduce secondary market liquidity; indeed, some studies (e.g., Boutabba & Rannou, 2022) find that green bonds in general can have tighter spreads but also lower trading liquidity because they reside in sticky portfolios. Sovereign green bonds have largely traded in line with conventional government bonds in terms of liquidity, thanks to their usually large size and integration into benchmark indices, but there have been instances (especially early on) where slightly smaller free float made them a bit less liquid. Germany's twin bond mechanism directly addresses this by allowing market makers to exchange green for conventional, thereby arbitraging any liquidity differences.

Critically, credibility mechanisms like external reviews and clear use-of-proceeds disclosure have proven economically meaningful in sustaining investor reception. All sovereign green bond issuers have published frameworks outlining eligible sectors and governance. Many have also sought certification or alignment with international standards—e.g., Denmark's 2025 green bond was the first to formally align with the EU Green Bond Standard and came with a Sustainable Fitch review confirming adherence to both ICMA principles and the EU standard. This high level of transparency and third-party scrutiny reduces investor concerns about "greenwashing" and is likely one reason sovereign green bonds consistently price near or slightly better than conventional bonds (a poorly credible framework might deter investors and eliminate any greenium). Empirical research across green bonds finds that issues with external verification tend to enjoy better pricing (lower yield) than those without. Sovereigns have generally been exemplary in this regard: as of end-2024, 100% of sovereign green bonds came with at least one external review (Second Party Opinions or SPOs), and many also incorporate ongoing review of impact reports by independent bodies. This robust verification regime likely contributes to tighter spreads. Additionally, because sovereign green bonds undergo parliamentary or public oversight in many countries (the approved projects often appear in budget documents), investors gain extra assurance. In effect, sovereign issuance has helped improve overall market quality—evidence from one IMF working paper suggests that after a sovereign debut, corporate issuers in that country more frequently obtain external reviews and improve their reporting, raising the bar for private issuance. Investors, aware of this dynamic, may reward sovereign issues for setting a gold standard.

Another aspect of performance is secondary market behavior and resilience. During the COVID-19 induced market turmoil of March 2020, for example, sovereign yields spiked across the board as liquidity dried up. There is little evidence that green bonds were spared from this sell-off; they behaved much like conventional bonds of similar duration and credit. However, as markets normalized and central banks intervened, green bonds bounced back strongly. By late 2020 and 2021, green bonds (sovereign and non-sovereign) were keeping pace with conventional bonds in performance, with no penalty on liquidity. Data from bond indices show that green bond indices and broad market indices track closely, with any performance differentials driven more by duration and sector composition than the green factor. For sovereigns, this means issuing green debt did not adversely affect their market; if anything, it added a slight diversification benefit. For instance, the FTSE World Green Bond Index (which includes sovereign green bonds) aligned closely with the global aggregate index over 2018–2024, suggesting that green bonds have similar risk/return profiles to vanilla bonds. The difference is that, as noted in LSEG analysis, portfolios of green bonds can be somewhat more sensitive to interest rate rises because they often have a higher concentration of long-dated government bonds (as many sovereign green bonds are long maturities). This is a technical nuance: green bonds as a subset had longer duration, so they underperformed slightly in rising rate environments, but that's not due to credit or liquidity issues, just interest rate exposure. Overall, sovereign green bonds have shown remarkable resilience, even amid macroeconomic headwinds and geopolitical tensions in 2022–2023, continuing to attract inflows when other segments saw outflows.

Market Behavior in Crises and Debt Restructuring Contexts

The dual nature of sovereign green bonds—as both an investment product and a policy tool—has been underscored during periods of crisis. During the COVID-19 pandemic, governments worldwide faced urgent financing needs for economic stimulus and healthcare. Rather than sidelining green finance, many policymakers embraced the idea of a "green recovery", channeling stimulus toward sustainable infrastructure and climate-friendly projects. Sovereign green bonds played a role in this narrative. In 2020, even as overall bond issuance spiked with mostly conventional debt, some countries either launched or expanded green bond programs as part of their recovery strategy. Germany's inaugural green bonds in 2020 were embedded in its €130 billion climate-friendly stimulus plan—the timing signaled that green investments were core to Germany's recovery spending. The EU's NextGeneration EU program, although funded partly by conventional bonds, devoted 30% of its expenditures to climate and led the European Commission to become a major green bond issuer by late 2021. Thus, the crisis accelerated certain sovereign green issuances rather than halting them.

Market data from 2020–2021 suggests that green bonds did not suffer a disproportionate penalty in the COVID-19 market volatility; if anything, they benefited from the strong subsequent recovery in fixed income markets and from investor rhetoric about "building back better". By 2021, green bond issuance (sovereign and otherwise) hit record highs, reflecting pent-up demand and policy support. A telling statistic: green bonds comprised about 6.9% of all bonds issued in the EU in 2024, up from 5.3% in 2023, a continuation of growth even after the pandemic peak. Sovereign issuance specifically remained robust through the pandemic and afterward—for instance, 2021 saw debut green bonds from the UK, Serbia, Spain, and others despite ongoing economic uncertainty, indicating that governments and investors maintained focus on climate finance. One reason is that many institutional investors, such as pension funds, have long-term horizons and welcomed the chance to invest in recovery bonds that also met ESG criteria. Additionally, central bank actions (like the ECB's asset purchases) indirectly supported sovereign green bonds by including them in quantitative easing programs, thereby stabilizing prices. In short, the COVID-19 crisis did not derail the sovereign green bond market; if anything, it reinforced the rationale for linking debt financing with resilient, sustainable investments.

In the context of sovereign debt distress and restructuring, the role of green bonds is more nascent but potentially transformative. Traditionally, when countries undergo debt restructuring, creditors exchange or write down conventional debt for new instruments—increasingly, proposals have emerged to incorporate climate or nature outcomes into these deals. One model is the "debt-for-nature swap", pioneered in the late 1980s, where a portion of a country's external debt is forgiven or bought back in exchange for the country committing local funds to conservation projects. These have been applied in over 30 countries, restructuring about $2.6 billion of debt and redirecting $1.2 billion to environmental programs as of 2021. Recent years saw a revival of such mechanisms with a climate focus. For example, in 2018 the Republic of Seychelles executed a novel debt-for-ocean-nature swap: with support from The Nature Conservancy (TNC), it exchanged $21 million of its sovereign debt for a commitment to fund marine conservation, alongside issuing the world's first "blue bond" to invest in sustainable fisheries. In 2021, Belize restructured a portion of its external commercial debt by refinancing it into a $364 million Blue Bond (backed by TNC and the US International Development Finance Corporation), in return for committing to protect 30% of its ocean territory. This effectively bought back Belize's Eurobond at a deep discount (post default) and replaced it with a lower-interest blue bond with conservation conditions, yielding both fiscal relief and environmental gains. Similarly, in 2022, Barbados included climate resilience clauses in its restructured debt and undertook a debt conversion with TNC to fund a coral reef trust—importantly, the new bonds have natural disaster contingencies (hurricane clauses) and are partly aimed at funding climate adaptation.

These examples illustrate how sovereign green or blue bonds can be integrated into debt workouts. The concept of a "sovereign green bond swap" in a restructuring is essentially that creditors agree to accept a new green bond (potentially at lower interest or longer maturity) in exchange for old debt, with the understanding that the proceeds of the new bond will go into climate investments or resilience, often under the monitoring of international institutions. This can make a restructuring more palatable by delivering funding for critical climate needs and signaling to markets a commitment to future sustainability (potentially attracting ESG investors to the new bond). For debtor nations, it's a way to unlock climate finance while reducing debt service. Multilateral development banks and the IMF have shown interest in facilitating such arrangements. The IMF in 2023 launched a "Resilience and Sustainability Trust" (RST) that provides affordable long-term financing to countries undertaking climate-related reforms, which can complement debt restructuring efforts for climate-vulnerable states.

China's experience is crucial in this arena, given China's status as the largest bilateral creditor to developing countries. Many low-income countries with Chinese loans faced debt challenges exacerbated by COVID-19 and climate disasters, leading to calls for China to participate in debt relief initiatives. Chinese policymakers and researchers have begun to explore debt-for-climate swaps as a solution. In 2021, policy research from Chinese institutions suggested that China could convert portions of its loans under the Belt and Road Initiative (BRI) into debt relief tied to debtor countries' commitments to nature conservation and climate action. The idea is framed as a "triple-win"—alleviating debt distress, funding green projects, and enhancing China's image as a responsible creditor. For instance, instead of demanding full repayment, China might allow a country to spend some of what it would have paid on solar farms or forest protection at home, counting that as repayment. While concrete cases are still limited, there are promising signs: China reportedly supported a small debt-for-nature swap in Pakistan in 2022 (allowing Pakistan to redirect debt payments to flood resilience projects), and has signaled openness to similar ideas for countries like Zambia and Sri Lanka as part of broader G20 Common Framework discussions. However, Chinese officials also emphasize that any swaps must respect debtor sovereignty and be done on a case-by-case basis, and they often advocate for multilateral grants or contributions to co-finance the swaps (to avoid China solely bearing the cost). There are also calls for an international platform or standards for such climate swaps, to which China could contribute, possibly through the establishment of a global green debt fund.

The COVID-19 period also spurred innovation in climate contingency clauses in sovereign bonds. Some countries (e.g., Barbados, Grenada) have pioneered clauses that pause debt payments in event of natural disasters—effectively embedding a form of resilience. While not "green bonds" per se, these clauses are in the spirit of aligning debt service with climate shocks. As climate change intensifies the frequency of hurricanes, floods, and other catastrophes, such features could become more common and have been championed by groups like the IMF and Commonwealth Secretariat.

In crises, sovereign green bonds are not just luxury instruments for good times; they can be critical tools in bad times as well. During COVID-19, they helped frame stimulus in sustainable terms and maintained investor engagement. In debt crises, they offer creative avenues for relief that also address climate and nature—an increasingly pressing need as vulnerable countries juggle debt burdens with the costs of climate adaptation. These trends suggest a future where the lines between debt management and climate finance blur: we may see more "debt-for-climate" swaps, climate resilience bonds, and other hybrids become part of sovereign debt restructuring packages. The case of Belize's blue bond, for example, showed that creditors (with guarantees) were willing to accept a lower payoff if it achieved measurable environmental conservation—essentially taking a haircut in exchange for nature outcomes. Such models could potentially be expanded (with international support) to larger economies. The challenge is scaling these niche deals into systematic options without undermining credit discipline. The opportunity, however, is significant: it opens a pathway to align the trillions in sovereign debt restructuring needs with the trillions needed for climate investment, creating synergy instead of competition for scarce fiscal resources.

Governance of Sovereign Bonds

The sovereign green bond market does not exist in a vacuum; it is shaped by the regulatory and normative frameworks of each region. Approaches to defining "green" and ensuring the integrity of sovereign green bonds vary, with Europe, China, and the US representing three distinctive paradigms of governance:

Europe: Taxonomy Alignment and the European Green Bond Standard

The EU has been at the forefront of developing formal green finance regulations. Building on the success of European sovereign issuers, the EU moved to create a common high-standard label. In 2023, the EU adopted the European Green Bond Regulation, which introduces an official "European Green Bond" label for bonds (including sovereign bonds) that meet stringent criteria. Key among these is the requirement that at least 85% of proceeds be allocated to projects aligned with the EU Taxonomy for sustainable activities. This taxonomy provides science-based technical screening criteria for what counts as a substantial contribution to climate mitigation, adaptation, etc., in various sectors. By tying green bonds to the taxonomy, the EU aims for consistency and credibility—investors can be assured that a EuGB funds projects that meet robust environmental standards. The regulation also mandates standardized template reporting and the use of EU-registered external reviewers (with oversight by the European Securities and Markets Authority, ESMA). Notably, the EuGB Standard is voluntary—sovereigns (and corporates) can choose to use it or continue with existing market standards (like ICMA's GBP). However, it is expected to become a mark of best practice. Denmark became the first sovereign to issue under the EuGB Standard in 2025, structuring its debut green bond as a twin and following the EU template. Other European sovereigns are likely to migrate their frameworks to align with the taxonomy over time; many had already been informally aligning (e.g., France's and Netherlands' use-of-proceeds broadly fit taxonomy categories). Europe's regulatory push reflects a philosophy that label credibility should be buttressed by law and supervision—a reaction to concerns about greenwashing. For sovereign issuers, this means more rigorous upfront work (ensuring taxonomy compliance of projects, enhanced disclosure) but promises a boost in investor confidence and possibly broader eligibility (some institutional investors may only want EuGB-labelled bonds once available).

European sovereigns also coordinate through bodies like the EU Sovereign Green Bond Club, an informal grouping to share best practices. By 2024, as noted, most EU governments had issued green bonds, and several (e.g. Germany, Sweden, Denmark) explicitly reference the EU Taxonomy in their frameworks. Additionally,

European sovereigns benefit from the ECB's monetary policy tilt toward green: the ECB now holds a sizeable portfolio of sovereign green bonds (within its broader holdings) and has pledged to preferentially reinvest in green bonds when feasible, under its climate initiative. While the effect of this on pricing is still being studied, it underscores Europe's whole-of-policy approach. In summary, Europe's model is one of regulatory-led standardization—using taxonomy and official standards to enhance the market's integrity. This approach, as **Chap. 3** noted, raises the floor on credibility and may gradually be emulated elsewhere.

China: Catalog-Based Definitions and State Guidance

China's green bond market historically operated under a different model: one of centrally coordinated but flexibly applied guidelines. Instead of a taxonomy legislated by parliament, Chinese regulators (the People's Bank of China, National Development and Reform Commission, etc.) have issued "Green Bond Endorsed Project Catalogues" that list eligible project categories. The most recent update in 2021 was a significant one—it removed fossil-fuel-related projects like "clean coal", bringing Chinese definitions closer to international norms. This shows China's responsiveness to global standards and the desire to make its green bonds more acceptable to foreign investors. Still, China's approach remains somewhat distinct: it allows certain projects (like large hydro dams or "clean" coal retrofits) that Europe's taxonomy might exclude, although the gap has narrowed. For sovereign context, China's first sovereign green bonds in 2023 adhered to a Sovereign Green Bond Framework (2025) that presumably builds on the national Catalogue and also references the Common Ground Taxonomy (a China-EU collaborative taxonomy for cross-border comparability). Chinese sovereign and policy bank issuers have typically obtained external verifications from approved Chinese verifiers, and increasingly from international SPO providers as well, to satisfy global investors.

In terms of governance, Chinese issuance is often tied to Five-Year Plan priorities. The government uses green bonds as a tool to channel funding to strategic green industries (renewables, EV infrastructure, etc.). The state influence means that credibility is reinforced by policy alignment—investors take comfort if a bond is known to fund projects under China's nationally determined climate targets or its massive ecological programs. However, it also means the line between green bonds and fiscal policy is blurred: for example, some local government special bonds are essentially green bonds financing water treatment or subway systems, without being labeled as such. China's focus has been on rapid scaling with adequate (if not perfect) standards, and indeed it achieved enormous green issuance (mostly by corporates and local governments) before even issuing a sovereign green bond itself. Now that it has a sovereign green bond framework, it signals top-level endorsement, which may spur even more local issuance.

One unique aspect in China is the role of state-owned banks and investors: many green bonds (sovereign or not) are bought by domestic banks, partly fulfilling policy guidance to support green finance. This captive demand ensures successful placement but can raise questions about market pricing efficiency. Nonetheless, China's move to internationalize—selling its sovereign green bonds in London—indicates a desire to meet global investor expectations on transparency. Overall, China's model can be seen as administrative guidance plus iterative improvement of standards. The government regularly refines the catalog, coordinates among regulators, and participates in international forums (like the IPSF's Common Ground initiative) to gradually converge definitions. Unlike the EU, where a legal framework compels disclosure templates, in China much is handled through policy directives and market self-discipline under regulators' eyes. The credibility of Chinese sovereign (and other) green bonds will likely increase as it continues to eliminate controversial categories and increase disclosure—the 2021 Catalog was a big step in that direction, praised by outside observers for its clarity. If China scales up sovereign issuance, one could envision it formalizing a taxonomy in law, but as of 2025, it relies on these detailed guidelines.

US: Voluntary Frameworks and Market-Driven Credibility

The US presents a contrasting case in that the federal government has not yet issued a sovereign green bond (often to the surprise of observers, given the size of US Treasury markets). Climate and sustainable finance in the US sovereign context have taken other routes—for example, via fiscal measures like the Inflation Reduction Act of 2022—but not through labeled treasury bonds. One reason is that the US Treasury traditionally issues the simplest, most liquid debt instruments and might see segmentation by label as complicating its market. Another is political: labeling debt for climate could be contentious domestically, as climate policy divides political parties. Instead, the action in US green bonds has been at sub-sovereign levels (state and municipal bonds) and corporate issuance. Many US states and cities have issued green municipal bonds for infrastructure—e.g., New York's MTA green bonds for transit—benefitting from tax-exemption and catering to socially responsible municipal investors. The federal government indirectly supports this through tax policy (municipal interest is tax-free), but the labeling is voluntary.

US issuers, whether municipal or corporate, typically adhere to ICMA's GBP and hire SPO providers to bolster credibility. There is no national taxonomy or mandatory standard. The Securities and Exchange Commission (SEC) has been inching toward stricter anti-greenwashing rules (like ensuring ESG fund names match their holdings), but as of 2025 there is no prescriptive regime for green bonds. Thus, the governance is market-driven: investors demand transparency, and issuers provide it to attract capital. This works reasonably well for high-quality issuers (e.g., Apple's and Google's corporate green bonds set good practice in reporting), but it can lead to heterogeneity. For a future US sovereign green bond (if one were proposed), the Treasury would likely use an approach similar to other sovereigns—a use-of-proceeds framework, probably referencing existing federal definitions (perhaps using the EPA's definitions of clean energy, etc.) or even piggybacking on the EU Taxonomy for international credibility. They would also likely get an SPO to assure investors, given the absence of US official standards. Notably, in early 2023, the US Treasury did hire an ESG advisor and began consulting on climate-related disclosure for federal debt, hinting at initial steps that could, in time, lead to green issuance. Some legislation has been floated (e.g., a proposed "Climate Forward Bonds" act), but nothing has passed.

One voluntary framework in the US worth noting is the Climate Bond Initiative's standards being used by some municipal issuers, and the fact that US investors often refer to the UN SDGs in marketing their sustainable municipal bonds (for example, a city might label a water infrastructure bond as advancing SDG6 and SDG13). These softer references fill the gap of a taxonomy. Additionally, states like California and New York have set up green bond guidelines or are considering state-level taxonomies for state issuance, which could influence the landscape if federal standards remain absent.

The credibility of US green bonds thus relies on reputation and liability: issuers know that false claims could lead to investor lawsuits or SEC enforcement (fraud provisions apply). We've seen the SEC fine a few entities for misleading "green" statements. This regulatory backdrop—general anti-fraud law rather than specific green bond rules—is a more ex post approach, catching egregious cases, whereas Europe's is ex ante, preventing them via standards. Both aim to protect investors, but the US way puts more onus on investor diligence and market reputation.

Other Regions

Other regions fall somewhere between these models. The UK, post-Brexit, has essentially followed the European approach in practice (its Green Gilt framework mirrors ICMA and was reviewed by a second-party opinion, and it is developing a UK Taxonomy similar to the EU's). Japan initially was market-driven, but the government put out Green Bond Guidelines (non-binding) to encourage standardization, and now with GX bonds, there is more government direction. Latin America has largely used ICMA principles (e.g., Chile's bonds have SPOs, and Chile aligned its framework with the SDGs and Paris Agreement goals). African issuers like Nigeria and Egypt have worked closely with development institutions (World Bank, etc.) to craft frameworks, effectively importing global standards.

Label Credibility

In terms of label credibility, one sees convergence: even without formal regulation, most sovereign issuers globally voluntarily follow the core tenets of the GBP—clear use of proceeds, external review, allocation and impact reporting. Many also incorporate elements of the EU Taxonomy or other taxonomies as reference. For example, Indonesia references both its national green criteria and ASEAN regional standards in its sukuk documentation, to assure a broad base of investors. Nigeria's framework was developed with the assistance of the African Development Bank and aligned with ICMA and the country's climate plan. These efforts suggest a de facto global coherence is emerging. Bodies like the International Organization of Securities Commissions (IOSCO) and the Network for Greening the Financial System (NGFS) have advocated for consistent climate disclosure for sovereign issuers. IOSCO's 2025 report on sustainable bonds recommended that sovereign issuers be transparent about how projects align with international goals, which is pushing even voluntary regimes toward rigor.

One challenge in sovereign context is additionality—skeptics sometimes argue that sovereign green bonds just relabel spending that would have happened anyway (governments could finance those projects with normal bonds). Regulatory standards like the EU's attempt to address this by requiring detailed allocation reporting and taxonomy metrics, effectively forcing governments to demonstrate the environmental impact of the spending. While additionality in a strict sense (new projects only because of the bond) is hard to assess, the label does ensure transparency and can influence budgetary decisions—for instance, if a ministry knows it can raise money via a green bond, it might prioritize green projects in budget requests. Over time, as a country issues multiple green bonds, there is evidence of a "ring-fencing" effect: budgets allocate more to eligible green expenditures to keep the program going, arguably increasing green fiscal spending margin. In Chile's case, the government explicitly linked its sustainable bond program to its NDC climate targets, creating a policy feedback loop.

In summary, governance regimes differ but are gradually converging in expectations. The EU's strict taxonomy and supervision, China's evolving catalog and coordination, and the US's market-driven norms all aim to uphold the credibility of the sovereign green label. The differences often reflect broader regulatory philosophies: precautionary harmonization in the EU vs. pragmatic flexibility in China vs. market self-regulation in the US. Each has pros and cons. What is clear is that investors globally value consistency and comparability—hence the push for common definitions (like the Common Ground Taxonomy effort). For sovereign issuers, aligning with high standards is beneficial: it can expand the investor base and potentially lower borrowing costs. That is why even absent formal rules, many have voluntarily adopted best practices like obtaining independent verification and committing to impact reporting (for example, almost all sovereign green bond issuers have joined the GBP's reporting forums, and countries like Spain and Colombia have published detailed impact reports referencing harmonized frameworks supported by the GBP group).

Conclusion

Sovereign green bonds have rapidly moved from novelty to an integral component of climate finance and sovereign debt management. As documented in this chapter, nations across the development spectrum are leveraging these instruments to direct capital toward the net-zero transition and other environmental objectives. Sovereign green bonds are not merely rebranded government debt; rather, they represent an important financial innovation at the nexus of public policy and capital markets. Their growth and performance to date yield several insights:

First, sovereign green bonds serve as an effective commitment device for governments. By issuing debt tied to specific climate-related expenditures and subject to ongoing reporting, sovereigns lock in a measure of accountability and focus for their climate spending. This addresses, in part, the credibility problem that often plagues government climate promises. Investors have shown they value this commitment—evidenced by strong demand and modest yield benefits—but they also will hold issuers to account. If a sovereign were to renege on its green commitments or misuse funds, it would face reputational damage and loss of market access beyond just the green niche. In this way, sovereign green bonds help mitigate information asymmetry: investors gain clearer line-of-sight into how their funds further climate goals, and governments gain credibility by transparently showcasing projects and outcomes. The "green" label is backed by formalized processes (frameworks, reviews, audits) that in effect create a higher standard of disclosure than is required for regular budget spending. This has spillover benefits for public financial management and trust.

Second, the sovereign green bond market has confirmed that environmental objectives and prudent debt management can be mutually reinforcing. Countries like France, Germany, and Chile have integrated green bonds into their financing strategies without increasing borrowing costs; indeed, often reducing them slightly. While the average greenium is small, it is persistently present under the right conditions—especially where credibility mechanisms (taxonomies, external verification, rigorous reporting) are strong. This underscores a policy message: good climate governance can translate into tangible financial advantages. Conversely, where frameworks are seen as weak or political commitment is doubtful, the market will price that in (either by no greenium or even a "brown" premium). Thus, sovereign green bonds incentivize improved climate governance. Notably, sovereign issuance has also helped build out the market ecosystem: it catalyzes local currency green bond markets, provides benchmark yield curves, and encourages the development of local verification providers and green rating methodologies. In emerging markets, the sovereign green bond often unlocks the market for state-owned enterprises and corporates to follow. For example, Nigeria's sovereign green bond paved the way for Nigerian banks to issue green bonds; Indonesia's sovereign sukuk set a template for domestic corporate sukuk. Sovereigns thereby act as market makers and standard setters.

Third, differences in regional regulatory approaches, while significant now, may diminish over time as global norms solidify. The EU's highly standardized model might become a de facto reference for many investors globally (especially those who operate under EU Sustainable Finance Disclosure rules). China's adjustments to its definitions and its participation in global taxonomy dialogues suggest convergence. International institutions (IMF, World Bank) are promoting common reporting frameworks for sovereign ESG debt. Over the next decade, we may see something akin to an international accord on green bond reporting for sovereigns, possibly under the G20 or IMF, which could facilitate comparisons (already, organizations like the CBI and OECD track sovereign bonds and encourage best practices). Harmonization will reduce transaction costs for investors and help smaller or new issuers come to market more easily (they can adopt an off-the-shelf standard rather than invent their own). One risk, however, is over-standardization—some flexibility is needed to account for national circumstances (for instance, not all countries have the same "green" opportunities; what's transitional in one may be green in another's context). The balance of market-based innovation and regulatory oversight will continue to be tested. Europe's introduction of the EuGB label, for example, will be watched closely: if sovereign issuers adopt it in droves, it will validate a regulated approach; if they shy away due to rigidity, it will indicate that voluntary standards might be preferable in some cases. Early indications (like Denmark's embrace) are optimistic.

Additionally, sovereign green bonds are poised to play a creative role in addressing the twin crises of climate change and debt distress in developing economies. The idea of using debt instruments to achieve climate co-benefits is gaining traction, and sovereign green bonds could be at the center of this trend. The chapter's exploration of debt-for-nature swaps and climate-linked restructurings highlights a future pathway where sustainability objectives are embedded in sovereign debt solutions. This is still at an experimental stage, but the urgency of climate action and the reality of rising debt vulnerabilities (exacerbated by climate shocks) make it likely that what is now novel could become mainstream. A plausible scenario is that multilateral lenders and creditor nations agree on frameworks to swap debt relief for green commitments, with new sovereign green (or blue) bonds issued as part of restructuring packages. If these can be backed by guarantee facilities or insurance (to improve credit for investors), we could unlock substantial financing. China's participation is a wildcard but also a linchpin—as a major creditor, its willingness to incorporate such innovations could scale the concept significantly. Sovereign green bonds thus might evolve from standalone market instruments to building blocks of comprehensive climate-financial deals.

Finally, the presence of a sovereign green bond market has deep implications for the relationship between investors and sovereign issuers. Investors are increasingly viewing climate risk as credit risk. By issuing green bonds, sovereigns signal that certain portions of their budgets are aligned with climate goals, implicitly indicating lower risk in those activities (e.g., investments in renewable energy are future-proofed against carbon regulation compared to investments in coal). Some research even suggests sovereign green bond issuance correlates with improved overall ESG scores or climate policy performance for countries, though causality is hard to establish. What is clear is that investors are now scrutinizing sovereigns on climate action—for instance, BlackRock and other large asset managers regularly engage with governments on climate policy, something virtually unheard of a decade ago. Green bond reporting provides a concrete entry point for such dialogue, allowing investors to ask, "What was the impact of project X funded by your green bond? How does it advance your 2030 goals?" This dynamic could enhance accountability and ambition over time, as governments realize that failing to deliver on the green projects could tarnish their reputation and even increase their cost of capital. On the flip side, investors might start differentiating between sovereigns more on climate performance—possibly rewarding those who issue green bonds and meet targets with better credit terms (already anecdotal evidence of certain green funds under-weighting sovereigns with poor climate scores exists).

In conclusion, sovereign green bonds embody the idea that financial innovation can be harnessed for public good without sacrificing market rigor. They channel the immense resources of global capital markets toward sustainable development needs, all while fitting into the risk-return frameworks that investors require. The chapter has shown that from conception to implementation, success has hinged on credibility: transparent use of proceeds, robust verification, diligent reporting, and integration with policy. Where these factors are present, sovereign green bonds have thrived, enjoying tight pricing and repeat issuance. The market's growth from one bond in 2016 to hundreds of billions in a few years is a testament to this instrument's adaptability and appeal. Challenges remain—ensuring true environmental impact, expanding issuance in low-income countries, refining standards—but the trajectory is clearly toward scaling up. As the world faces a financing gap for climate change imperatives, sovereign green bonds are poised to be a cornerstone of how countries raise and direct capital to meet the Paris Agreement and SDGs. They symbolize a shift in sovereign finance: from simply funding government operations to strategically shaping investment for a sustainable future. In doing so, they not only provide finance but also embed environmental accountability into the heart of government budgeting and investor decision-making—a lasting institutional innovation in the transition to net-zero.

References

Ando, S., Fu, C., Roch, F., & Wiriadinata, U. (2023). How large is the sovereign greenium? In *IMF Working Papers*, WP/23/80.

Boutabba, M. A., & Rannou, Y. (2022). Investor strategies in the green bond market: The influence of liquidity risks, economic factors and clientele effects. *International Review of Financial Analysis, 81*, 102071.

CBI. (2016). *Poland wins race to issue first green sovereign bond (market note).* Climate Bonds Initiative.

Chavarría-Flores, A., & Warren, P. (2024). Sovereign climate bonds: Policy innovation for just transitions in developing countries. *Journal of Climate Finance, 7*, 100041.

Das, N., Pradhan, R. P., & Janjua, L. R. (2026). Climate commitments and market risks: Analysing the drivers of sovereign green bond issuance in India. *Finance Research Letters, 90*, 109365.

Löffler, K. U., Petreski, A., & Stephan, A. (2021). Drivers of green bond issuance and new evidence on the "greenium". *Eurasian Economic Review, 11*(1), 1–24.

London Stock Exchange. (2025). *Ministry of Finance of the People's Republic of China launches inaugural sovereign green bonds issuance*. London Stock Exchange.

Lupo-Pasini, F. (2022). Sustainable finance and sovereign debt: The illusion to govern by contract. *Journal of International Economic Law, 25*(4), 680–698.

Ministry of Finance. (2017). *Green bond report on the use of proceeds (sovereign green bond allocation/reporting).* Government of Poland.

Nevatia, V. (2026). Sovereign green bonds: Risk-mitigating sustainability instruments in emerging markets. *Energy Economics, 155*, 109173.

Owusu-Mante, S., Chi, K. H.-K., & Gopalakrishnan, T. (2025). Sovereign green bonds in practice: Effectiveness as a climate finance instrument in emerging economies. *Climate Policy*, 1–15.

World Bank. (2025). *Labeled sustainable bonds market update—June 2025*. World Bank.

Zhou, P., Jin, S., Mazouz, K., & Ding, W. (2025). Choices and effects of different green labels in the EU bond market. *Journal of Business Ethics, 200*(1), 207–229.

Chapter 5
Investing in Green Bonds

Introduction

Previous chapters of this book have established green bonds as a central institutional instrument within climate finance. We have moved from conceptual foundations (**Chap. 1**), through the role of standards and regulation in sustaining market credibility (**Chap. 2**), to issuer-side dynamics in corporate and sovereign green bond markets (**Chaps. 3** and **4**). Together, these chapters emphasize how green bonds mobilize capital for the net-zero transition by linking debt finance to defined environmental expenditures under increasingly formalized disclosure regimes. What remains underexplored so far is the investor-facing question: how green bonds behave within portfolios, and whether they offer distinctive risk-management or hedging benefits beyond their environmental purpose.

This chapter addresses that gap. Its focus shifts from issuance and governance to investment strategy, with particular attention to the role of green bonds as hedging instruments in diversified portfolios. The chapter asks how they perform relative to conventional bonds and other asset classes under different market conditions, and whether they contribute to downside protection, volatility reduction, or diversification when financial stress or climate-related shocks materialize. This perspective is especially relevant for institutional investors—pension funds, insurers, sovereign wealth funds, and central bank reserve managers—whose mandates require careful balancing of return objectives, risk constraints, and long-term liabilities.

The motivation for a more technical, portfolio-oriented analysis is twofold. First, green bonds have matured from a niche ethical product into a sizable and liquid segment of global fixed-income markets. Green bond indices, exchange-traded funds, and dedicated mandates are now widely used by asset managers, making questions of correlation structure, duration exposure, and hedging effectiveness unavoidable. Second, climate change is increasingly recognized not only as an environmental externality, but also as a source of financial risk. Transition risk, physical risk, and

P. Zhou, D. Guo, *Climate Finance in the Net-Zero Transition*, Contributions to Finance and Accounting, https://doi.org/10.1007/978-981-92-0827-2_5

policy uncertainty all have the potential to affect asset prices across markets. In this context, green bonds are often assumed—sometimes implicitly—to provide partial insurance against climate-related shocks or broader market stress. Whether this assumption is empirically justified is a question that requires careful analysis rather than intuition.

Building on the analytical foundations of earlier chapters, this chapter treats green bonds as financial assets first and climate instruments second, without losing sight of their dual nature. Conceptually, green bonds are not a separate asset class in a strict sense; they are conventional debt instruments distinguished by the use of proceeds and associated disclosure obligations. Their cash flows, credit risk, and interest-rate sensitivity are therefore largely comparable to those of conventional bonds issued by the same entities. Any hedging benefit must arise not from contractual differences, but from differences in investor clientele, market segmentation, regulatory treatment, or behavioral responses under stress. Identifying and disentangling these channels is central to the analysis that follows.

The chapter is structured around three interrelated questions. First, how do green bond indices behave relative to conventional bond indices across market cycles, particularly during periods of heightened volatility? Second, do green bonds exhibit lower correlations with riskier assets—such as equities or high-yield credit—thereby offering diversification and hedging benefits in mixed-asset portfolios? Third, are any observed hedging properties stable across regions and market structures, or do they depend on institutional contexts such as Europe's Taxonomy-based framework, China's policy-guided market, or more market-driven environments like the US?

Methodologically, the chapter draws on index-level evidence and comparative international analysis, consistent with the applied orientation of the attached technical study. Rather than focusing on individual bond pricing or issuer behavior, the emphasis is on portfolio-level outcomes: volatility, drawdowns, correlations, and tail behavior. This approach complements the issuer- and market-design perspectives developed earlier in the book by translating them into metrics that matter directly for asset allocation and risk management. In doing so, the chapter speaks not only to academic debates on green finance performance, but also to practical investment decisions faced by institutional investors operating under regulatory and fiduciary constraints.

Importantly, the chapter does not assume that green bonds necessarily dominate conventional bonds in a risk-return sense. The objective is more modest and more precise: to assess whether green bond investments can contribute to portfolio resilience, particularly in environments where climate policy uncertainty, energy price shocks, or macro-financial stress interact. If green bonds exhibit hedging properties, these may arise from their investor base, longer duration profiles, or association with public-sector issuers and regulated utilities—factors that are themselves shaped by the institutional frameworks discussed in previous chapters. Conversely, if hedging benefits are weak or context-dependent, this has direct implications for how climate-aligned investment strategies should be designed and evaluated.

By situating green bonds within a rigorous portfolio and hedging framework, this chapter advances the book's overarching argument: climate finance cannot be understood solely through labels, standards, or issuance volumes. It must also be evaluated through the lens of financial functionality. Green bonds will only scale sustainably if they satisfy both environmental objectives and the risk-management needs of investors. The analysis that follows therefore bridges climate finance and modern portfolio theory, showing how green bonds operate not just as instruments of transition finance, but as components of contemporary investment strategy.

Literature

This section builds on earlier discussion of how standards, external review, and taxonomy alignment underpin the credibility of labeled debt instruments and shape pricing and demand in primary and secondary markets. From an investor perspective, those features matter because they affect (1) expected excess returns via any "greenium" and liquidity premium, and (2) the stability of correlations with other assets that ultimately determine diversification and hedging value. The recent literature has therefore shifted from asking whether green bonds are priced differently to asking when, and through which channels, green bonds improve portfolio outcomes—especially during episodes of elevated macro, geopolitical, and climate-policy uncertainty.

Green Bonds as Portfolio Assets

A first-order question is whether green bonds behave as a distinctive portfolio component rather than conventional bonds with a label. The emerging consensus is that green bonds share the dominant drivers of bond returns—duration, credit risk, and currency risk—yet may exhibit *partial distinctiveness* because of clientele effects, segmentation, verification practices, and climate-policy sensitivity.

Evidence on pricing and credibility supports this view. Flammer (2021) shows that corporate green bonds can function as commitment devices and are associated with environmentally relevant corporate actions, indicating that the green label may be economically meaningful beyond marketing. Fatica et al. (2021) document that pricing differentials depend on issuer type and market frictions, implying heterogeneity in how "green" information is capitalized into yields. These results are consistent with the book's earlier argument that standards, external review, and taxonomy alignment mitigate information asymmetry and can influence both demand and secondary-market outcomes.

Beyond average pricing, connectedness and horizon-specific behavior matter for portfolio design. Ferrer et al. (2021) use time-frequency connectedness analysis and show that the dependence structure of green bonds with other assets differs across investment horizons, suggesting that strategic (long-horizon) allocation may differ from short-horizon tactical positioning. For index investors, this implies that the portfolio role of green bond indices depends on both macro regimes and the intended rebalancing horizon.

Green Bonds as Hedging and Safe-Haven Assets

A second strand of research asks whether green bonds can hedge equity risk, serve as safe havens in crises, or protect against climate-policy uncertainty. The literature increasingly evaluates these properties through time-varying correlation models, connectedness frameworks, and hedging effectiveness metrics, often comparing green bonds directly with conventional bonds.

A key contribution is the explicit comparison of green versus conventional bonds under different uncertainty regimes. Dong et al. (2023) find that both conventional and green bonds can act as safe havens when geopolitical risk is high, but green bonds show stronger safe-haven performance under elevated economic policy uncertainty and climate policy uncertainty, improving hedging effectiveness in those states. This result is particularly relevant for transition-aware investors because climate policy uncertainty is a plausible driver of cross-asset repricing as decarbonization pathways become more contested.

Evidence also suggests sector heterogeneity on the equity side. Chopra and Mehta (2023) report that green bonds can hedge multiple US stock sectors and that safe-haven behavior is especially pronounced for high-emission sectors and during crisis conditions such as the COVID-19 period. This supports the idea that green bonds may hedge *specific* equity risks tied to transition exposure rather than providing only generic bond-like diversification.

Other studies operationalize these relationships into implementable portfolio strategies. Abuzayed and Al-Fayoumi (2023) translate dynamic dependence into optimal weights and hedge ratios, showing that green bonds can generate meaningful diversification and hedging gains in multi-asset portfolios during stress periods. Complementing this, Jin et al. (2020) connect green bond allocation to carbon-finance risk management by showing that green bond indices can hedge carbon market risk using dynamic hedge ratio approaches, highlighting a channel through which green bond exposure may be valuable for investors facing climate-policy and carbon-pricing risk.

Finally, crisis sensitivity and cross-country context are central for the reliability of hedges. Guo and Zhou (2021) show that hedging effectiveness can shift across pre- and post-COVID regimes, reinforcing that green bond hedging is time-varying and potentially fragile in tail states. China-focused evidence similarly indicates regime dependence: Xu et al. (2024) find that connectedness between green bonds and other domestic investment channels fluctuates materially during pandemic stress, while portfolio exercises still support a hedging role for Chinese investors. More recent geopolitical shocks also matter; Wang et al. (2025) document that conflict-related risk can influence green bond market stability, underscoring that green bonds are not insulated from global risk episodes.

What Remains Unresolved

Despite rapid growth in the evidence base, three unresolved issues are particularly salient for a technical and practical chapter focused on green bond index investing and hedging.

Implementability at the index level Much of the literature relies on aggregate proxies and correlation-based evidence, while investors implement exposures through indices and funds with embedded duration, currency, issuer-composition, and rebalancing rules. Translating dependence patterns into robust, investable strategies—including stress-tested hedge ratios and rebalancing frequency—remains a key gap.

Identification of incremental "green" hedging channels Even when green bonds hedge equities, it is not always clear whether the incremental benefit is driven by "greenness" (e.g., climate-policy sensitivity, investor clientele, institutional demand) or by conventional bond channels (e.g., duration-driven flight-to-quality). Papers that explicitly compare green and conventional bonds under climate-policy uncertainty provide more credible evidence of an incremental channel (e.g., Dong et al., 2023), but broader identification remains limited.

Cross-country heterogeneity and regime dependence Evidence from the US, China, and global indices suggests that hedging properties vary with market structure and shock type rather than being universal. This motivates the chapter's scenario-based, international-comparative approach: investors should expect hedging performance to differ across jurisdictions and episodes, reflecting differences in regulation, investor base, and index composition.

Taken together, the literature supports a pragmatic conclusion aligned with earlier chapters: green bonds can add portfolio value as risk-management tools in certain regimes, but their effectiveness is context-dependent and must be evaluated with implementable index constraints in mind.

Model

Returns of any assets, including green bonds, corporate bonds, stocks, oil index and dollar index, can be modeled in the following general form. The subscript g denotes green bonds, i denotes any other asset, and t is time. To be general, we allow both mean and volatility to change over time.

$$r_{gt} = \mu_{gt} + \xi_{gt}, \text{where } \xi_{gt} \equiv \sigma_{gt}\varepsilon_{gt} \tag{5.1}$$

$$r_{it} = \mu_{it} + \xi_{it}, \text{where } \xi_{it} \equiv \sigma_{it}\varepsilon_{it} \tag{5.2}$$

The mean component (μ_{vt}) of any asset ($\nu = g, i$) can be modeled as an ARMA(p, q) process. To write the model in an elegant form, econometricians usually use polynomials of lag operator L, such as $\boldsymbol{\phi}(L;p) = \phi_1 L + \ldots + \phi_p L^p$ and $\boldsymbol{\psi}(L;q) = \psi_1 L + \ldots + \psi_p L^p$, to express the ARMA model:

$$\mu_{vt} = \phi(L;p)\mu_{vt} + \psi(L;q)\xi_{vt} \tag{5.3}$$

Similarly, the volatility component (σ_{vt}^2) of the model is assumed to exhibit a threshold generalized autoregressive conditional heteroskedasticity (TGARCH). The polynomials $\boldsymbol{\alpha}(L;m)$, $\boldsymbol{\beta}(L;n)$, and $\boldsymbol{\gamma}(L;s)$ are defined in a similar way for the GARCH(m), ARCH(n), and TARCH(s) terms.

$$\sigma_{vt}^2 = \alpha_0 + \alpha(L;m)\sigma_{vt}^2 + \beta(L;n)\xi_{vt}^2 + \gamma(L;s)\xi_{vt}^2\Big|_{\xi_{vt}<0} \tag{5.4}$$

Nothing is new up to this point. Equations (5.1)–(5.4) are time-series models widely applied in finance literature since 1980s. To extend this simple model, as we summarized in the literature section above, there are four directions. If the focus is on the tail dependence between ϵs, then we arrive at the quantile-based approach. If we are more interested in the mean dependence, then we have MGARCH. If the research embarks on the temporal variation of the dependence, then TVP-VAR is a good choice. If one wants to capture all features to a certain degree, then the copula approach is the optimal choice. Therefore, we will adopt the copula approach as the baseline in this paper.

In the copula approach, joint distributions between ϵ_{gt} and ϵ_{it} are obtained in two steps in the light of Sklar's theorem (1959). The theorem states that every multivariate cumulative distribution function (CDF) $F(\bullet)$ of a set of jointly distributed random variables (say, ϵ_{gt} and ϵ_{it}) can be expressed in terms of the marginal CDFs ($F_g(\epsilon_{gt})$ and $F_i(\epsilon_{it})$) and a copula function ($C(\bullet)$) to link the marginals:

$$F(\varepsilon_{gt}, \varepsilon_{it}) = C\left(F_g(\varepsilon_{gt}), F_i(\varepsilon_{it})\right) \tag{5.5}$$

Copulas provide a more complete description of dependence between two or more random variables than linear correlation coefficient (Patton, 2006). Thus, the copula approach deals with the interdependence between random variables via ϵs rather than via μs as opposed to MGARCH and TVP-VAR. The distributional dependence is therefore the core of the copula approach.

In the first step of the copula approach, marginal CDFs ($F_g(\epsilon_{gt})$ and $F_i(\epsilon_{it})$) can be separately estimated. This feature grants great flexibility in practice—the underlying marginals can have different distributions and/or different parameters, without having to conform with the restrictions if a multivariate distribution is directly applied to model the dependence of assets. In the green bond literature, it is well established that a Student's t distribution (with a fat tail) tends to be the most appropriate marginal distribution (Reboredo, 2018), so we are going to use t distributions for the marginals.

Turning to the second step of specifying copula models, we largely follow the classical approach developed by Patton (2006). The tail dependence of the lower and upper ends of marginal CDFs can be formulated as:

$$\tau_L = \lim_{x\to 0} \Pr\left(F_g\left(\varepsilon_{gt}\right) \leq x \middle| F_i\left(\varepsilon_{it}\right) \leq x\right) = \lim_{x\to 0} \frac{C(x,x)}{x} \tag{5.6}$$

$$\tau_U = \lim_{x\to 1} \Pr\left(F_g\left(\varepsilon_{gt}\right) \geq x \middle| F_i\left(\varepsilon_{it}\right) \geq x\right) = \lim_{x\to 1} \frac{1-2x+C(x,x)}{1-x} \tag{5.7}$$

The two tail dependence measures τ_L and τ_U describe the probability that both assets are in their lower or upper joint tails, i.e., during extreme events like the financial crisis and the COVID pandemic. There are many different copulas with different features of tail dependence. We discuss the most popular and relevant ones here.

- **Gaussian/Normal copula**. It does not allow for tail dependence of the underlying marginal distributions, so both tail dependence measures τ_L and τ_U are equal to zero. Dependence is simply measured by Pearson's correlation coefficient $-1 \leq \rho \leq 1$.
- **Student's t copula**. It has a fat tail, so tail dependence is possible. The symmetry of the t distribution implies an equal lower and upper tail dependence $\tau_L = \tau_U$ which depends on the two copula parameters, the correlation coefficient ρ and the degree of freedom ν.
- **Clayton copula**. It is an asymmetric distribution with greater lower tail dependence $\tau_L > 0$ than upper tail dependence $\tau_U = 0$. There is only one parameter of the Clayton copula $\vartheta \geq 1$, where $\vartheta = 1$ means independence.
- **Rotated Clayton copula**. It is the reverse of the Clayton copula, so it allows for positive upper dependence $\tau_U > 0$ but zero lower dependence $\tau_L = 0$. In practice, one can simply transform the data to swap the tails before estimation.
- **SJC copula**. It allows for asymmetric tail dependence $\tau_L \neq \tau_U$ and the two measures can be estimated directly.

In addition to the copulas described above, Gumbel copula is also popular, but it is close to Clayton copula. They, together with their rotated counterparts, are called the Archimedean copulas (Creal et al., 2011).

To capture time variation of copulas, an autoregressive conditional density in the spirit of Hansen (1994) is usually used. The advantage of this method, relative to alternatives, regime switching method for example, is that it is more efficient and parsimonious in parameterization. Assume the time-varying parameters in copulas ($\theta_t \equiv \rho_t | \tau_{Lt} | \tau_{Ut}$) are summarized by an ARMA-type process (Patton, 2006).

$$\theta_t = \Lambda\left(a + b\theta_{t-1} + c\frac{1}{K}\sum_{k=1}^{K} H\left(\varepsilon_{g,t-k}, \varepsilon_{i,t-k}\right)\right). \tag{5.8}$$

In Eq. (5.8), $\Lambda(\bullet)$ is a logistic transformation to keep measures of tail dependence within defined domains. $H(\bullet)$ is product of normal quantile functions for normal copula, product of t quantile functions for t copula, absolute difference function for Clayton, Gumbel, and SJC copulas. According to Patton (2006), the length of lags $K = 10$ is chosen, which corresponds to 2 working weeks for daily data.

Results

Following the convention of the green bond literature, we select bond market, stock market, energy market, and forex market to study the dependence of green bond market. We will compare our results of the US, the EU, and China which play significant roles in global green bond issuance.

Data Description

The sample period is set from July 2014 to February 2022. For the China-focused analysis, the choice of data proceeds in two steps. First, for the green bond investment variable, we select a representative green bond index to reflect the increasingly index-based asset allocation practices of international investors. Although China's financial market offers more than a dozen major green bond indices, this chapter uses the China Bond Green Bond Index. The rationale is that the index provider is a key financial market infrastructure institution in China's interbank bond market and has explicitly aimed to support both "genuine greenness" and "green use of proceeds" in the green bond market. The index methodology embeds green standards aligned with China's "dual carbon" strategy while incorporating sustainable development and ESG principles. In empirical analysis, the China Bond Green Bond Index (CNGB) is used to capture the evolving direction of China-EU standards convergence. It is also designed to be consistent with relatively stringent international green bond standards, thereby helping to mitigate risks of greenwashing and "pseudo-green" labeling.

Second, to characterize other investable asset markets in China, the bond market is proxied by the yield to maturity on China Bond 10-year government bonds (CNB). The equity market is represented by the Shanghai Stock Exchange Composite Index (CNS). Forex market movements are measured by returns on the USD/CNY exchange rate (CFN). Given the current stage of RMB internationalization—where RMB pricing and settlement in global oil markets remain limited and

China largely remains a price-taking net importer—international oil price exposure faced by the Chinese market is proxied by Brent crude oil prices (CNO).

For Europe, we use daily data for the Bloomberg MSCI Green Bond Index (EUGB) from the same sample period. The European bond market is proxied by 10-year European government bonds (EUB). The equity market is represented by a major European stock market index provided by Refinitiv (EUS). Forex market volatility is measured by the EUR/USD exchange rate (EUF). As a key commodity closely related to green bond performance through macro and energy-transition channels, European energy price dynamics are captured using Brent crude oil prices (EUO).

For the US, we use daily data for the Barclays MSCI Green Bond Index (USGB) from August 2014 to February 2022. The US bond market is proxied by 10-year US government bonds (USB). The equity market is represented by the Dow Jones Industrial Average (USS). Forex market movements are measured by the US dollar index (USF). Energy price variation is proxied by West Texas Intermediate (WTI) crude oil prices (USO), which is preferred over Brent in this context because it more directly reflects US oil market conditions, whereas Brent incorporates broader non-US market dynamics.

Tables 5.1, 5.2, and 5.3 show descriptive statistics of data for China, the EU, and the US. Figures 5.1, 5.2, and 5.3 visualize the joint distributions among assets. Across the three regions, there is a set of common "stylized facts" that motivate the modeling strategy adopted later.

First, all daily return series have means close to zero, while the Jarque-Bera (JB) statistics are large across assets, indicating strong departures from normality and the presence of fat tails. Second, the ADF statistics are strongly negative in all cases, supporting return stationarity. Together, these properties imply that linear-Gaussian dependence measures are likely to be incomplete, and that volatility dynamics and tail behavior should be modeled explicitly (hence the later use of conditional heteroskedasticity in the marginals and tail-sensitive dependence models).

Table 5.1 Descriptive statistics of data (China)

China	CNGB	CNUB	CNUS	CNUF	CNUO
Mean	0.0002	−0.0001	0.0001	0.0000	0.0006
Max	0.0083	0.0367	0.0576	0.0186	0.2102
Min	−0.0089	−0.0568	−0.0849	−0.0099	−0.2440
Stand. dev.	0.0009	0.0080	0.0137	0.0021	0.0259
JB	2.04E + 04	1.00E + 03	4.27E + 03	3.97E + 03	1.57E + 04
ADF	−26.51	−37.22	−40.73	−39.25	−41.69
Corr.	**CNGB**	**CNUB**	**CNUS**	**CNUF**	**CNUO**
CNGB	1				
CNB	−0.5103	1			
CNS	−0.0587	0.1342	1		
CNF	−0.0181	0.0431	−0.0467	1	
CNO	−0.024	0.0343	−0.0074	0.0121	1

Table 5.2 Descriptive statistics of data (EU)

EU	EUGB	EUB	EUS	EUF	EUO
Mean	0.0001	0.0001	0.0002	0.0000	−0.0006
Max	0.0113	0.0148	0.0840	0.0308	0.2102
Min	−0.0194	−0.0160	−0.1148	−0.0237	−0.2440
Stand. dev.	0.0023	0.0025	0.0107	0.0049	0.0259
JB	3.51E + 03	1.76E + 03	1.32E + 04	5.61E + 02	1.46E + 04
ADF	−39.70	−40.32	−42.88	−43.15	−42.40
Corr.	**EUGB**	**EUB**	**EUS**	**EUF**	**EUO**
EUGB	1				
EUB	0.8791	1			
EUS	−0.048	0.0271	1		
EUF	−0.0988	−0.1132	−0.1527	1	
EUO	−0.0668	−0.036	0.3268	0.0037	1

Table 5.3 Descriptive statistics of data (US)

US	USGB	USB	USS	USF	USO
Mean	0.0001	0.0005	0.0005	0.0001	−0.0012
Max	0.0104	0.4074	0.0938	0.0252	0.3766
Min	−0.0235	−0.2703	−0.1198	−0.0207	−3.0597
Stand. dev.	0.0021	0.0326	0.0111	0.0046	0.0827
JB	1.14E+04	7.67E+04	3.16E+04	2.42E+03	8.29E+07
ADF	−41.99	−44.10	−52.87	−56.38	−32.09
Corr.	**USGB**	**USB**	**USS**	**USF**	**USO**
USGB	1				
USB	−0.7718	1			
USS	−0.1366	0.3834	1		
USF	−0.0622	−0.0252	−0.1701	1	
USO	−0.0422	0.1098	0.1625	−0.0745	1

A second feature is the pronounced cross-asset heterogeneity in volatility and extremes, which is informative for portfolio construction and hedging. Equity indices (CNUS/EUS/USS) are more volatile than green bond indices, while oil returns (CNUO/EUO/USO) display the largest extreme movements, particularly in the US sample where the minimum oil return is exceptionally large in magnitude. This combination—relatively low-volatility green bond indices versus highly non-Gaussian commodity returns—creates scope for diversification in normal times, but also raises the possibility that dependence structures become regime-dependent in stressed markets, especially through tail events in energy prices.

Third, the correlation matrices point to a consistent but region-specific pattern in how green bond indices relate to core asset classes. In China and the US, green bonds are negatively correlated with the conventional bond proxy (CNGB-CNUB ≈ −0.51; USGB-USB ≈ −0.77), whereas in the EU green bonds are strongly

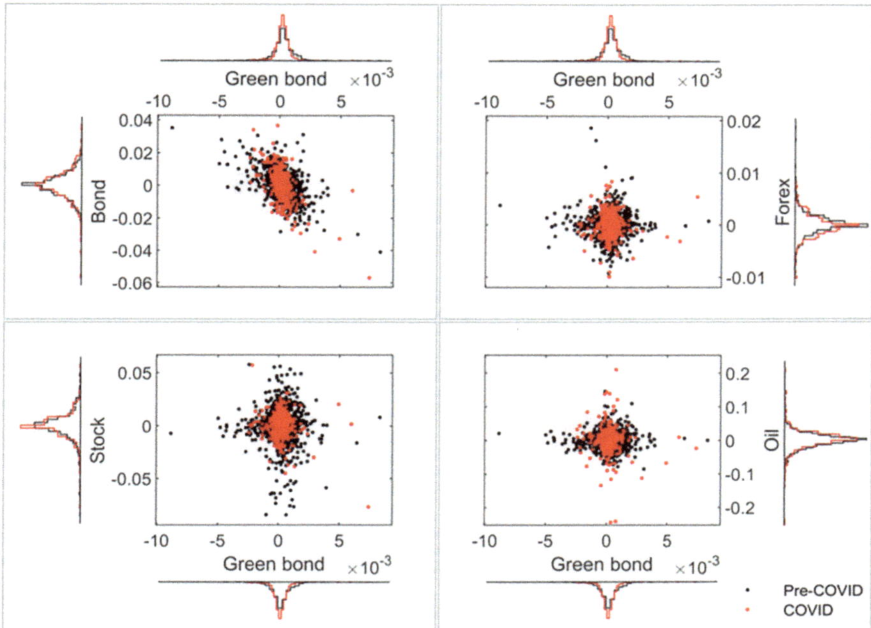

Fig. 5.1 Scatter plots between green bonds and other assets (China)

positively correlated with the government bond proxy (EUGB-EUB ≈ 0.88). This divergence matters for interpretation: in the EU, green bond indices behave more like conventional duration exposure, implying that hedging performance may resemble that of standard sovereign fixed income; in China and the US, the negative green-bond correlation suggests either measurement differences in the bond proxy or a more complex interaction between rates, index composition, and market structure that could materially affect hedge ratios. Beyond bonds, green bonds exhibit only weak correlations with equities and commodities in all three regions (generally small negatives), and modest links with forex proxies. These low contemporaneous correlations are consistent with diversification potential, but the combination of fat tails and crisis-prone commodities implies that hedging assessments should be based on time-varying and tail-sensitive dependence rather than unconditional correlations alone.

Tail-Risk Metrics

To evaluate whether green bond index investing provides downside protection—especially during market stress—this chapter relies on three tail-risk measures that have become standard in the empirical literature: Value at Risk (VaR), Conditional

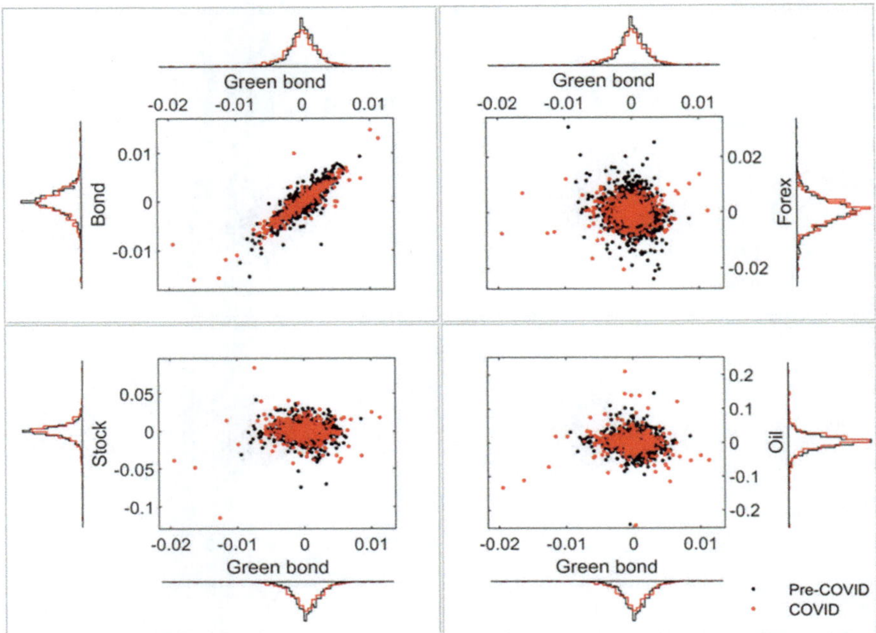

Fig. 5.2 Scatter plots between green bonds and other assets (EU)

Value at Risk (CoVaR), and Delta CoVaR (ΔCoVaR). VaR provides a direct measure of an asset's left-tail loss under a specified probability level (e.g., the 5% quantile). Operationally in our setting, VaR is obtained by ranking each asset's historical daily returns and identifying the return at the relevant lower quantile, which represents the "bad state" outcome for that asset. While VaR captures standalone tail risk, it is silent on tail dependence—that is, how losses in one market coincide with, or transmit to, losses in another.

CoVaR addresses this limitation by quantifying the downside risk of an asset conditional on a stress event in another asset (or in the same asset), thereby providing a tractable measure of tail co-movement and potential risk spillovers (Girardi & Ergün, 2013; see also Adrian & Brunnermeier, 2016). In practice, the conditioning event can be defined as another asset being below its own VaR threshold, allowing CoVaR to capture "how bad outcomes cluster" across markets. Building on CoVaR, ΔCoVaR summarizes the incremental tail risk contribution associated with stress: it is the difference between CoVaR under a stress condition and CoVaR under a baseline (normal) condition, typically assessed at a high confidence level (e.g., 95%). To facilitate interpretation across markets and assets, ΔCoVaR is often scaled by the baseline CoVaR, yielding a marginal contribution measure that is comparable across environments with different unconditional risk levels (Shahzad et al., 2018).

The VaR results in Table 5.4 first provide a disciplined way to compare how the pandemic-period shock altered tail risk across asset classes and regions. A key

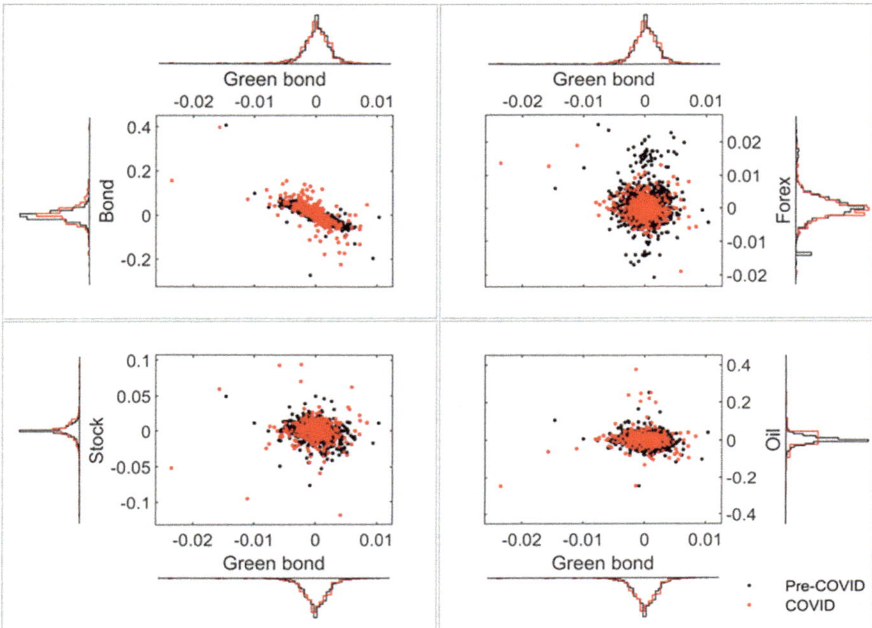

Fig. 5.3 Scatter plots between green bonds and other assets (US)

empirical regularity is that green bond indices and forex returns exhibit relatively limited VaR shifts across China, the EU, and the US, suggesting that these two markets were comparatively less sensitive—at least in left-tail terms—to the pandemic shock than equities and energy-related commodities. By contrast, equity-market VaR rises sharply in China, consistent with a pronounced deterioration in stock-market downside risk. Commodity-related tail risk also moves materially, although the direction differs across regions, underscoring that "global shocks" can still map into heterogeneous tail outcomes once local market structure and investor base are considered.

The CoVaR and ΔCoVaR results then shift the focus from how risky each asset is to how green bonds behave when other markets are in distress—which is precisely the relevant criterion for hedging and safe-haven discussions. The sign of the conditional green-bond VaR under stress provides an intuitive reading of hedging direction. In China, the conditional tail outcomes of green bond returns are positive when other assets are in stress, implying that exposure to the China green bond index has substantial potential to offset extreme downside outcomes elsewhere—i.e., green bonds behave as an effective tail hedge against multiple asset classes. In the EU, the evidence is more state-dependent: the hedging role of green bonds appears stronger pre-pandemic, while under pandemic stress the conditional tail behavior vis-à-vis euro-area bonds and the exchange rate can turn unfavorable, indicating that green bonds may not uniformly deliver tail protection in the most adverse

Table 5.4 Tail-risk metrics of assets of the three economies

	VaR at 5%		CoVaR at 5%		ΔCoVaR	
Assets	Pre-COVID	COVID	Pre-COVID	COVID	Pre-COVID	COVID
CNGB	−0.12%	−0.07%	−0.24%	−0.14%	−10.9289	−9.007
CNB	−1.23%	−1.36%	0.14%	0.11%	5.6242	5.337
CNS	−2.20%	−1.73%	0.04%	0.07%	1.0438	3.6379
CNF	−0.34%	−0.34%	0.02%	0.02%	−0.1571	0.1384
CNO	−3.63%	−4.04%	0.04%	0.05%	1.1504	1.7781
EUGB	−0.33%	−0.46%	−0.47%	−0.73%	−28.7144	148.7859
EUB	−0.36%	−0.48%	−0.42%	−0.69%	−25.8885	148.8076
EUS	−1.57%	−1.87%	0.06%	−0.06%	4.4791	4.5589
EUF	−0.80%	−0.70%	0.08%	−0.22%	5.2228	−1882.89
EUO	−3.69%	−4.04%	0.04%	0.00%	2.0295	−1.3668
USGB	−0.30%	−0.36%	−0.44%	−0.66%	−28.879	−84.959
USB	−3.39%	−5.68%	0.38%	0.33%	21.182	68.304
USS	−1.45%	−1.94%	0.15%	−0.11%	10.97	−15.796
USF	−0.73%	−0.48%	0.02%	0.11%	0.7858	120.08
USO	−3.84%	−4.49%	0.10%	−0.02%	6.9129	−14.49

states. The US results again suggest a qualified hedging role: green bonds retain positive conditional tail behavior for several conditioning assets, but the protective pattern is weaker against equities and energy commodities, and—similar to the EU—the pre-pandemic period appears more supportive of a hedging interpretation than the pandemic period.

Finally, ΔCoVaR provides a quantitative lens on how the marginal hedging contribution changes from normal times to stress times. The evidence indicates that the pandemic shock does not mechanically reduce the hedging value of green bonds; rather, the marginal tail interaction intensifies in several cases, consistent with a "crisis amplification" in tail dependence that can either strengthen or weaken hedge properties depending on the market. Empirically, the hedging contribution improves in China across multiple conditioning assets; in the EU it improves for several key assets (including bonds and equities); and in the US the improvement is more selective (notably for bonds and forex), while the overall hedging effect is the one most likely to weaken under pandemic stress. These heterogeneous patterns motivate the chapter's next step: formally testing tail dependence and state-contingent co-movement using a copula-based framework, rather than relying solely on reduced-form tail statistics.

Marginal Distributions

The marginal dynamics specified in Eqs. (5.1)–(5.4) are estimated for each asset, with lag orders selected by AIC and BIC from a flexible grid—ARMA orders p, $q \in \{0,1,2,3,4,5\}$and volatility orders m, n, $s \in \{0,1,2\}$. The results (Table 5.5) indicate substantial heterogeneity in mean dynamics across assets and regions, consistent with the view that short-run return predictability is weak and asset-specific. In particular, euro-area equities (EUS) display no dynamic terms in the conditional mean, implying that once standard filtering is applied, their mean process is effectively white noise over the sample period.

By contrast, volatility dynamics are pervasive and robust. Across all assets in China, the EU, and the US, the conditional variance equations feature statistically significant ARCH and GARCH components, providing strong evidence of conditional heteroskedasticity and volatility clustering. This finding justifies modeling volatility explicitly rather than treating it as constant, and it also motivates the later use of time-varying dependence measures, given that cross-asset correlations often co-move with volatility. Moreover, leverage terms are significant across regions, implying asymmetric volatility responses: negative shocks tend to generate larger increases in conditional volatility than positive shocks of comparable magnitude. This asymmetry is particularly relevant for hedging analysis because downside states—rather than average conditions—are precisely where portfolio insurance is most valuable.

Finally, the marginal return distributions exhibit pronounced fat tails. To accommodate this, the innovations are modeled with a Student's t distribution. The estimated degrees of freedom are uniformly below 8 across all assets, indicating heavy tails far from the Gaussian benchmark (with the t distribution approaching normality only at much higher degrees of freedom). Importantly, China's green bond index tends to have even lower degrees of freedom than its counterparts, implying comparatively thicker tails and greater exposure to extreme outcomes. This combination—volatility clustering, leverage effects, and heavy-tailed innovations—supports the chapter's empirical strategy of pairing flexible marginal models with dependence structures designed to capture tail co-movement, rather than relying on linear correlation measures that are ill-suited to crisis-period behavior.

Copulas

Based on the estimated marginal models, we construct standardized residuals and use them to identify the dependence structure between green bond returns and each comparator asset. This two-step approach reduces the risk that cross-asset dependence is mechanically driven by unmodeled serial correlation or volatility clustering in the individual series. Table 5.6 reports results for a set of widely used static

Table 5.5 Estimation results of marginal distributions

Mean	CNGB	CNB	CNS	CNF	CNO	EUGB	EUB	EUS	EUF	EUO	USGB	USB	USS	USF	USO
AR(1) ϕ_1	0.2834	0.3283*	−0.1591*	0.9937**	−0.4721**	−0.0553**	−0.4494**		−0.1294	−0.5305**	0.4165**	−0.8435**	1.3372	0.0258	0.3680
AR(2) ϕ_2	1.0978*	−0.7726*	0.7827*	−1.0126**	−0.9068**	0.0206**	−0.5520**		1.4665	0.1641*	−0.4455**	−0.9612**	0.0498	0.1093*	0.3813*
AR(3) ϕ_3	0.1597	−0.3387*	−0.1102*	0.8864**		0.9092**	−0.8789**		0.2958*	0.8309**	0.9085**		−0.3870	−0.3035**	0.6773*
AR(4) ϕ_4	−0.6907		−0.8155*						−0.7396	0.0541**	0.0787**			−0.5893*	−0.5887
AR(5) ϕ_5	0.1493*		−0.0430**							0.0563**	−0.0236**			0.3792*	
MA(1) ψ_1	0.1055	−0.1863*	0.1471*	−0.9684*	0.4485**	0.05015**	0.4625**		0.1247	0.5063*	−0.4703**	0.8254**	−1.3921	−0.0711	−0.3817
MA(2) ψ_2	−1.0278	0.6797*	−0.7675*	1.0267**	0.8760**	−0.0026**	0.5629**		−1.5000	−0.2060**	0.5152***	0.9515**	0.0372	−0.0950*	−0.3773*
MA(3) ψ_3	−0.5181	0.4804*	0.1047*	−0.8767*	−0.0202**	−0.9056**	0.8924**		−0.3052*		−0.9406**		0.3559	0.2914**	−0.6843**
MA(4) ψ_4	0.4441		0.7814*		−0.0249**	0.0384**	0.0248**		0.7703					0.5608*	0.6245
MA(5) ψ_5														−0.4376	

Variance	CNGB	CNB	CNS	CNF	CNO	EUGB	EUB	EUS	EUF	EUO	USGB	USB	USS	USF	USO
Constant α_0	0***	0***	0**	0***	0***	0	0***	0***	0***	0***	0***	0**	0***	0***	0***
GARCH(1) α_1	0	0.8797**	0.9107 **	0	0.8909**	0.8841**	0.1077	0.4523	0.9501***	0.8895**	0.8689**	0.9549 ***	0.8494**	0.0046**	0.7343**
GARCH(2) α_2	0.3625*			0.7415		0	0.7109	0.3461			0				
ARCH(1) β_1	0.4211	0.0744*	0**	0.1187**	0.0241**	0.0502***	0.0314**	0**	0.0432**	0.0327**	0.0779**	0.0167***	0**	0.0358**	0.0691**
ARCH(2) β_2	0.0809*	0.0399*	0.0783**	0.0569**			0.0592**						0.0087**		
Leverage(1) γ_1	−0.0360	0.0094*	0.0734*	0.0930**	0.1199**	0.0506**	0.0040**	0.3550*	−0.0040**	0.1156**	0.0111**	0.0563**	0.2924*	1.0000	0.1885*
Leverage(2) γ_2	0.3069	−0.0399*	−0.0582*	0.0726**			0.0619**						−0.0087*		

Variance	CNGB	CNB	CNS	CNF	CNO	EUGB	EUB	EUS	EUF	EUO	USGB	USB	USS	USF	USO
DoF ν	2.6485	4.9418	3.8765	3.6124	5.4616	5.8628	5.2611*	5.7712	7.9883	5.3762	6.2263	7.5806	3.4638	2.9004	2.9976
No. of obs.	1859	1859	1859	1859	1859	1859	1859	1859	1859	1859	1859	1859	1859	1859	1859
AIC	−21,526.0	−12,665.9	−11,316.8	−17,561.1	−8863.6	−17,778.8	−17,320.7	−12,514.5	−14,802.5	−9131.7	−18,091.1	−8789.7	−12,975.3	−15,691.1	−8964.6
BIC	−21,432.6	−12,594.5	−11,228.9	−17,484.2	−8803.2	−17,712.5	−17,237.8	−12,481.3	−14,730.6	−9059.8	−18,019.2	−8739.9	−12,903.4	−15,608.1	−8892.6

Notes: significance * 10% ** 5% *** 1%

Table 5.6 Estimation results of static copulas

		CNB	CNS	CNF	CNO	EUB	EUS	EUF	EUO	USB	USS	USF	USO
Normal	ρ	−0.478***	−0.046*	−0.02	−0.004	0.8668**	−0.1035*	−0.0944	−0.1173	−0.400***	−0.054**	−0.597***	−0.01
	$\tau_L = \tau_U$	0	0	0	0	0	0	0	0	0	0	0	0
	AIC	−466.4	−1.82	1.248	1.965	−2623.6	−17.69	−21.97	−19.11	−318.07	−3.374	−805.21	1.812
Student's t	ρ	−0.457***	−0.050**	−0.02	−0.001	0.8818**	−0.1218	−0.0898*	−0.1221	−0.427***	−0.063**	−0.612***	−0.005
	DoF ν	4.375***	8.816***	99.99***	28.28***	4.723***	8.016***	4.651***	9.619***	4.423***	7.036***	4.041***	8.619***
	$\tau_L = \tau_U$	0.0126	0.0093	0	0	0.0052	0.0256	0.0248	0.0243	0.0144	0.0166	0.0059	0.0124
	AIC	−533.5	−19.864	3.539	2.103	−2984.8	−78.16	−31.30	−36.25	−416.34	−36.7	−913.11	−19.51
Clayton	ρ	0.0001	0.0001	0.0001	0.0001	0.0001	0.0001	0.0001	0.0134	0.0001	0.0001	0.0001	0.0134
	τ_L	0	0	0	0	0	0	0	0	0	0	0	0
	AIC	2.132	2.014	2.01	2.007	2.195	2.031	2.126	1.334	2.099	2.001	2.166	1.639
Rotated	ρ	0.0001	0.0043	0.0001	0.0182	0.0001	0.0001	0.0001	0.0082	0.0001	0.0001	0.0001	0.0082
Clayton	τ_U	0	0	0	0	0	0	0	0	0	0	0	0
	AIC	2.128	1.962	2.005	1.438	2.116	2.001	2.016	1.215	2.096	2.007	2.16	1.875
SJC	τ_U	0	0***	0***	0	0	0***	0	0**	0	0***	0	0**
	τ_L	0	0***	0***	0***	0	0***	0	0	0	0***	0	0
	AIC	59.776	8.082	8.798	5.983	52.182	8.161	8.253	4.154	49.982	8.261	74.253	4.551

Notes: significance * 10% ** 5% *** 1%

copulas—Normal, Student's *t*, Clayton, Rotated Clayton, and SJC—allowing both robustness checks and model selection.

A central distinction in the copula framework is between the *linear association* captured by the copula correlation parameter $\rho$and *tail dependence* captured by $\tau_L$and τ_U. The Normal copula implies $\tau_L = \tau_U = 0$ by construction, meaning that extreme co-movements are not systematically more likely than what is implied by average dependence. By contrast, the Student's *t* copula allows for *symmetric* tail dependence, $\tau_L = \tau_U > 0$, and therefore can capture joint extremes that occur more frequently than under Gaussian dependence.

The estimates highlight two economically meaningful patterns. First, most estimated ρvalues are negative, suggesting that in "typical" market conditions adverse movements in many conventional assets tend to coincide with relatively favorable green bond returns. This is consistent with a hedging interpretation in normal times. Second, once tail dependence is allowed for, the preferred Student's *t* copula implies $\tau_L = \tau_U > 0$ for most asset pairs. In other words, even when average dependence is negative, the probability of *joint extreme outcomes* is non-negligible: when another asset experiences a rare and severe negative shock, green bonds are more likely than a Gaussian benchmark would predict to also fall sharply. This distinction matters for risk management because portfolio insurance is most valuable precisely in left-tail states; negative unconditional correlations can therefore overstate hedge reliability if tail dependence rises in crises.

The asymmetric copulas play a mainly diagnostic role. The Clayton and Rotated Clayton copulas impose one-sided tail dependence (lower-tail only or upper-tail only, respectively), yet they are generally not strongly supported in this application. The SJC copula, which permits asymmetric tail dependence, can be statistically significant in some cases, but the implied tail dependence magnitudes are typically small. Overall, the evidence favors dependence structures that are heavy-tailed but broadly symmetric, consistent with the notion that systemic shocks tend to raise joint extremes across markets in a relatively balanced way rather than producing strongly one-sided co-movement.

Using AIC for model selection, the Student's *t* copula is preferred for most green bond-asset pairs, indicating that allowing for fat-tailed joint behavior materially improves fit relative to the Normal copula. Two exceptions stand out: for CNF (the RMB exchange rate proxy) and CNO (oil exposure in the China set), the Normal copula is preferred, implying limited evidence of tail dependence beyond linear association in these pairs. Substantively, this suggests that green bond dependence with RMB forex and with oil (in the China specification) may be closer to Gaussian-like co-movement, potentially making hedging performance against extreme forex or oil movements more stable than for assets whose dependence is characterized by heavy-tailed joint risks.

Taken together, the static copula results support a nuanced interpretation of green bonds as hedging instruments. Green bonds tend to provide diversification benefits in normal times (negative ρ for many pairs), yet their crisis protection cannot be inferred from unconditional correlation alone because tail dependence is often positive under the best-fitting copula. This motivates the chapter's subsequent emphasis on tail-risk metrics (VaR/CoVaR) and on time-varying dependence models, which are better suited to capturing regime shifts around major stress episodes such as COVID-19.

Static copulas provide a useful benchmark, but the dependence patterns are likely to shift around major stress episodes. The chapter therefore extends the analysis to time-varying copulas, where both the correlation parameter $\rho_t$and tail dependence measures (τ_{Lt}, τ_{Ut}) evolve over time. Given that Student's t copulas dominate model selection for most pairs, the dynamic analysis focuses primarily on time-varying Student's t specifications, while retaining Normal copulas for cases such as the China forex pairing where tail dependence is empirically weak. The dynamic results (Table 5.7) further reinforce the qualitative cross-regional contrasts observed in the surfaces: China and the US often share similar green bond-bond dynamics, while the EU remains distinct; the US dependence is typically more unstable for equities and forex; and China's green bond-forex linkage is comparatively stable and weak. Finally, although allowing time variation increases parameterization, improvements in fit (as reflected in information criteria for most pairs) indicate that dynamic copulas capture economically meaningful regime shifts—an important consideration when the sample includes extended crisis observations.

To compare dependence structures across regions in an intuitive way, we plot the estimated copula surfaces in 3D mesh form. In these plots, stronger curvature near the corners indicates greater tail dependence (i.e., a higher likelihood of joint extremes), while a flatter surface suggests weak dependence and limited tail co-movement. Assuming Student's t copulas for comparability (with Normal copulas as exceptions where supported by estimation), the surfaces reveal both cross-market similarities and important structural differences.

The China-US comparison (Fig. 5.4) shows strong convergence in the dependence of green bonds with conventional bonds and equities. For green bonds versus "brown" bonds, the two copula surfaces are almost indistinguishable, and both exhibit visible tail dependence at low and high quantiles. This implies that, in both markets, extreme shocks in the conventional bond segment are more likely to coincide with extreme outcomes in green bonds than a purely Gaussian dependence structure would predict. For green bonds versus equities, the two countries again exhibit highly similar surfaces, but with "thicker" tails than in the bond pairing—consistent with the idea that equity stress is more likely to coincide with joint tail events even when average correlations remain modest.

Differences emerge most clearly in forex and oil. For the US, the green bond-USD index pairing produces a dependence pattern broadly comparable to those observed for bonds and equities. In China, by contrast, the green bond-RMB exchange-rate pairing is close to flat, consistent with a Normal-copula-type structure (i.e., limited tail dependence). This suggests that tail co-movement between green bonds and forex is weaker in China than in the US. For oil, both countries show qualitatively similar patterns, but China's surface is flatter, implying weaker joint tail behavior. A plausible interpretation is that China's oil exposure (proxied by Brent) reflects an externally priced global commodity where China is largely a price taker, which can reduce the tightness of tail linkages between domestic financial

Table 5.7 Estimation results of time-varying copulas

		CNB	CNS	CNF	CNO	EUB	EUS	EUF	EUO	USB	USS	USF	USO
Normal	ρ	−0.98***	0.6717*	0.638	0.675	0.4642***	−0.9258	0.9844***	−0.2783**	0.835***	−0.149	0.979***	0.684***
	a	−0.989***	−0.178*	−0.076	−0.031	−0.9754**	−0.1666	−0.3358	−0.4591	−0.989***	−0.011	−0.236***	0.0017
	b	−0.136***	0.077	0.3804**	−0.51***	−0.0731	0.1295	0.4098	0.1013**	0.0319	0.051***	−0.079***	0.400***
	c	0.3321***	−1.93***	−1.97***	−0.675	0.4642***	−0.9258**	0.9844***	−0.2783**	−0.388***	1.638***	2.013***	−1.996***
	AIC	−471.92	2.148	2.398	−1.967	−2623.6	−17.69	−21.97	−19.11	−313.09	−4.5049	−808.96	−6.5371
Student's t	ρ	−0.98***	−0.599	0.018	0.654	0.8950	−0.9024	0.9822	0.2532	0.357	−0.156	0.967	0.660
	ν	4.468***	8.566***	99.81***	31.12***	2.3853**	5.4149***	10.8512**	13.4236*	4.484***	7.096***	3.964***	9.489***
	a	−1.200**	−0.150	−0.078	−0.02	4.6570**	−0.2450	−0.3100**	−0.0075	−1.906***	−0.012	−3.108***	0.004
	b	−0.05	0.139	0.3533***	−0.48***	−0.0180	0.0629***	0.2652	−0.0176**	0.031	0.047***	−0.091	0.274***
	c	−0.285***	−1.30***	−2.007***	−0.664***	−2.0710**	−0.0461**	−1.7277**	1.9828**	−2.411***	1.728***	−2.570***	−1.996***
	AIC	−535.37	−15.5094	4.2018	−1.5362	−2985.2	−75.29	−34.38	−37.19	−412.46	−41.11	−914.79	−24.04

Notes: significance * 10% ** 5% *** 1%

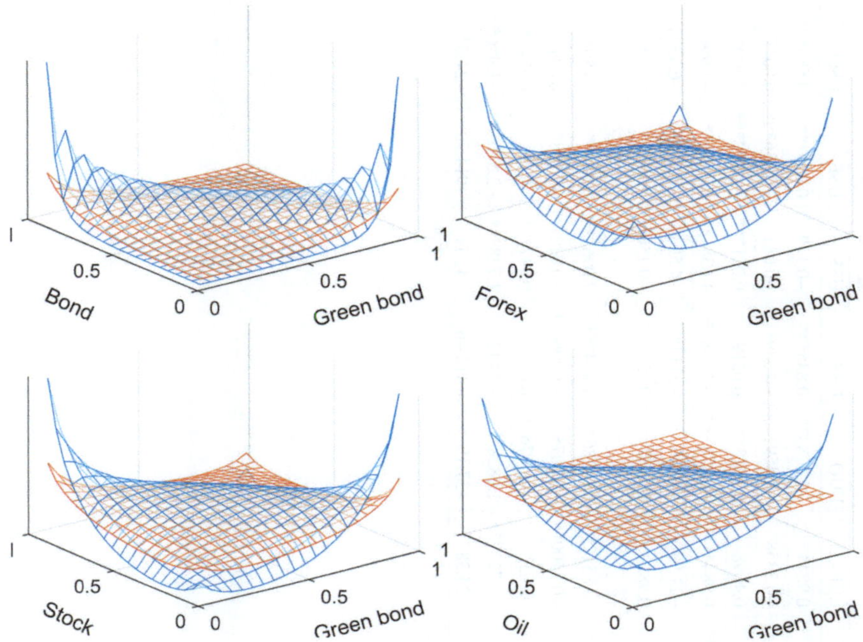

Fig. 5.4 Copulas between green bonds and other assets (China vs. US)

assets and oil return extremes relative to the US (where WTI is more closely tied to domestic market conditions).

The China-EU comparison (Fig. 5.5) highlights that the main cross-regional differences arise from bond-market linkages. For green bonds versus conventional bonds, the copula surfaces differ markedly. The EU surface indicates stronger same-direction tail co-movement between green bonds and conventional bonds, whereas China's surface is more consistent with green bonds behaving differently from the broader bond segment in tail states. This distinction is economically important: if green bond indices in the EU are more tightly embedded in conventional duration risk and sovereign-rate dynamics, then their incremental hedging contribution against bond-market stress may be limited, even if they remain useful for hedging other portfolio risks.

By contrast, green bonds versus equities look much more similar between China and the EU. Both surfaces display tail dependence in the lower and upper quantiles, suggesting that severe equity market moves are associated with an elevated probability of joint extreme outcomes in green bonds. This cross-market similarity is consistent with the idea that equity stress episodes are more synchronized internationally than bond-market episodes, making the green bond-equity dependence structure more comparable across regions than the green bond-bond structure.

In forex, the EU pairing (green bonds with EUR/USD) resembles the equity-like dependence structure more than China's pairing does; China's green bond-RMB

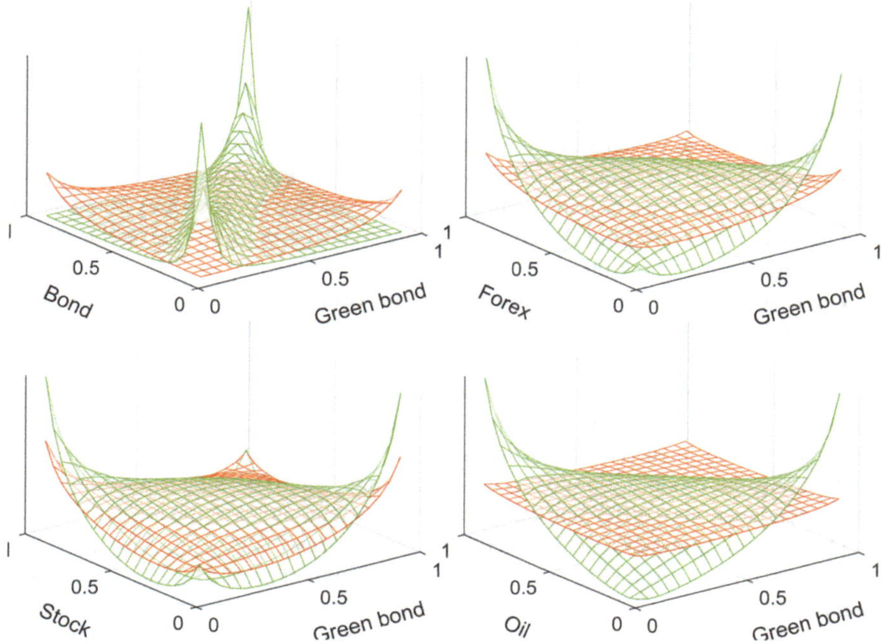

Fig. 5.5 Copulas between green bonds and other assets (China vs. EU)

forex surface remains relatively flat. In commodities, the EU-China comparison resembles the US-China comparison: dependence patterns are broadly similar, but China's surface is flatter, again indicating weaker tail integration between domestic green bonds and internationally priced oil shocks.

Two implications follow directly from these cross-regional patterns.

1. The largest regional heterogeneity is in green bond-bond dependence. The EU stands out for stronger co-movement between green bonds and conventional bonds, while China and the US appear closer in several bond-related pairings. This matters for portfolio construction because bond dependence affects hedge ratios and the extent to which green bonds deliver *incremental* diversification beyond standard sovereign or duration exposures.
2. Tail dependence with equities is present across regions. Despite differences in regulation and market structure, green bond-equity copulas show non-negligible tail features in China, the EU, and the US. This supports a cautious interpretation of "safe haven" claims: green bonds may hedge in normal times (especially if average dependence is weak or negative), but joint tail outcomes remain possible during severe equity stress.

Robustness

The copula results in the previous section indicate statistically meaningful tail dependence between green bonds and several comparator assets. To verify that these findings are not an artifact of parametric specification, we conduct two robustness checks based on quantile-oriented, largely nonparametric dependence measures. These approaches provide complementary evidence because they characterize dependence across the joint distribution rather than relying on a particular copula family and parameterization.

The first approach computes **quantile correlations**, which measure association conditional on particular quantiles of the marginal distributions (Patton, 2006). Intuitively, instead of summarizing dependence through a single unconditional correlation, quantile correlation allows the strength and sign of dependence to vary across the distribution—especially in the lower tail where hedging and safe-haven properties matter most. This is particularly useful in the present context because the earlier marginal modeling points to heavy tails and volatility clustering, suggesting that dependence may differ markedly between normal and extreme states.

The second approach uses **exceedance correlations** following Ang and Chen (2002). Given a specified exceedance threshold (often expressed relative to a mean plus/minus a multiple of the standard deviation), exceedance correlation measures the correlation between two assets conditional on both experiencing unusually large positive moves (upper exceedances) or unusually large negative moves (lower exceedances). This method is more flexible than tail dependence in a single copula sense because it allows direct comparison of co-movement in "good" versus "bad" extreme states and can reveal asymmetry in how assets interact during stress.

Together, these two methods serve as nonparametric (or semi-nonparametric) alternatives to copulas for characterizing dependence. Their main advantage is robustness to functional-form misspecification: because they do not impose a specific copula family, they reduce concerns about model-driven tail dependence. In addition, quantile-based diagnostics capture dependence beyond the extreme tails, allowing us to assess whether copula-implied tail features are consistent with broader distributional patterns.

Figures 5.6 and 5.7 summarize these robustness checks for China-US and China-EU comparisons, respectively. Overall, the quantile-based robustness checks display qualitative consistency with the copula findings in Table 5.6. Most notably, the quantile correlation profiles exhibit broadly symmetric tail behavior (upper vs lower tails) for many asset pairs, which is compatible with the Student's *t* copula structure that implies symmetric tail dependence. At the same time, exceedance correlations highlight *state asymmetry*—stronger co-movement in downside exceedances—providing an additional layer of evidence that hedging effectiveness may deteriorate in crises, even if average dependence is favorable in normal times.

However, these nonparametric approaches also have limitations that are important for interpretation. Exceedance correlation can be sensitive to small-sample variation in the tails: when thresholds are extreme, the number of exceedance

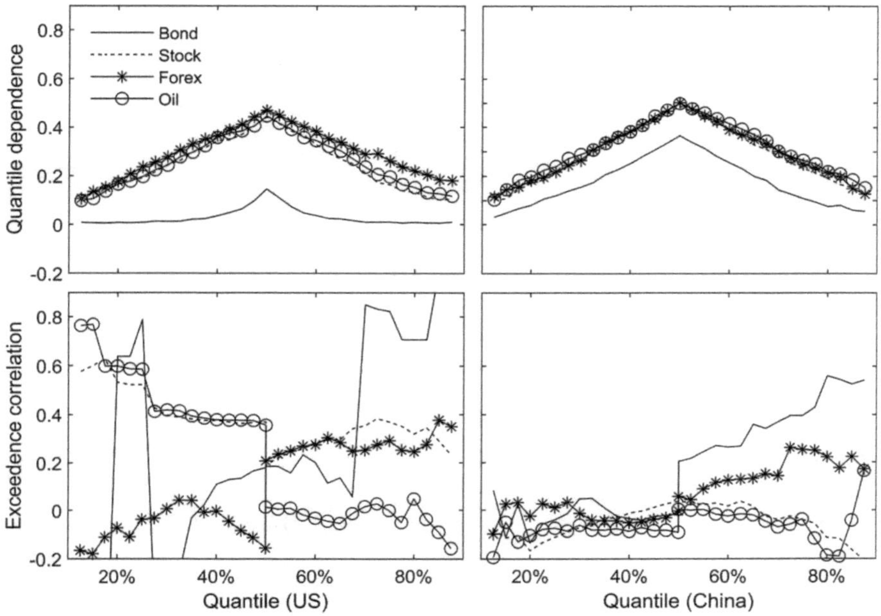

Fig. 5.6 Quantile dependence and exceedance correlation (China vs. US)

observations shrinks, making the estimates noisier and sometimes unstable. More broadly, quantile-based measures do not "filter out" dynamic effects as explicitly as the copula strategy built on marginal residuals; they therefore may inherit noise from volatility clustering and other time-series features. By contrast, the copula approach benefits from the preceding marginal modeling step, which controls for mean and volatility dynamics and typically yields more stable dependence estimates.

Taken together, these robustness checks reinforce the chapter's main message. Green bonds often appear to offer diversification benefits in typical market conditions, but dependence strengthens in downside states and exhibits marked asymmetry. This supports the use of tail-aware frameworks—copulas, VaR/CoVaR metrics, and time-varying dependence models—when assessing the hedging and safe-haven properties of green bond index investing.

Investment Performance Evaluation

The results show that the correlations between green bonds and other financial assets are significant, time-varying, and quantile-dependent. How can we make use of this information in investment practice? To evaluate the potential role of green bonds as safe-heaven assets to hedge against rare risks, it is common to calculate the

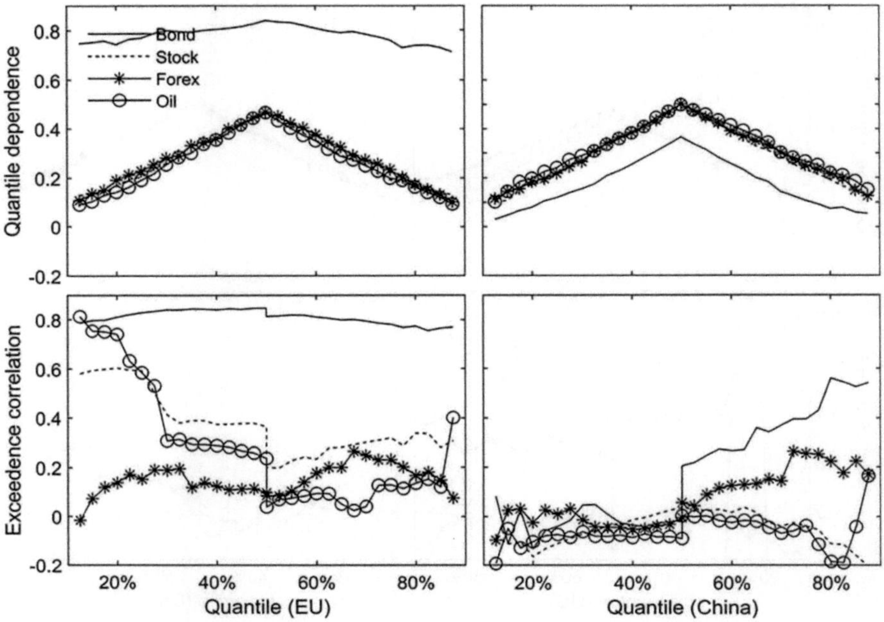

Fig. 5.7 Quantile dependence and exceedance correlation (China vs. EU)

optimal hedging weight (HW) and evaluate the hedging effectiveness (HE) of green bonds in a portfolio.

Heading Weight

We follow Jin et al. (2020) and adopt the Theory of Minimum Variance Heading Ratio (Johnson, 1960). Assume a portfolio is composed of an asset and a green bond index. The return of the hedged portfolio, r_{ht}, and its variance, $V(r_{ht})$, depend on the HW of green bond index (w_{gt}):

$$r_{ht} = \left(1 - w_{gt}\right) r_{it} + w_{gt} r_{gt}. \tag{5.9}$$

$$V\left(r_{ht}\right) = \left(1 - w_{gt}\right)^2 V\left(r_{it}\right) + w_{gt}^2 V\left(r_{gt}\right) + 2\left(1 - w_{gt}\right) w_{gt} \operatorname{cov}\left(r_{it}, r_{gt}\right) \tag{5.10}$$

To minimize the variance of the hedged portfolio, take partial derivative of $V(r_{ht})$ with respect to w_{gt} to obtain the optimal HW (w_{gt}^*):

$$\frac{\partial V(r_{ht})}{\partial w_{gt}} = 0 \rightarrow w_{gt}^{*} = \frac{V(r_{gt}) - \mathrm{cov}(r_{it}, r_{gt})}{V(r_{it}) + V(r_{gt}) - 2\,\mathrm{cov}(r_{it}, r_{gt})}. \tag{5.11}$$

Note that if $w_{gt}^{*} > 0$, then the hedged portfolio contains a long position of green bonds. If $w_{gt}^{*} < 0$, then the portfolio is hedged by holding a short position of green bonds. Covariance and variance terms are conditional forecasts based on the estimated marginal distribution of TGARCH models.

Figure 5.8 reports the time-varying optimal hedging weight w_{gt}^{*} for green bonds against each selected financial asset across China, the EU, and the US. Interpreted in portfolio terms, w_{gt}^{*} summarizes how much green bond exposure is required—at each point in time—to minimize risk when hedging a position in the corresponding asset. The dynamic profile therefore provides a practical complement to the copula and tail-risk evidence: it translates changing dependence into implementable hedging positions.

Two broad patterns emerge. First, at the cross-country level, green bonds exhibit a relatively consistent and close relationship with conventional bonds in all three regions, both before and after COVID-19. This stability implies that the bond market and the green bond market are largely driven by similar macro-financial forces, most plausibly interest-rate expectations, monetary policy shocks, and the broader

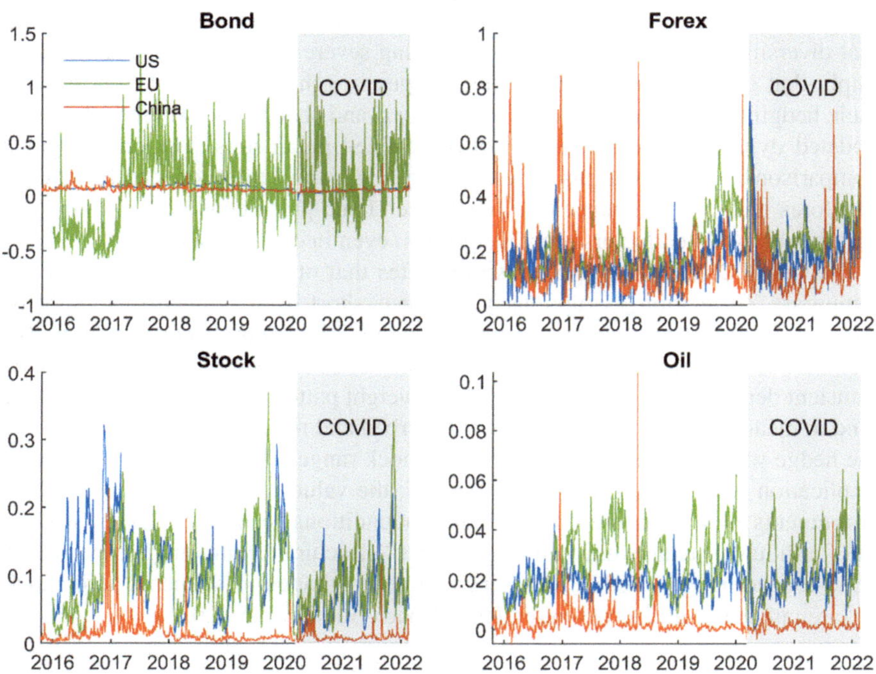

Fig. 5.8 Optimal hedging weights of green bonds in the three economies

discount-rate channel. It also suggests that hedging a conventional bond exposure with green bonds (or vice versa) is comparatively predictable over time: optimal hedge weights fluctuate, but they do so within a relatively stable range and with similar dynamics across China, Europe, and the US. From an investment standpoint, this reinforces the view that green bond indices—especially those with substantial sovereign and quasi-sovereign components—often embed duration risk comparable to traditional government bond benchmarks, so their hedging interaction is less sensitive to region-specific idiosyncrasies than for other asset classes.

Second, the green bond relationship with non-bond markets is markedly more heterogeneous across regions, and the heterogeneity becomes particularly visible around the onset of the pandemic. For equities and forex, the time-varying hedge weights diverge across China, the EU, and the US, indicating that the covariance structure between green bonds and these markets is more regime- and institution-dependent. This is consistent with earlier dependence results: equity and forex markets differ substantially across regions in terms of investor base, policy management, and exposure to global risk factors, so the green bond hedge ratio is less likely to be "portable" across jurisdictions.

A prominent feature is the temporary weakening of co-movement during the early phase of COVID-19, which manifests as shifts in optimal hedge weights. In the short run, the pandemic appears to have reduced the correlation between green bonds and several financial assets, implying less stable hedging effectiveness. Put differently, when tail-risk conditions intensify, green bonds do not always preserve their normal-time hedging role—consistent with the broader empirical regularity that diversification benefits can weaken during severe market stress. This does not imply that green bonds are ineffective hedges in general; rather, it indicates that their hedging contribution is *state-contingent*, and that hedge weights should be updated dynamically rather than treated as fixed parameters. The cross-regional comparison suggests that this "stress decoupling" is most pronounced for equities and forex and less pronounced for bond-green bond pairs, consistent with the idea that duration-related factors remain dominant even in crisis episodes.

Beyond COVID-19, Fig. 5.8 also indicates that other major shocks can cause temporary correlation disruptions and hence short-lived adjustments in hedge weights. Episodes such as the escalation of the US-China trade conflict from 2018 onward and the sharp oil price collapse in early 2020 are associated with visible but transient departures from prevailing hedge-weight patterns. Importantly, the effects tend to mean-revert—once the shock is absorbed and market functioning stabilizes, the hedge weights return toward their pre-shock ranges. This reinforces a practical implication for investors and risk managers: the value of green bonds as hedging instruments is not captured by a single unconditional estimate. Rather, hedging design should be adaptive, combining a stable "structural" component (especially in bond-related hedges) with a time-varying overlay that adjusts when macro shocks or rare tail events alter cross-asset dependence (Guo & Zhou, 2021).

Hedging Effectiveness

From Eq. (5.11), it is straightforward that the diversification benefit of a hedged portfolio depends on the correlation between the underlying assets and the variances of them. To better quantify the diversification benefit of green bonds, it is useful to have a metric to summarize the hedging effect. Ku et al. (2007) propose a measure termed hedging effectiveness based on risk reduction:

$$HE \equiv \frac{V(r_{it}) - V(r_{ht})}{V(r_{it})}. \tag{5.12}$$

Table 5.8 compares the optimal hedging weights (HW) and hedging effectiveness (HE) of green bonds across China, Europe, and the US, before and during the COVID period, for four hedging targets—conventional bonds, equities, forex, and oil. Three broad messages stand out.

First, Europe differs structurally from China and the US in the bond segment. Before COVID, Europe shows a negative HW (−1.28%) and HE (−9.54%) for conventional bonds, indicating that—under the estimated dependence structure—green bonds did not provide an effective hedge for European bond exposure in normal times. During COVID, Europe's HW rises sharply to 19.22%, while HE moves close to zero (−0.35%). This pattern is consistent with the earlier copula evidence that European green bonds are tightly linked to the broader bond complex: when green bonds and conventional bonds co-move strongly, the incremental risk reduction from using one to hedge the other can be limited, and the optimal hedge position may even switch sign depending on the prevailing covariance structure. By contrast, both China and the US display positive HEs for bond hedging in both periods, but with a clear decline during COVID (China: 12.93% → 10.08%; US: 17.36% → 10.16%), suggesting that tail-risk episodes reduce—but do not eliminate—the hedging contribution of green bonds against bond-market risk.

Second, green bonds hedge equity risk most strongly in the US and Europe, but the benefit weakens during COVID across all regions. Pre-COVID equity HEs are

Table 5.8 Hedging weights and hedging effectiveness before and after COVID

		China		Europe		US	
		Pre-COVID	COVID	Pre-COVID	COVID	Pre-COVID	COVID
Bond	HW	6.34%	4.95%	−1.28%	19.22%	8.33%	4.95%
	HE	12.93%	10.08%	−9.54%	−0.35%	17.36%	10.16%
Stock	HW	1.53%	1.11%	9.72%	8.94%	11.61%	7.53%
	HE	3.00%	2.21%	18.67%	17.23%	22.71%	14.83%
Forex	HW	20.96%	12.66%	18.82%	26.50%	17.41%	21.45%
	HE	19.57%	21.24%	33.02%	43.48%	30.82%	32.83%
Oil	HW	0.33%	0.17%	2.45%	2.55%	1.92%	1.95%
	HE	0.66%	0.35%	4.91%	5.10%	3.86%	3.92%

highest in the US (22.71%) and Europe (18.67%), and substantially lower in China (3.00%). This suggests that, in normal times, green bond indices in the US and Europe offer a more meaningful diversification channel against equities, likely reflecting deeper market integration and a more established investor base. During COVID, equity HEs decline in all three regions (China: 3.00% → 2.21%; Europe: 18.67% → 17.23%; US: 22.71% → 14.83%). This aligns with the general crisis stylized fact that cross-asset correlations can rise and hedges become less reliable. Still, the equity HEs remain positive, implying that green bonds continue to contribute to risk reduction even under severe stress, albeit less than in normal conditions.

Third, forex is the segment where hedging strengthens during COVID, especially in Europe. In all three regions, forex HEs are large and increase from pre-COVID to COVID (China: 19.57% → 21.24%; Europe: 33.02% → 43.48%; US: 30.82% → 32.83%). Europe not only has the highest forex HE in both periods, but also the largest increase during COVID. This indicates that, relative to other markets, forex shocks create a stronger hedging role for green bonds under tail-risk conditions—consistent with the interpretation that heightened macro uncertainty and policy risk amplify cross-market hedging capacity through safe-asset demand and rebalancing channels. The corresponding HWs also rise in Europe and the US (Europe: 18.82% → 26.50%; US: 17.41% → 21.45%), while China's HW falls (20.96% → 12.66%) even as HE rises—suggesting that in China a smaller green-bond hedge position achieves larger incremental risk reduction, plausibly reflecting changing covariance rather than a simple scaling of exposure.

A related, more mechanical point is that oil hedging effects are positive but modest everywhere, reflecting that energy prices have large idiosyncratic components and may transmit to financial assets through multiple channels. Oil HEs are small in China and decline during COVID (0.66% → 0.35%), while Europe and the US show slightly higher and stable oil HEs (Europe: 4.91% → 5.10%; US: 3.86% → 3.92%). This pattern is consistent with the idea that oil-price dynamics are more directly priced into European and US financial assets (and hence into green bond indices) than into China's domestic green bond index, where international oil shocks may be less tightly integrated.

Taken together, the results indicate that COVID as a tail-risk episode generally weakens green-bond hedging performance against bonds and equities, while strengthening hedging performance in forex markets, particularly in Europe. Importantly, comparing pre- and during-COVID HEs should be interpreted as a comparison between normal-time hedging and hedging under extreme uncertainty, rather than as a simple "improvement versus deterioration" metric. In that sense, the persistence of positive HEs in most cases supports the practical relevance of green bond indices as hedging instruments, while the cross-regional differences—most notably Europe's bond-market behavior—underscore that hedging performance is shaped by market structure and the degree to which green bonds are embedded in conventional fixed-income risk factors.

Conclusion

This chapter attempts to answer a practical question that follows naturally from the earlier, institution-focused chapters: how should investors use green bond indices in portfolio construction, and do green bonds provide hedging benefits—especially under tail risk? Using index-based evidence for China, Europe, and the US, the results support a cautious but actionable conclusion: green bonds can contribute meaningfully to portfolio risk management, but their hedging value is state-contingent and region-specific, and it cannot be inferred from unconditional correlations alone. Three empirical messages are robust across methods.

- Green bond markets exhibit pronounced nonlinearity in both marginal behavior and joint dependence. Across regions and assets, returns are stationary but strongly non-Gaussian—characterized by volatility clustering, leverage effects, and heavy tails. This is not a technical footnote; it directly motivates tail-aware risk management. Models built on constant variance or normal innovations would understate the likelihood of extreme outcomes and mischaracterize diversification benefits precisely when investors care most about protection.
- Dependence between green bonds and other assets differs sharply between normal states and crisis states. Copula estimates indicate statistically meaningful tail dependence for most asset pairs—best captured by Student's t structures—while many linear correlation parameters are negative. This combination is economically important: green bonds may hedge "ordinary" fluctuations (negative average co-movement) yet still share joint downside extremes with other markets when systemic risk rises. Quantile-based robustness checks support this reading—tail dependence is broadly symmetric in quantile correlations, while exceedance correlations show clear asymmetry, with stronger co-movement in bad tail events than in good tail events. In practical terms, green bonds are not uniformly "safe havens" in a strict sense, but they can remain useful hedges that require dynamic calibration.
- The cross-regional comparison highlights that market structure matters most for the bond channel, while equity and forex channels are more regime-sensitive. Europe stands out for the strong integration of green bonds with conventional bonds, which limits the incremental hedging contribution of green bonds against bond-market risk in some states. China and the US show more comparable patterns for bond-related dependence, whereas green bond relationships with equities and forex differ across regions, particularly around the onset of COVID. Dynamic hedge-weight results reinforce this: hedging effectiveness against bonds and equities generally weakens under pandemic tail risk, but forex hedging effectiveness rises across regions, especially in Europe. This points to a simple investment lesson—green bonds can play distinct hedging roles depending on the risk being hedged and the jurisdiction in which the hedge is implemented.

Policy implications follow directly from the chapter's central empirical message: green bonds can support portfolio resilience, but their hedging capacity is state-contingent and differs across market structures. This has concrete consequences for how policymakers should frame the role of green bonds within both climate policy and financial stability.

First, the evidence suggests that green bonds should be treated as part of the financial system's risk architecture rather than as a separate "impact" niche. The presence of tail dependence and crisis-state co-movement implies that green bond markets can absorb shocks, transmit shocks, or move with broader markets depending on conditions. For regulators and central banks, this argues for incorporating green bond exposures into macro-financial monitoring, stress testing, and risk dashboards—particularly for large institutional investors and intermediaries that hold green bond indices as core allocations. In practical terms, the supervisory question is not whether green bonds are greener than conventional bonds, but whether concentrated positions in green indices could amplify—or dampen—systemic stress when correlations shift under tail risk.

Second, the institutional agenda around standards and disclosure takes on an additional rationale beyond environmental credibility. When the "green" label is trusted, investor demand is more stable, pricing is less fragile, and the market is less vulnerable to sudden repricing during stress. Conversely, if investors suspect greenwashing or weak post-issuance accountability, they may withdraw precisely when risk rises, amplifying volatility and weakening hedging reliability. Taxonomy clarity, credible external review, and consistent post-issuance reporting therefore serve a dual function: they reduce informational frictions that matter for environmental integrity, and they reduce label-related uncertainty that can destabilize demand in adverse states. This is also where international coordination matters. The chapter's cross-regional findings imply that comparability and convergence—particularly between major jurisdictions—can improve investor confidence and facilitate more stable cross-border allocation.

Third, the chapter's focus on index-based allocation underscores that policy should not treat "market growth" as synonymous with "market usability". Hedging and risk management depend on liquidity and secondary-market functioning. When green bond markets are thin or fragmented, index investing can become pro-cyclical: prices gap in stress, turnover spikes, and hedges become expensive exactly when needed. Policies that support market depth—through transparent issuance pipelines, improved trading transparency, stronger market-making incentives, and well-designed repo and collateral infrastructures—can materially improve the implementability of dynamic hedging strategies. From a policy perspective, this is a climate finance analogue of a familiar lesson in bond markets: the social value of an instrument rises when it can be traded efficiently under stress, not only when it can be issued in large volumes.

Additionally, the results suggest a need for more disciplined communication to investors about what green bonds can and cannot do in crises. The empirical evidence does not support an unconditional safe-haven narrative; instead, it points to hedging benefits that vary by asset class, by region, and by market regime. If policy and industry messaging oversells crisis protection, subsequent disappointment could undermine investor trust and slow market development. A more sustainable approach is to encourage standardized disclosure of stress-period performance for green bond indices and funds—covering drawdowns, tail correlations, and hedging effectiveness during major shocks—so that climate-aligned products compete on both sustainability criteria and risk transparency. This would also help align fiduciary processes with climate objectives by making risk trade-offs explicit rather than assumed.

Finally, transition-finance policy should recognize that scalable green bond markets require compatibility with investor risk constraints. The chapter's evidence indicates that green bonds can support diversified portfolios and, in some settings, provide meaningful hedging value; however, that value is not automatic and can weaken under tail events for certain hedging targets. This means that policy frameworks aiming to expand green bond issuance should pay at least as much attention to the demand side as to labeling and supply. Market design that enhances credibility and liquidity will make green bonds easier to hold through cycles, supporting the long-horizon capital that the transition requires. In that sense, strengthening the microstructure and governance of green bond markets is not a peripheral technicality—it is a core condition for mobilizing stable private capital toward net-zero investment at scale.

References

Abuzayed, B., & Al-Fayoumi, N. (2023). Diversification and hedging strategies of green bonds in financial asset portfolios during the COVID-19 pandemic. *Applied Economics, 55*(36), 4228–4238.

Adrian, T., & Brunnermeier, M. K. (2016). CoVaR. *American Economic Review, 106*(7), 1705–1741. https://doi.org/10.1257/aer.20120555

Ang, A., & Chen, J. (2002). Asymmetric correlations of equity portfolios. *Journal of Financial Economics, 63*(3), 443–494.

Chopra, M., & Mehta, C. (2023). Going green: Do green bonds act as a hedge and safe haven for stock sector risk? *Finance Research Letters, 51*, 103357.

Creal, D., Koopman, S. J., & Lucas, A. (2011). A dynamic multivariate heavy-tailed model for time-varying volatilities and correlations. *Journal of Business & Economic Statistics, 29*(4), 552–563.

Dong, X., Xiong, Y., Nie, S., & Yoon, S.-M. (2023). Can bonds hedge stock market risks? Green bonds vs conventional bonds. *Finance Research Letters, 52*, 103367.

Fatica, S., Panzica, R., & Rancan, M. (2021). The pricing of green bonds: Are financial institutions special? *Journal of Financial Stability, 54*, 100873.

Ferrer, R., Shahzad, S. J. H., & Soriano, P. (2021). Are green bonds a different asset class? Evidence from time-frequency connectedness analysis. *Journal of Cleaner Production, 292*, 125988.

Flammer, C. (2021). Corporate green bonds. *Journal of Financial Economics, 142*(2), 499–516.

Girardi, G., & Tolga Ergün, A. (2013). Systemic risk measurement: Multivariate GARCH estimation of CoVaR. *Journal of Banking & Finance, 37*(8), 3169–3180. https://doi.org/10.1016/j.jbankfin.2013.02.027

Guo, D., & Zhou, P. (2021). Green bonds as hedging assets before and after COVID: A comparative study between the US and China. *Energy Economics, 104*, 105696.

Hansen, B. E. (1994). Autoregressive conditional density estimation. *International Economic Review, 35*(3), 705–730.
Jin, J., Han, L., Wu, L., & Zeng, H. (2020). The hedging effect of green bonds on carbon market risk. *International Review of Financial Analysis, 71*, 101509.
Johnson, N. L. (1960). An approximation to the multinomial distribution: Some properties and applications. *Biometrika, 47*(1/2), 93–102.
Ku, Y.-H. H., Chen, H.-C., & Chen, K.-H. (2007). On the application of the dynamic conditional correlation model in estimating optimal time-varying hedge ratios. *Applied Economics Letters, 14*(7), 503–509.
Patton, A. J. (2006). Modelling asymmetric exchange rate dependence. *International Economic Review, 47*(2), 527–556.
Reboredo, J. C. (2018). Green bond and financial markets: Co-movement, diversification and price spillover effects. *Energy Economics, 74*, 38–50. https://doi.org/10.1016/j.eneco.2018.05.030
Shahzad, S. J. H., Arreola-Hernandez, J., Bekiros, S., Shahbaz, M., & Kayani, G. M. (2018). A systemic risk analysis of Islamic equity markets using vine copula and delta CoVaR modeling. *Journal of International Financial Markets, Institutions and Money, 56*, 104–127. https://doi.org/10.1016/j.intfin.2018.02.013
Wang, A., Ding, S., & Cui, T. (2025). Green bond market stability and Russia Ukraine conflict: The role of green inclusive finance. *Research in International Business and Finance, 74*, 102734.
Xu, D., Hu, Y., Corbet, S., & Lang, C. (2024). Return connectedness of green bonds and financial investment channels in China: Implications for hedging and regulation. *Research in International Business and Finance, 70*, 102329.

Part III
Blue Finance and the Ocean Economy

Chapter 6
Blue Finance

Introduction

Climate finance has expanded from a niche ethical agenda into a policy-relevant component of global capital markets, with green bonds and related instruments becoming a prominent vehicle for mobilizing capital toward climate objectives on land. Yet a large share of climate stability, biodiversity integrity, and socio-economic resilience is mediated through oceans, coasts, and water systems. The ocean economy itself is sizeable: OECD estimates suggest that global ocean-economy gross value added doubled in real terms from $1.3 trillion in 1995 to $2.6 trillion in 2020, highlighting both its macroeconomic importance and the policy imperative to safeguard the natural capital on which that production depends (OECD, 2025).

At the same time, the financing gap for sustainable ocean outcomes remains large. A widely cited landscape scan estimates that achieving SDG14 ("Life Below Water") would require around $175 billion per year, yet reported investment over 2015–2019 was just below $10 billion in total, implying persistent underinvestment relative to stated global commitments (World Economic Forum, 2022). Blue finance has emerged in response to this gap. It refers to the set of financial instruments, institutional arrangements, and policy frameworks that mobilize and allocate capital toward activities that support the sustainable use, protection, and restoration of oceans, coasts, and water-related systems, while managing the environmental and social risks embedded in ocean-linked economic activity. This chapter clarifies the concept and boundary of blue finance, compares it with green finance, explains its economic and policy rationale, presents a typology of instruments, and reviews documented global cases that illustrate how blue finance is being operationalized in practice.

P. Zhou, D. Guo, *Climate Finance in the Net-Zero Transition*, Contributions to Finance and Accounting, https://doi.org/10.1007/978-981-92-0827-2_6

Definition

Blue finance is best understood as a specialized branch of climate finance that targets the water-ocean-coastal nexus. It overlaps with green finance, but it is not merely "green finance applied to the sea". The difference is not cosmetic; it arises from the economics of marine natural capital and from the institutional complexity of managing common-pool resources and spatially connected ecosystems.

A practical definition consistent with market guidance is that blue finance funds projects and activities that deliver measurable benefits for ocean health and sustainable ocean economies—typically through use-of-proceeds structures (blue bonds and loans), blended finance platforms, and debt operations linked to conservation outcomes. This framing is consistent with the World Bank's early sovereign blue bond work (notably Seychelles), and with the growing guidance architecture designed to reduce definitional ambiguity and limit "blue washing" (World Bank, 2018; IFC, 2022; ICMA, 2023).

A helpful way to formalize the comparison with green finance is to focus on domain boundary, market failures, bankability, measurement, and governance. Table 6.1 summarizes the key differences in a way that is relevant for both policy design and investor due diligence.

This comparison implies a central proposition: while green finance can often scale through relatively standardized project finance and capital markets, blue finance frequently requires institution building (monitoring capacity, enforcement, and coordinated coastal governance) as a precondition for credible investment pipelines.

The rationale for blue finance can be framed through three intersecting lenses—underinvestment due to market failures, systemic risk and macroeconomic exposure, and development constraints tied to fiscal capacity and debt sustainability.

First, the persistent SDG14 financing gap points to a classic underinvestment problem. Where benefits are public or diffuse—biodiversity, coastal protection, ecosystem resilience—private actors cannot capture the full social return, leading to capital scarcity even when the social net present value is positive. The World Economic Forum's estimate of $175 billion per year needed for SDG14, contrasted with sub-$10 billion invested over 2015–2019, provides a stark indicator of the scale of the gap (World Economic Forum, 2022).

Second, blue finance is increasingly tied to systemic and macro-financial considerations. Ocean-linked production is not marginal; OECD's quantification of ocean-economy GVA ($2.6 trillion in 2020) suggests that disruptions to ocean health can propagate to growth, employment, and fiscal revenues (OECD, 2025). For small island and coastal states, the transmission is often stronger because tourism, fisheries, and port logistics are large shares of GDP and forex earnings. In such contexts, investing in coastal resilience and sustainable ocean governance can reduce fiscal volatility and protect long-run debt service capacity.

Third, blue finance has a distinct development rationale because many high-exposure countries face constrained fiscal space. This is where sovereign liability

Table 6.1 Comparison between green finance and blue finance

	Green finance	Blue finance	Notes
Primary domain	Decarbonization, energy transition, climate mitigation/adaptation (often land-based)	Oceans, coasts, and water systems; marine biodiversity; pollution pathways to oceans	Determines eligible project categories and risk frameworks
Dominant market failures	Carbon externality; technology diffusion barriers; stranded asset risk	Common-pool resources (fisheries); public goods (biodiversity); cross-boundary pollution; weak property rights	Blue projects often need stronger governance and monitoring
Typical revenue model	Often clearer cash flows (PPAs for renewables, energy savings, transport guarantees)	Frequently mixed cash flows with non-market benefits (ecosystem services, resilience)	Greater reliance on blended finance and public support
Measurement	CO_2 metrics and energy indicators relatively standardized (though still debated)	Ecological indicators often local and complex (habitat quality, fish stock status, nutrient loads)	Higher MRV cost and higher reputational risk if claims are weak
Credibility risks	Greenwashing via loose eligibility or weak reporting	Blue-washing is acute because many ocean-linked projects have mixed impacts	Necessitates strict eligibility, safeguards, and disclosure
Common instruments	Green bonds/loans dominate; taxonomy-driven regulation increasingly important	Blue bonds/loans plus debt-for-nature swaps, guarantees, and resilience finance are central	Instrument mix reflects bankability and sovereign constraints

Sources: OECD (2025) on the ocean economy scale; World Economic Forum (2022) on SDG14 gap; World Bank (2018) on early sovereign blue bond precedent. *MRV* Measurement, Reporting, and Verification

management instruments—particularly conservation-linked debt conversions—become prominent. Belize's 2021 transaction illustrates this logic: the IMF reports that Belize financed the repurchase of a large external commercial debt instrument at a discount and issued $364 million in "blue bonds", with insurance support; the transaction embedded marine conservation commitments while improving the sovereign's debt profile (IMF, 2022). The Nature Conservancy's case documentation describes the same $364 million scale and reports associated conservation financing and policy commitments (TNC, 2021).

Typology

Blue finance instruments can be organized around economic function—capital mobilization, risk reduction, incentive alignment, and credibility assurance. In practice, five channels dominate: (1) labeled debt instruments (blue bonds and loans), (2) blended finance and guarantees, (3) debt-for-nature swaps and

Table 6.2 Typology of blue finance

Channel	Common instruments	Typical uses	Credibility
Labeled use-of-proceeds	Blue bonds; blue loans	Sustainable fisheries and aquaculture; wastewater and pollution control; coastal resilience infrastructure	Clear eligibility criteria; proceeds tracking; reporting; external review; safeguards against mixed impacts
Blended finance and guarantees	MDB guarantees; concessional tranches; catalytic facilities	Early-stage projects; public-good-heavy investments (MPAs, restoration); scaling private participation	Transparent additionality; risk-sharing rationale; pipeline governance; measurable outcomes
Conservation-linked debt operations	Debt-for-nature swaps; debt conversions with marine commitments	Debt relief or reprofiling tied to conservation and long-term funding commitments	Legal enforceability; monitoring institutions; transparent conservation targets and financing flows
Natural capital and ecosystem service finance	Outcome-based payments; conservation trust funds; (context-specific) blue carbon-linked finance	Mangrove/reef restoration; watershed-coast pollution reduction	Robust MRV; permanence and leakage controls; benefit-sharing and local rights protection
Risk transfer and resilience finance	Parametric insurance; resilience bonds; risk pools	Disaster risk management; incentives for risk-reducing nature-based solutions	Credible hazard models; transparent triggers; integration with adaptation investment plans

Sources: Conceptual synthesis anchored in documented blue bond and debt conversion practice (World Bank, 2018; IMF, 2022; TNC, 2021). *MRV* Measurement, Reporting, and Verification

conservation-linked debt conversions, (4) payments for ecosystem services and natural capital finance, and (5) insurance and resilience finance.

The underlying point is that blue finance's institutional environment often makes risk-sharing and conditionality more central than in many green-finance applications. Table 6.2 presents a structured typology with illustrative uses and the principal credibility requirements.

This typology suggests a practical interpretation: blue finance is less likely to be dominated by a single instrument class (as green finance often is by green bonds). Instead, blue finance scales through ecosystems of instruments that jointly solve a bankability problem—particularly via guarantees, concessional capital, and institutionalized monitoring.

Case Studies

Blue finance in practice clusters around a small number of repeatable "deal archetypes". The first archetype is the sovereign use-of-proceeds blue bond, typically used by small coastal and island states to fund fisheries reform and marine resource governance, often with multilateral credit enhancement to reduce borrowing costs. The second is the conservation-linked debt conversion (debt-for-nature), where a sovereign refinances external debt at lower effective cost and commits part of the resulting fiscal space to long-horizon marine conservation, usually through a dedicated fund with monitoring and enforcement provisions. The third is the corporate or utility blue bond (or blue-labeled loan) financing upstream infrastructure—especially sanitation and wastewater—because marine ecosystem outcomes frequently depend on land-based pollution control rather than marine spending alone.

Together, these three archetypes illustrate the economic logic of blue finance: capital mobilization is typically conditional on (1) risk-sharing mechanisms (guarantees, insurance, concessional tranches) and (2) credibility infrastructure (eligible-use definitions, monitoring, and enforceable governance commitments). The case studies below are selected because each is widely documented by primary policy and transaction sources, and each demonstrates a distinct pathway through which blue finance can plausibly scale.

Case Study 1. Seychelles Sovereign Blue Bond

Seychelles is frequently treated as the proof-of-concept for sovereign blue bonds because it combined a labeled bond structure with multilateral de-risking and a clear policy objective around sustainable fisheries and marine resource management. In October 2018, Seychelles launched what the World Bank described as the world's first sovereign blue bond, raising $15 million with a 10-year maturity (World Bank, 2018). The transaction embedded a World Bank partial guarantee of $5 million and a Global Environment Facility concessional loan of $5 million to subsidize coupon costs, explicitly addressing the sovereign's borrowing-cost constraint.

From an economic perspective, the Seychelles structure is most informative not because of scale—$15 million is modest—but because it illustrates how blended finance can change the feasible set of sovereign environmental investments. A World Bank case study later reports that integrating the $5 million partial credit guarantee reduced Seychelles' borrowing cost by at least 2 percentage points per year, while the GEF concessional financing further lowered the net borrowing cost by over 3 percentage points per year (World Bank, 2025). The implication is that credit enhancement can materially improve affordability for small states where fiscal space is limited and where commercial borrowing rates are inconsistent with the long-run payoff profile of ocean governance investments.

The bond's use-of-proceeds orientation also matters. In green finance, use-of-proceeds bonds frequently fund projects with readily quantifiable outputs (installed capacity, emissions reductions). For blue bonds, use-of-proceeds often funds policy and institutional measures—fisheries governance, monitoring capacity, and marine management—where the benefits accrue over time and are partly public. The Seychelles transaction therefore highlights a core feature of blue finance: for many countries, the binding constraint is not the absence of "projects", but the absence of affordable capital to finance the institutional foundations of a sustainable blue economy.

In addition, Seychelles demonstrates an early institutional model for credibility. The bond was supported by recognizable multilateral institutions and required transparency around eligible activities and reporting, thereby reducing reputational risk for investors. This credibility function is not a secondary feature; it is central because many ocean-linked investments can generate mixed impacts if safeguards are weak.

Seychelles represents the archetype of a sovereign blue bond whose effectiveness depends on a layered capital structure—market finance plus multilateral guarantee plus concessional finance—combined with policy-anchored use-of-proceeds. It is representative of how blue finance can work where the primary objective is building governance capacity and sustainable resource management rather than financing large infrastructure.

Case Study 2. Belize Debt Conversion

Belize's 2021 transaction is widely cited as a flagship of conservation-linked sovereign liability management. It illustrates how blue finance can operate through debt restructuring rather than through conventional project or budget finance. The IMF reports that Belize used financing to buy back a $553 million external commercial "superbond" at a discounted price of 55 cents on the dollar, and financed this by issuing $364 million in "blue bonds" arranged and underwritten by Credit Suisse, with insurance support from the US International Development Finance Corporation (IMF, 2022). The IMF also notes the macroeconomic context: the superbond represented the entirety of Belize's external commercial debt and was equivalent to around 30% of GDP, illustrating why the transaction was macro-relevant rather than marginal.

Primary transaction documentation emphasizes the dual objective: improve debt metrics while locking in a conservation funding stream and legally binding conservation commitments. The Nature Conservancy's case study reports that the refinancing savings enabled Belize to create an estimated $180 million in conservation funding over 20 years, composed of annual cashflows and an endowment capitalized through the financing structure, and that Belize committed to place 30% of its ocean area under protection by 2026, with a participatory marine spatial planning process and the establishment of an independent conservation fund (TNC, 2021). A

DFC press release similarly highlights the conservation commitment, stating that Belize agreed to increase biodiversity protection zones from 15.9% to 30% of its ocean.

Economically, Belize demonstrates a logic that is increasingly salient for climate and nature finance: when sovereign borrowing costs are high and fiscal capacity is limited, the most scalable "investment" may be a balance-sheet intervention that reduces debt service and redirects fiscal space into long-run natural capital stewardship. In effect, the transaction internalizes part of the global public-good value of marine conservation by embedding it into the sovereign's financing costs and into legally enforceable commitments tied to the refinancing.

At the same time, Belize also illustrates governance and credibility challenges. The effectiveness of conservation-linked debt operations depends on enforceability, institutional capacity, and transparency over time. Transaction documentation therefore places weight on governance mechanisms—dedicated conservation funding structures, reporting requirements, and binding policy commitments—because these are the channels through which financial engineering translates into ecological outcomes (TNC, 2021). This underscores a broader point: conservation-linked debt structures are not purely financial; they are hybrid instruments where policy conditionality and monitoring are integral to the contract.

Belize represents the archetype of a sovereign debt conversion that uses credit enhancement and structured intermediation to reduce debt service and finance conservation, embedding explicit commitments on ocean protection. It is representative of how blue finance can scale in high-debt, high-exposure contexts where conventional project finance is constrained.

Case Study 3. SABESP Blue Bond

A recurring challenge in blue finance is that marine outcomes frequently depend on upstream, land-based infrastructure. Pollution control, especially sewage and wastewater treatment, often delivers ocean and coastal benefits through reduced nutrient loading, pathogen exposure, and contaminant flows into rivers and coastal zones. This logic has underpinned a growing segment of blue-labeled issuance in which the "blue" category is justified by pollution-prevention pathways rather than by direct marine spending.

In January 2026, IDB Invest announced financing for SABESP (São Paulo's water and sanitation utility) to accelerate universal sanitation. The announcement states that the project is expected to expand sewage collection and treatment coverage in São Paulo from 85% to 99% by 2029, benefiting 2.5 million people, and describes the financing as "the largest Blue Bond issuance in history", reaching \$1.35 billion (IDB Invest, 2026). The same source frames the "blue" labeling explicitly around wastewater management and pollution prevention, positioning sanitation finance as a pathway to improved water ecosystem outcomes.

The SABESP case is economically important for two reasons. First, it shows how blue finance can enter larger-scale capital market territory by attaching the "blue" label to infrastructure with measurable outputs and relatively stable cash-flow foundations. Compared with many marine conservation projects, sanitation has clearer project economics, identifiable beneficiaries, and well-established performance metrics (coverage, treatment capacity, pollutant load proxies). Second, it provides a pragmatic answer to a common critique of blue finance—namely that "ocean projects" are too small or too hard to monetize. By treating wastewater and pollution control as "blue-eligible", the market can mobilize larger amounts of capital while maintaining an environmentally defensible causal link to ocean health.

However, the credibility requirement remains strict. For sanitation-linked blue finance to be more than relabeling, it must demonstrate that proceeds are allocated to eligible investments and that reporting is consistent with pollution reduction pathways rather than broad, non-falsifiable claims about "ocean health". IDB Invest's framing—explicitly linking the label to wastewater management and pollution prevention—suggests an effort to ground the blue designation in a measurable causal chain.

SABESP represents the archetype of corporate or utility blue issuance where the environmental thesis is pollution prevention and improved water quality, with relatively strong measurability and scalability. It is representative of a likely growth corridor for blue finance—large, bankable infrastructure aligned with ocean outcomes via land-to-sea pathways.

The three case studies—Seychelles' blended sovereign blue bond, Belize's conservation-linked debt conversion, and SABESP's sanitation-focused blue issuance—illustrate that blue finance is not a single market with a uniform instrument, but a family of arrangements designed to overcome distinct constraints. The common thread is that blue finance projects tend to face a dual hurdle: the economics of bankability (cash flows, risk premia, debt sustainability) and the economics of credibility (measurement, enforceability, and the avoidance of blue-washing). The evidence also suggests that the constraints are not symmetric across instrument types. Sovereign use-of-proceeds issuance is often constrained by borrowing costs and limited fiscal space; debt conversions are constrained by transaction complexity and governance enforceability; and corporate "blue" sanitation instruments are constrained by definitional discipline and the rigor of impact reporting. A policy section that follows from these cases should therefore treat blue finance less as a "labeling exercise" and more as market design under conditions of high externalities, institutional fragility, and cross-sector coordination problems.

A central challenge is that "blue" has an unusually wide semantic boundary. Oceans and coasts touch shipping, ports, tourism, offshore energy, aquaculture, real estate, sanitation, and land-based pollution control. This breadth creates an obvious incentive for issuers to adopt a blue label even where net ecological benefits are ambiguous or where environmental safeguards are weak. The SABESP case shows why this is not merely a theoretical concern. The issuance is framed as blue because wastewater and sanitation improvements reduce downstream marine pollution. This causal chain is plausible and policy-relevant, but it is only credible if reporting stays tightly aligned to that pathway—coverage expansion, treatment capacity, reductions in untreated discharge—rather than using diffuse narratives about "ocean health" that cannot be verified (IDB Invest, 2026). In other words, the scalability of sanitation-linked blue finance is also its credibility risk: once the market accepts upstream infrastructure as blue, the eligibility boundary must be governed carefully to prevent category inflation.

Policy implication. Regulators and standard setters should treat blue labeling as an eligibility-and-safeguards regime, not as a branding device. A practical approach is to require that every blue-labeled instrument disclose (1) the eligible category, (2) the causal pathway to ocean outcomes, and (3) the safeguards for potential negative externalities. IFC's blue finance guidelines provide a usable starting point for operational eligibility and exclusions, and can be adopted into national sustainable finance taxonomies or supervisory expectations (IFC, 2022, 2025). For market participants, ICMA's practitioner guidance similarly emphasizes the need for clear use-of-proceeds definitions and reporting consistent with recognized guidance (ICMA, 2023).

Blue finance is more intensive in terms of Measurement, Reporting, and Verification (MRV) than much of climate mitigation finance. Carbon metrics are imperfect but comparatively standardized; marine ecosystem outcomes are spatially heterogeneous and often slow-moving. This is evident in the contrast between the cases. SABESP's sanitation outcomes are measurable at relatively low cost—coverage rates, treatment capacity, and compliance with wastewater standards—making the blue label more auditable (IDB Invest, 2026). By contrast, Seychelles' and Belize's core objectives are tightly linked to governance, enforcement, and ecological states (fisheries sustainability, MPAs), which require baseline ecological assessments, monitoring capacity, and institutional continuity over time (World Bank, 2018; IMF, 2022; TNC, 2021). In conservation-linked debt operations, MRV becomes central because the transaction's legitimacy depends on whether fiscal savings translate into durable marine protection rather than short-lived commitments.

Policy implication. Governments and MDBs should treat MRV infrastructure as enabling public capital that crowds in private finance by reducing information asymmetry and reputational risk. In practical terms, this means investing in (1) fisheries monitoring and enforcement capacity, (2) coastal ecosystem baselines and periodic ecological surveys, and (3) transparent reporting platforms that allow investors to observe both allocation and outcomes over time. For regulators, a feasible minimum standard is staged disclosure: early reporting on allocation and implementation milestones, followed by outcome reporting on pre-specified indicators at longer horizons. This is consistent with the logic of use-of-proceeds instruments and the governance-heavy nature of sovereign conservation finance.

The Seychelles case provides direct evidence that sovereign blue bonds can be financially feasible when credit enhancement reduces borrowing costs. The World Bank reports that Seychelles' blue bond was supported by a World Bank partial guarantee and GEF concessional finance, and later case documentation reports that the guarantee reduced borrowing costs by at least two percentage points per year and concessional finance reduced the net cost further (World Bank, 2018, 2025).

This matters because many countries most dependent on ocean assets—SIDS and low- to middle-income coastal states—also face relatively high sovereign risk premia. Without de-risking layers, blue bonds may either be too expensive or too small to be meaningful.

Belize reinforces the same theme through a different mechanism. The IMF emphasizes that the country's external commercial debt was large relative to GDP, and that the conversion created debt service savings while embedding conservation commitments (IMF, 2022). In this structure, the "financing" objective is inseparable from debt sustainability: blue finance becomes a way of reshaping the sovereign balance sheet while funding conservation.

Policy implication. Blue finance strategies for vulnerable sovereigns should be built around explicit risk-sharing and fiscal feasibility, not only around project identification. This suggests a role for (1) partial credit guarantees, (2) political risk insurance, and (3) concessional tranches that reduce coupon burdens and extend maturities, particularly for first-time issuers. MDBs and DFIs are not peripheral in this environment; they are often the anchor institutions that make sovereign blue issuance feasible at scale (World Bank, 2018; IMF, 2022). A policy corollary is that scaling blue finance in low-capacity states is partly a question of scaling these de-risking facilities and standardizing documentation to reduce transaction costs.

Conservation-linked debt conversions are attractive because they can unlock large conservation funding relative to direct project finance, but they are also high-friction transactions. Belize's deal involved complex intermediation, legal design, and insurance support, and the conservation commitments relied on institutional arrangements such as a dedicated fund and monitoring structures (IMF, 2022; TNC, 2021). These features are essential for credibility, yet they also create replicability barriers: legal and advisory costs, negotiation time, and institutional requirements are non-trivial.

Policy implication. If debt conversions are to become a scalable pillar of blue finance, the next stage is standardization and pipeline development. This includes templates for conservation commitments, monitoring protocols, and fund governance, and a clearer division of labor between sovereigns, conservation partners, insurers, and creditors. Multilateral institutions can accelerate replication by offering technical assistance and by publishing standardized frameworks that reduce the fixed costs of negotiating bespoke deals. However, policy design should also recognize limits: debt conversions are not universally appropriate, and their suitability depends on debt structure, creditor composition, and domestic governance capacity.

The cases imply that blue finance's effectiveness depends on institutional capacity at least as much as on capital volume. Seychelles used proceeds in the context of a broader fisheries and marine governance agenda, supported by multilateral oversight and reporting requirements (World Bank, 2018). Belize embedded conservation outcomes into a contractual structure supported by a conservation fund and monitoring requirements, indicating that institutional arrangements were integral to the financial deal rather than an add-on (TNC, 2021; IMF, 2022). These are examples of what can be called institutional additionality: the financing does not only fund activities; it helps create or strengthen governance mechanisms that make outcomes durable.

Policy implication. Blue finance strategies should explicitly finance institutions—monitoring agencies, enforcement capacity, and governance bodies—rather than treating them as exogenous. This implies that eligible expenditure categories in sovereign blue bonds should include institutional capacity building, and that impact reporting should include governance milestones (patrol capacity, compliance rates, enforcement actions, transparent budget execution) alongside ecological outcomes. For conservation-linked debt operations, enforceability and transparency should be treated as non-negotiable design conditions because the market legitimacy of these instruments depends on observable compliance.

Blue finance frequently fails not because the financial instrument is poorly designed but because the policy interface is fragmented. Sanitation is a clear example: the "blue" outcome is produced through urban infrastructure, environmental regulation, municipal implementation, and water governance. SABESP's case underscores how marine outcomes are mediated by land-based systems and by institutions outside marine ministries (IDB Invest, 2026). Similarly, fisheries outcomes require coordination among environment agencies, fisheries regulators, local authorities, and trade/traceability systems.

Policy implication. Blue finance should be embedded in integrated "land-to-sea" policy frameworks, such as watershed management, coastal zone planning, and pollution control systems. Practically, this means building blue project pipelines through cross-ministry mechanisms that include finance ministries (for debt sustainability), environment ministries (for safeguards and MRV), and sectoral agencies (water utilities, fisheries authorities). Without coordination, the result is often a pipeline of projects that are either not financeable or not credible.

Conclusion

Blue finance has moved from an aspirational concept to a set of implementable financing arrangements that respond to a clear and persistent gap: oceans and water systems are central to climate stability, biodiversity, and coastal livelihoods, yet they remain structurally underfinanced relative to need. The evidence reviewed in this chapter points to a financing problem that is not simply about mobilizing more capital, but about designing financial and policy architectures that can overcome distinctive market failures—common-pool resource dynamics, public-good benefits, cross-boundary externalities, and high monitoring costs. In this respect, blue finance should be understood as a specialized branch of sustainable finance with a different constraint set from many green finance applications.

The cases examined provide concrete lessons about what works and why. Seychelles demonstrates that sovereign blue bonds can be feasible when affordability constraints are addressed through layered de-risking—partial guarantees and concessional elements that reduce borrowing costs and align repayment horizons with the long-run payoff profile of ocean governance. Belize shows that conservation-linked debt conversions can be macro-critical, transforming sovereign liability structures while embedding measurable and enforceable marine protection commitments and long-horizon conservation funding. SABESP highlights a scalable pathway in which blue finance is operationalized through land-to-sea linkages, financing sanitation and wastewater infrastructure with clear output metrics and credible causal pathways to marine outcomes. Taken together, these cases imply that blue finance scales through at least three distinct channels—use-of-proceeds sovereign issuance, conservation-linked debt operations, and blue-labeled infrastructure finance—each with its own risk profile, transaction costs, and credibility requirements.

A central conclusion is that credibility is not a secondary issue; it is the market's binding constraint. Blue finance is particularly exposed to blue-washing because the boundary of "ocean-related" activity is broad and many projects can carry mixed environmental effects. This creates a strong case for definitional discipline and enforceable safeguards, anchored in eligibility frameworks, transparent proceeds management, and staged reporting that distinguishes allocation from outcomes. Equally, the chapter's evidence underscores that robust measurement, reporting, and verification is a public-good input to market growth: without ecological baselines, monitoring systems, and institutional capacity to enforce rules, blue finance risks expanding labels faster than it improves ocean health. For policymakers and MDBs, investing in MRV infrastructure and governance capacity is therefore a form of catalytic finance that can crowd in private capital by reducing information asymmetry and reputational risk.

The policy agenda implied by the chapter is pragmatic. Scaling blue finance requires a pipeline approach: integrating land-to-sea policy planning, building credible project preparation capacity, and deploying risk-sharing instruments strategically where private capital would otherwise remain on the sidelines. For high-debt and high-exposure sovereigns, conservation-linked debt conversions may offer large leverage, but only when transaction templates, monitoring frameworks, and governance arrangements are sufficiently standardized to reduce fixed costs and ensure enforceability. For larger-scale market growth, sanitation and pollution-control financing—when tightly linked to measurable marine outcome pathways—appears to be a promising corridor for scaling, precisely because it can combine bankability with auditability. Across all channels, the long-run success of blue finance will depend on whether it can maintain environmental integrity while reducing the cost of capital for credible ocean-positive investments.

Overall, the chapter supports a broader proposition for climate finance in the carbon-neutral transition: oceans and water systems must be treated as core financial and policy domains rather than peripheral environmental concerns. Blue finance offers a means to operationalize that shift, but its expansion will be sustainable only if it remains grounded in rigorous definitions, credible MRV, and governance arrangements that can translate financial innovation into durable ecological and socio-economic outcomes.

References

ICMA. (2023). *Bonds to finance the sustainable blue economy: A practitioners' guide*. International Capital Market Association.

IDB Invest. (2026). *IDB invest finances SABESP to accelerate universal sanitation in São Paulo*. IDB Invest.

IFC. (2022). *Guidelines for blue finance*. International Finance Corporation.

IFC. (2025). *Guidelines for blue finance—Version 2.0*. International Finance Corporation.

IMF. (2022). *Belize: Swapping debt for nature*. International Monetary Fund.

OECD. (2025). *The ocean economy to 2050*. Organisation for Economic Co-operation and Development.

TNC. (2021). *Belize debt conversion for marine conservation: Case study*. The Nature Conservancy.

World Bank. (2018). *Seychelles launches world's first sovereign blue bond*. World Bank.

World Bank. (2025). *Case study—Blue bond Seychelles*. World Bank.

World Economic Forum. (2022). *SDG14 financing landscape scan: Tracking funds to realize sustainable outcomes for the ocean*. World Economic Forum.

Chapter 7
Financing the Ocean Economy

Introduction

The ocean economy, also known as the blue economy, is best understood as the set of market activities—and the enabling natural and institutional capital—that depends on oceans, seas, and coasts. It spans shipping and ports, fisheries and aquaculture, coastal and marine tourism, offshore energy, marine manufacturing and services, and the public infrastructure that makes coastal settlement and trade possible (OECD, 2025). In scale, it is no longer peripheral: OECD estimates suggest that global ocean-economy gross value added doubled in real terms from $1.3 trillion in 1995 to $2.6 trillion in 2020.

It is tempting to treat the ocean economy as simply "the green economy applied to the sea", but that analogy breaks down quickly. The green economy is typically framed around decarbonization, resource efficiency, and low-carbon growth, with many investments anchored in measurable physical outputs and relatively standardized metrics (for example, renewable capacity and emissions reductions). The ocean economy, by contrast, is built on a natural capital base that is spatially connected and often governed as a common-pool resource (Table 7.1). The economic consequences are familiar to environmental economics: benefits are diffuse, property rights and enforcement are uneven, and marginal private returns often fail to reflect marginal social returns. As a result, the ocean economy can expand in GDP terms while drawing down the biological and coastal systems that make that production sustainable.

Blue finance—introduced earlier in this book as a specialized branch of sustainable finance—sits at the point where these features become financially binding. The practical issue is not only that ocean-positive projects are underfunded, but that investors face a compounded problem: many high-impact interventions generate public benefits (coastal protection, biodiversity integrity, fish stock resilience) while also requiring costly monitoring and enforceability. The financing gap is

P. Zhou, D. Guo, *Climate Finance in the Net-Zero Transition*, Contributions to Finance and Accounting, https://doi.org/10.1007/978-981-92-0827-2_7

Table 7.1 Comparison between the green economy and the blue economy

	Green economy	Blue/ocean economy	Notes
Market failures	Carbon externality; technology diffusion; stranded asset risk	Common-pool resources; cross-boundary spillovers; public-good benefits	Greater need for enforceable governance and MRV
Revenue model	Often clearer user-pay cash flows (PPAs, efficiency savings)	Frequently mixed cash flows and non-market benefits	More reliance on blended finance, guarantees, and policy conditionality
Measurement	CO_2 and energy metrics relatively standardized	Ecological indicators spatially heterogeneous, slow-moving	Higher credibility risk; reporting must be tightly specified
Policy interface	Often sectoral (energy, transport)	Land-to-sea coordination (wastewater, fisheries, coastal planning)	Blue bond frameworks must describe causal pathways clearly
Integrity risk	Greenwashing via vague eligibility	Blue washing amplified by broad ocean adjacency	Standards and exclusions become first-order

Sources: OECD (2025); World Economic Forum (2022); ICMA (2023); IFC (2025)

correspondingly stark. A widely cited landscape scan estimates that achieving SDG14 would require about $175 billion per year, yet between 2015 and 2019 "just below" $10 billion in total was invested.

In this setting, blue bonds matter less as a branding innovation and more as an implementation technology. They are a way to channel debt finance toward ocean-economy priorities while imposing a governance discipline—use-of-proceeds definitions, safeguards, and MRV expectations—that investors can price and monitor. The "bond" form is also economically meaningful: it allows the ocean economy to be financed through the institutional plumbing of fixed income markets—benchmarks, mandates, and asset-liability frameworks—rather than relying only on project grants or concessional facilities.

Governance

Blue bond markets are emerging inside the broader sustainable debt ecosystem. This means they inherit the basic logic of use-of-proceeds markets—eligibility, tracking, reporting, and (often) external review—while adding ocean-specific requirements. The essential point is that "blue" is a wide semantic category; research suggests that without rigorous boundaries, almost any coastal infrastructure, shipping activity, or water-related investment can be narrated as ocean-adjacent, leading to risks of "blue-washing" (Sumaila et al., 2021). Standards exist to narrow that space, require explicit impact pathways, and reduce the incentive to relabel business-as-usual activities. Currently, two guidance architectures have become particularly influential for practitioners.

- ICMA's Bonds to Finance the Sustainable Blue Economy positions blue bonds as aligned with the established market architecture of sustainable bonds while emphasizing ocean-relevant eligibility categories and integrity expectations (ICMA, 2023).
- IFC's Guidelines for Blue Finance (Version 2.0, 2025) provide a more operational eligibility lens for "blue" activities and are designed to help market participants identify, structure, and scale investments linked to sustainable use of water and ocean resources (IFC, 2025).

Standards matter because they clarify what "responsible ocean finance" should look like at the level of financial institutions rather than individual transactions: UNEP's Sustainable Blue Economy Finance Principles (unveiled in 2018) articulate an ocean-specific set of commitments around ecosystem protection, compliance, risk management, and transparency (UNEP, 2018). In practice, these frameworks converge on a compact set of regulatory-relevant questions that investors and supervisors can use as a due diligence spine.

Eligibility and exclusions A credible blue bond framework does not only list "what is included", but explains why it is included. Ocean-related sectors routinely involve mixed impacts—for example, ports and shipping can reduce emissions intensity while still posing risks to habitats, water quality, and local communities. This creates a straightforward integrity condition: a blue framework must make tradeoffs visible rather than implied (Kabaklarlı et al., 2024).

Causal pathways For blue labeling to be economically meaningful, disclosure needs to move beyond adjacency ("near the ocean") to causality ("how the expenditure changes ocean outcomes"). This is particularly important for upstream land-based interventions, such as sanitation and wastewater finance, where the ocean outcome is mediated through pollution pathways (Rangel-Buitrago et al., 2024).

MRV as a market infrastructure Blue claims are often difficult to verify quickly. Standards therefore emphasize MRV not as an "impact add-on", but as a market condition for scaling. From an economic perspective, MRV reduces information asymmetry and reputational risk, which in turn lowers the risk premium demanded by investors and raises feasible issuance volumes (Hyun et al., 2023).

Enforceability and governance This is where blue bonds diverge most sharply from many green bond applications (March et al., 2024). For sovereign and conservation-linked structures, the commitment is partly policy performance over long horizons. Frameworks therefore place weight on governance arrangements—independent oversight, reporting schedules, and in some cases ring-fenced funds—because those mechanisms are what make intertemporal commitments credible.

The regulatory implication is subtle but important. Blue bond standards are not only "voluntary guidance". They function as a substitute for incomplete regulation in a market that would otherwise be vulnerable to category inflation. Policymakers that want blue bonds to scale with integrity therefore face a design choice: either embed these expectations into domestic sustainable finance taxonomies and supervisory practices, or accept that market growth will be constrained by credibility risk.

Implementation is where blue bonds become either catalytic finance or a thin label. A practical way to understand implementation is to follow the financing chain from "ocean-economy need" to "investable fixed-income product". In most jurisdictions, the binding constraint is not the absence of ocean problems, but the absence of an investable pipeline that is both bankable and verifiable. There are three recurring implementation mechanisms.

First, blue bonds often finance "institutions" as much as "assets". Ocean-economy productivity depends on governance capacity—monitoring fisheries, enforcing MPAs, managing coastal zones, and regulating pollution pathways. These are essential inputs with weak private appropriability. Blue bond proceeds can finance them, but only if the framework explicitly treats them as eligible and reports progress in observable ways.

Second, risk-sharing is frequently decisive. For many sovereigns and quasi-sovereigns, the social return on ocean stewardship may be high, yet the market borrowing cost is too high for the project's payoff profile. Credit enhancement and concessional layers are therefore not peripheral; they are the mechanism that makes the investment set feasible.

Third, ocean outcomes routinely depend on land-to-sea coordination. Wastewater and sanitation illustrate this cleanly: ocean health is often determined upstream, through municipal infrastructure and regulatory enforcement. Blue bond implementation succeeds when this coordination is made explicit and measurable, rather than assumed.

Case Studies

The cases below build directly on the deal archetypes discussed previously in **Chap. 6**—so the focus here is on what they reveal about implementation choices, scaling conditions, and investor relevance.

Case Study 1. Seychelles Sovereign Blue Bond

Seychelles is a foundational reference point because it shows how a sovereign blue bond can be feasible when borrowing-cost constraints are addressed through multilateral support. The World Bank reports that the bond had a ceiling value of $15 million and a 10-year maturity, supported by a $5 million partial guarantee from IBRD and a $5 million concessional loan from the Global Environment Facility to subsidize coupon payments.

Later case documentation provides a quantification of the cost-of-capital effect: integrating a $5 million partial credit guarantee lowered Seychelles' borrowing cost by at least 2 percentage points per year, and the concessional financing further lowered net borrowing costs by over 3 percentage points per year.

The economic importance is not the scale—$15 million is modest in global markets—but the implementation logic. It demonstrates how layered structures can convert an otherwise unaffordable sovereign investment into an investable instrument, allowing the sovereign to finance governance and policy capacity that underpin long-run fisheries productivity and resilience.

For investors, the case clarifies what "blue" means in sovereign issuance: the credit story remains sovereign, but the integrity story depends on proceeds governance, MRV, and credible institutional partners. For policymakers, it highlights a replicable mechanism: if the goal is to facilitate sustainable ocean-economy production in high-risk settings, scaling guarantees and standardizing documentation may matter as much as identifying projects.

Case Study 2. Belize Debt Conversion

Belize illustrates a different implementation pathway: the binding constraint is debt sustainability rather than project finance. The IMF reports that Belize bought back a $553 million external commercial debt instrument at a discounted price of 55 cents per dollar and financed this through the issuance of $364 million in "blue bonds", with insurance support from the US International Development Finance Corporation. The IMF also notes that the original debt represented the entirety of Belize's external commercial debt and was around 30 percent of GDP.

The implementation insight is that the "ocean outcome" is mediated through sovereign fiscal space and long-horizon governance commitments. In effect, a balance-sheet intervention becomes the financing channel for long-run natural capital stewardship.

For policymakers, the Belize model suggests that, in high-debt coastal states, the most scalable "investment" may be liability management that frees resources for marine protection. For investors, it shows why governance structures—dedicated funds, oversight, reporting—are not cosmetic: they are the mechanism that allows a macro-finance transaction to claim ecological additionality credibly.

Case Study 3. SABESP Blue Bond

SABESP's transaction is important because it shows how "blue" can scale when the financed activity has clearer outputs and cash-flow foundations. IDB Invest reports that the operation is expected to expand sewage collection and treatment coverage in São Paulo from 85% to 99% by 2029, benefiting 2.5 million people, and describes it as the largest blue bond issuance in history, reaching $1.35 billion.

This case operationalizes the land-to-sea logic: sanitation is financed as "blue" because wastewater management and pollution prevention are direct pathways to improved water ecosystems and reduced marine pollution.

For investors, the case suggests a growth corridor for blue bonds: bankable infrastructure where outcomes can be tracked with relatively standard indicators. For policymakers, it highlights a practical lesson: scaling blue finance may often mean scaling upstream infrastructure and regulation—because marine outcomes are frequently produced on land.

Conclusion

This chapter has treated blue bonds as an implementation instrument for the ocean economy rather than as a standalone product category. The ocean economy is large and increasingly policy-relevant, yet structurally prone to underinvestment because it rests on natural capital that is partly public, spatially connected, and costly to monitor (OECD, 2025). The funding gap for ocean outcomes remains substantial relative to global commitments (World Economic Forum, 2022). Blue bonds—when disciplined by standards and coupled with MRV and governance—offer a way to bring fixed income markets into the financing of the sustainable ocean economy.

Two implications follow for investors. First, credit risk remains conventional, but integrity risk is not. The investability of blue bonds depends on the credibility of eligibility, exclusions, and causal pathways, and on whether MRV is sufficiently robust to support claims over time (ICMA, 2023; IFC, 2025). Second, the most scalable opportunities may be those with measurable outputs and clear pollution or transition pathways—such as sanitation, ports, and shipping—provided the blue label is not allowed to drift into adjacency.

For policymakers, the key lesson is that blue bonds scale when the state invests in the market infrastructure of credibility. This means making standards operational, building MRV capacity, and—where affordability is binding—expanding the availability of guarantees, insurance, and concessional layers that align financing costs with long-horizon ocean returns. The cases also show that, in high-debt settings, blue finance may be most powerful when it operates through sovereign balance sheets (debt conversions) rather than through marginal project finance alone.

In short, blue bonds can facilitate the future ocean economy, but only if they are treated as governance-embedded finance: tight frameworks, credible MRV, and risk-sharing designs that convert high-social-return ocean stewardship into investable, monitorable, and scalable fixed income products.

References

Hyun, S., Park, D., & Tian, S. (2023). The price of frequent issuance: The value of information in the green bond market. *Economic Change and Restructuring, 56*(5), 3041–3063.

ICMA. (2023). *Bonds to finance the sustainable blue economy: A practitioners' guide*. International Capital Market Association.

IFC. (2025). *Guidelines for blue finance—Version 2.0*. International Finance Corporation.

Kabaklarlı, E., Ayvaz, Z., Petrova, M., Kotsev, I., & Kyriazi, Z. (2024). Economic, innovation and finance perspectives of sustainable blue economy: A focus on fisheries and aquaculture. In W. Leal Filho, A. L. Salvia, J. P. P. Eustachio, & M. A. P. Dinis (Eds.), *Handbook of sustainable blue economy* (pp. 1–36). Springer Nature Switzerland.

March, A., Evans, T., Laing, S., & Raguain, J. (2024). Evaluating the world's first sovereign blue bond: Lessons for operationalising blue finance. *Commodities, 3*(2), 151–167.

OECD. (2025). *The ocean economy to 2050*. Organisation for Economic Co-operation and Development.

Rangel-Buitrago, N., Galgani, F., & Neal, W. J. (2024). Addressing the global challenge of coastal sewage pollution. *Marine Pollution Bulletin, 201*, 116232.

Sumaila, U. R., Walsh, M., Hoareau, K., Cox, A., Teh, L., Abdallah, P., Akpalu, W., Anna, Z., Benzaken, D., Crona, B., Fitzgerald, T., Heaps, L., Issifu, I., Karousakis, K., Lange, G. M., Leland, A., Miller, D., Sack, K., Shahnaz, D., et al. (2021). Financing a sustainable ocean economy. *Nature Communications, 12*(1), 3259.

UNEP. (2018). *Sustainable blue economy finance principles*. United Nations Environment Programme Finance Initiative.

World Economic Forum. (2022). *SDG14 financing landscape scan: Tracking funds to realize sustainable outcomes for the ocean*. World Economic Forum.

Part IV
Carbon Trading and the Sustainable Development

Chapter 8
Carbon Finance

Introduction

Carbon finance translates an environmental externality into a financial variable that can be priced, traded, hedged, and governed. In economic terms, the appeal is straightforward: when greenhouse gas (GHG) emissions are costly to society but cheap to the emitter, markets will over-produce carbon-intensive goods and under-invest in abatement. Carbon finance attempts to correct this wedge by assigning a price to emissions (or to verified reductions/removals), thereby turning mitigation into an investable proposition and creating incentives for firms and households to substitute away from carbon-intensive activities. The scale of the policy and market response is now material. Carbon pricing instruments (carbon taxes and emissions trading systems—Emission Trading Systems or ETSs) cover roughly one quarter of global emissions, with policy discussions that could raise coverage further.

Carbon finance is best understood as a family of mechanisms rather than a single market. At its center sit compliance carbon markets (ETSs) and carbon taxes—tools designed to internalize the externality. Around that center has grown an ecosystem of tradable allowances, offset credits, derivatives, structured products, project finance, and disclosure regimes. The research literature reflects this broadening scope: carbon finance is increasingly analyzed alongside sustainable finance and market governance questions, and the newest strands emphasize digital market infrastructure and climate justice, consistent with a shift from "pricing carbon" to "building institutions that make pricing credible and investable".

Historically, the contemporary architecture of carbon finance is commonly traced to the late-1990s shift toward market-based international climate governance. The Kyoto Protocol, adopted in 1997, is widely treated as a turning point because it formalized cross-border flexibility through three mechanisms—international emissions trading, Joint Implementation, and the Clean Development Mechanism—thereby establishing the institutional foundations of what later became known as the

P. Zhou, D. Guo, *Climate Finance in the Net-Zero Transition*, Contributions to Finance and Accounting, https://doi.org/10.1007/978-981-92-0827-2_8

carbon market (UN, 1997). Building on this logic, the EU Emissions Trading System, launched in 2005 as the world's first international ETS, became the most influential compliance market and a practical template for subsequent cap-and-trade systems, while project-based crediting expanded through CDM-style approaches and associated verification and registry infrastructures. Carbon finance then evolved again under the Paris Agreement, adopted in 2015, which broadened mitigation governance through nationally determined contributions and introduced Article 6 as a framework for voluntary international cooperation and credit transfers; in doing so, it elevated questions of environmental integrity—especially the avoidance of double counting—and reinforced the centrality of governance, measurement, and verification as prerequisites for scaling international carbon market activity (UN, 2015).

Carbon finance overlaps with, but is distinct from, instruments such as green bonds and blue bonds. Green and blue bonds are predominantly use-of-proceeds instruments: they label debt capital for eligible expenditures (renewables, clean transport, coastal resilience, etc.), relying on standards, reporting, and verification for credibility. Carbon finance is instead price-of-externality finance: it attempts to make emissions (or reductions/removals) expensive enough that abatement becomes privately rational. The interaction, however, is increasingly tight. In practice, many transition projects combine both channels: a green bond can fund the capital expenditure, while expected carbon revenues (from allowance savings, credit generation, or avoided carbon taxes) improve project economics. At the portfolio level, carbon pricing is also becoming a major driver of transition risk and hence influences the risk-return profiles of green and conventional assets. This is consistent with the view that climate disclosure and sustainable debt standards reduce information frictions, while carbon pricing provides the economy-wide incentive that makes those disclosures financially binding.

The classic efficiency case for carbon pricing is well known: if marginal abatement costs differ across emitters, a uniform carbon price equalizes marginal costs and achieves a given reduction at minimum cost (relative to many command-and-control approaches). Yet the practical rationale for carbon finance goes beyond static efficiency. It includes:

- Dynamic incentives for innovation: credible price signals can shift R&D and investment toward low-carbon technologies and business models.
- Capital market integration: once carbon is priced, it becomes hedgeable and analyzable like other risk factors, allowing investors to manage transition exposure and allocate capital in ways that reinforce decarbonization.
- Fiscal and political economy channels: auction revenues can fund green public investment, reduce distortionary taxes, or compensate vulnerable households—choices that materially affect political durability.
- Institution building: the long-run effectiveness of carbon finance depends less on the theoretical elegance of pricing and more on monitoring, reporting, verification (MRV), enforcement, and governance credibility—topics that now dominate both policy debate and the empirical literature.

Prevailing Carbon Finance Systems

The ICAP ETS world map (Fig. 8.1) depicts emissions trading systems currently in force, under development or under consideration. As of January 2024, there are 36 ETSs in force. Another 14 are under development and expected to be in operation in the next few years. These include ETSs in Colombia, Türkiye, and Vietnam. 12 jurisdictions are also considering the role an ETS can play in their climate change policy mix. If a jurisdiction has multiple systems in force, it is depicted in blue, with the borders of the jurisdiction representing the layered systems (e.g. Germany and Guangdong). If, however, it has a system in force but is also developing an additional system, it is depicted in blue but also features a green border (e.g. the EU).

The performance of a carbon finance system depends on scope (what is covered), stringency (how tight the cap or tax is), price formation (market design and liquidity), and integrity (MRV, enforcement, and protection against manipulation and low-quality credits). These dimensions provide a consistent basis for comparing the EU's relatively centralized and tightening ETS, China's rapidly scaling but still evolving national ETS, and the US's fragmented landscape dominated by subnational compliance markets alongside federal tax incentives and a large voluntary ecosystem.

EU

The EU ETS remains the most influential compliance carbon market because it combines wide coverage with deep market infrastructure and a steadily tightening policy trajectory. It regulates roughly 45% of the EU's GHG output and has been

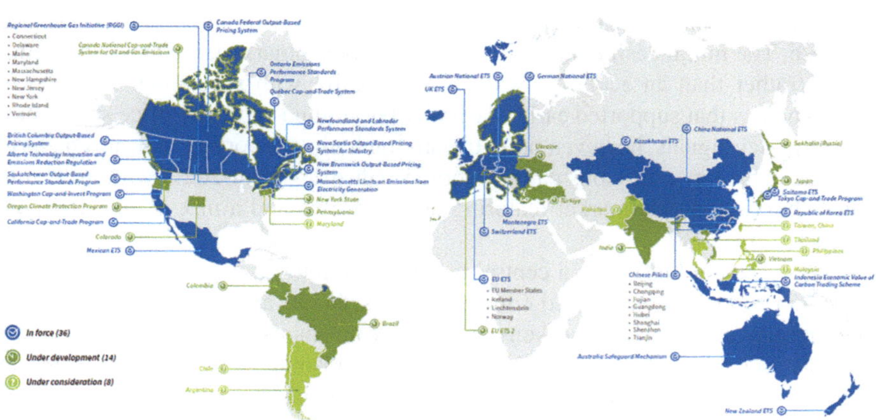

Fig. 8.1 ICAP emissions trading system worldwide. Source: International Carbon Action Partnership (ICAP)

repeatedly reformed to increase ambition and reduce surplus allowances. The Fit for 55 reforms align the EU ETS with a 2030 emissions-reduction goal for covered sectors on the order of 62% relative to 2005, strengthening the cap trajectory and accelerating decarbonization incentives.

A critical institutional development is that the EU ETS has increasingly expanded sectoral scope and tightened market management. From 2024, maritime emissions from large ships are included, reinforcing the EU's strategy of embedding carbon pricing into harder-to-abate sectors rather than relying solely on energy-sector decarbonization. In parallel, the EU has coupled carbon pricing with border measures and complementary regulations, aiming to reduce leakage risk and sustain political legitimacy. These choices illustrate a broader point: mature carbon finance systems tend to evolve into policy packages, where the ETS is the "price spine" and other instruments handle distributional, competitiveness, and technology constraints.

From a finance perspective, the EU ETS has also supported the development of allowance derivatives and risk-management practices. A deeper market permits compliance entities to smooth costs intertemporally and enables financial intermediaries to provide liquidity. Yet maturity also raises governance challenges—especially around market integrity, volatility, and the interface between compliance markets and offset credits. The EU's experience therefore offers two durable lessons for investors and policymakers: (1) credible long-run tightening is the main driver of decarbonization incentives; (2) credibility requires institutional capacity that goes well beyond simply launching a trading platform.

China

China's national ETS (launched 2021) is often described as the largest in the world by covered emissions because it began with the power sector and is being expanded stepwise. The initial design has relied heavily on benchmarked, intensity-style allocation (rather than an economy-wide absolute cap), with substantial free allocation—choices that supported early feasibility but limited short-run price stringency. Recent policy signals, however, point toward tightening: reporting indicates plans to introduce absolute emissions caps in certain industries from 2027, with an aim to establish a nationwide market featuring absolute caps and a mix of free and paid allowances by 2030.

This evolution highlights a central political economy trade-off. Intensity-based allocation can reduce perceived competitiveness shocks and protect growth objectives in early phases, but it weakens the scarcity mechanism that makes allowances valuable and prices informative. Moving toward absolute caps typically increases environmental effectiveness but raises distributional and competitiveness pressures, intensifying the need for complementary measures (targeted compensation, industrial policy, and credible enforcement).

Empirical work beyond the ETS itself also suggests that "carbon finance" in China is not only about allowance trading. Carbon finance is increasingly discussed as an integrated policy and financial ecosystem—linking carbon pricing, green finance reforms, and firm incentives for green efficiency and innovation. In the applied literature, carbon finance development is often associated with improvements in green economic efficiency and with broader "high-quality development" narratives (with heterogeneous results across regions and institutional contexts). The bibliometric evidence also underlines that China is now one of the major hubs of carbon finance research and policy experimentation, alongside Europe and the US.

A useful sectoral illustration comes from empirical research on industrial transformation in coastal and marine-related contexts. While not an ETS evaluation per se, the evidence base connects innovation efficiency and structural upgrading to environmental constraints and market mechanisms, reinforcing the broader argument that pricing and finance channels can shape industrial upgrading under binding ecological constraints.

The interpretation for carbon finance is that institutional complementarity matters: pricing signals are more likely to translate into real decarbonization when firms have access to finance, innovation capacity, and credible governance that rewards low-carbon upgrading.

US

In the US, carbon finance operates through a patchwork of subnational emissions trading systems rather than a single national ETS. This institutional fragmentation reflects long-standing federal political constraints, but it has not prevented meaningful carbon pricing from developing in several large jurisdictions. California's cap-and-trade program is often described as the most comprehensive and financially mature US allowance market because it is designed as an economy-wide system, covering roughly 80% of statewide GHG emissions across electric power, industry, and fuels (Congressional Research Services, 2024). Its fiscal significance is also substantial: by May 2024, cumulative auction revenues were approximately $28 billion, which California channels through the Greenhouse Gas Reduction Fund to finance climate-related programs with explicit distributional requirements for disadvantaged and low-income communities. Market design features—particularly quarterly auctions, banking provisions, and reserve mechanisms—shape price formation and reduce short-term cost shocks, while also creating a transparent schedule of compliance demand that supports forward planning. Auction data illustrate the degree to which prices respond to both policy expectations and market conditions: in the May 2024 joint auction, the current-vintage settlement price was $37.02 and the advance-vintage settlement price was $38.35, with all offered allowances sold, indicating continued demand for compliance instruments even as regulatory uncertainty periodically influences secondary-market sentiment (California Air Resources Board, 2025).

Alongside California, the Regional Greenhouse Gas Initiative (RGGI) provides the other major pillar of US allowance trading, although it is narrower in sectoral scope because it targets power-sector emissions in participating states. RGGI's quarterly auctions generate a consistent public-revenue stream and offer clear evidence of how price-containment tools operate in practice. In the second auction of 2024 (Auction 64), 16.1 million allowances cleared at $21.03 per short ton and generated $337.6 million in proceeds for reinvestment in programs such as energy efficiency, renewable energy, bill assistance, and abatement (RGGI, 2026). More broadly, market-monitoring evidence indicates that RGGI allowance prices increased materially in 2024: the volume-weighted average auction clearing price rose from $13.58 in 2023 to $20.17 in 2024, while option-implied volatility increased sharply in the second half of 2024 as cost-containment reserves were depleted, underscoring how institutional design affects both the level and the risk characteristics of carbon assets (RGGI, 2025).

These subnational systems create a distinctive US carbon finance profile. The price signal is real and investable in covered jurisdictions, yet the absence of a nationwide cap means that incentives vary across regions and sectors, complicating carbon-cost pass-through and hedging for firms operating nationally. The broader literature increasingly treats this fragmentation not merely as a political curiosity but as a defining structural feature shaping the interaction between carbon markets, complementary regulation, and private finance—an interpretation consistent with bibliometric evidence that positions the US as one of the main global centers of carbon finance research and market innovation despite the lack of a federal ETS (Roshid et al., 2025).

Governance

This section argues that carbon finance is ultimately an institutional project. Market-based pricing can only deliver decarbonization if the traded commodity (allowances or credits) is credible, scarce enough to matter, and protected from manipulation and low-integrity supply. The governance challenge is therefore not secondary—it is the mechanism that determines whether carbon finance is a credible "price of externality" or merely a symbolic market.

Compliance Markets

In compliance ETSs, the central governance question is whether the cap is binding and expected to tighten. If firms believe future caps will be relaxed when prices rise, they will under-invest in abatement and treat allowance purchases as a temporary compliance cost rather than a strategic transition signal. This is the familiar time-consistency problem in environmental policy, closely linked to commitment and credibility in macroeconomics. The EU's repeated reforms and tightening trajectory can be interpreted as an institutional attempt to strengthen commitment technology—making the long-run scarcity path more believable.

Allocation design is the second major governance frontier because it determines distributional incidence and political durability. Free allocation can reduce short-run opposition but can also generate windfall profits and weaken price pass-through incentives. Auctioning strengthens fiscal capacity and transparency but can intensify competitiveness pressures. In practice, jurisdictions often mix free allocation (especially for trade-exposed sectors) with partial auctioning and targeted compensation. The Chinese move from intensity benchmarks toward absolute caps, if sustained, would represent a shift toward stronger scarcity governance, but it also raises the importance of transparent allocation rules and enforcement capacity.

Market integrity governance increasingly resembles financial market regulation. As carbon allowances become financialized, issues such as insider trading, manipulation, and the role of intermediaries become more salient. The literature reflects this shift by increasingly treating carbon markets as hybrid institutions—part environmental policy, part financial market—requiring both environmental MRV and financial conduct oversight. The implication is that "good ETS governance" should be evaluated with tools familiar from finance: transparency rules, surveillance, position limits where appropriate, robust clearing and settlement, and credible penalties.

Voluntary Carbon Markets

Voluntary Carbon Markets (VCMs) are often justified as a way to mobilize private capital for mitigation beyond formal compliance obligations, especially in sectors where direct decarbonization is difficult or where nature-based solutions can generate co-benefits. Yet VCMs face a more severe governance challenge than ETSs because they typically rely on project-level claims about additionality, baselines, permanence, leakage, and MRV quality—dimensions that are difficult for buyers to verify.

A systematic review of empirical VCM evidence synthesizing 69 studies concludes that there is an urgent requirement for a policy framework for VCMs across regions and climate zones, emphasizing governance and transparency needs rather than treating VCMs as purely private ordering (Kochar et al., 2025). The review highlights that financial and socioeconomic dimensions—such as ROI and project profitability—are common evaluative lenses, and that co-benefits can materially affect both implementation and the marketability of credits, even when profitability is uncertain. It also documents systematic differences between Global North and Global South study patterns—consistent with broader concerns about distribution, land use opportunity costs, and the political economy of offset supply chains.

From an economic perspective, VCM integrity problems are a variant of the "lemons market" under asymmetric information: if buyers cannot distinguish high-quality from low-quality credits, average willingness to pay falls, high-quality supply exits, and the market can unravel. That logic explains why governance initiatives—standard-setting, verification, transparency platforms, and public oversight—are not optional extras but the conditions for market survival.

The VCM literature also underscores that land-use choices are central and contested. The review notes an inclination toward agroforestry projects relative to REDD mechanisms in parts of the empirical evidence base, and it emphasizes the importance of evaluating opportunity costs and land-use alternatives in a way that is financially, environmentally, and socially feasible. This aligns with a more general point: in carbon finance, "measurement" is not merely technical—it is political economy, because baselines and counterfactuals determine who is paid and for what.

Theoretical Perspectives

A useful way to analyze carbon markets is to treat them simultaneously as (1) instruments for correcting a welfare-theoretic market failure, (2) institutional arrangements that must be politically credible over time, and (3) financial markets in which prices, liquidity, and risk premia condition real investment responses. These lenses are complementary rather than competing. Together they explain why carbon markets that look similar on paper can generate very different price dynamics and decarbonization outcomes in practice.

The welfare-theoretic starting point is the Pigouvian logic of externality pricing: emissions impose social damages that are not reflected in private costs, so a price on carbon (or a binding cap that generates a market price) can align decentralized decisions with social objectives (Pigou, 1920). Within this frame, the main benchmark for evaluating a carbon market is cost-effectiveness—whether it achieves a given emissions constraint at minimum economic cost by equalizing marginal abatement costs across heterogeneous sources. In an idealized setting, this delivers a clean efficiency ranking relative to many prescriptive regulations. Yet the policy problem is not only one of static efficiency; it is also one of uncertainty. Here the prices-versus-quantities result provides an influential second benchmark. Under uncertainty about abatement costs and damages, the relative performance of carbon taxes and cap-and-trade depends on the slopes of marginal benefits and marginal costs and the structure of uncertainty (Weitzman, 1974). In climate policy, this logic has been extended to explain why real-world systems often converge toward hybrid designs—caps accompanied by banking, stability reserves, or soft price bounds that dampen cost shocks while maintaining a medium-term emissions trajectory (Aldy & Stavins, 2012; Goulder & Schein, 2013). The analytical implication is that "instrument choice" is rarely decisive in isolation; the design of the instrument—including rules that shape expectations about future scarcity—often dominates the welfare comparison (Schmalensee & Stavins, 2017).

A second perspective emphasizes institutions, commitment, and political economy. In this view, a carbon market is not simply a decentralized mechanism for finding the least-cost abatement; it is a state-backed governance system that creates and enforces a new form of scarcity. This draws attention to credibility and time consistency. If economic agents believe that policymakers will relax caps, expand free allocation, or weaken enforcement when prices become politically uncomfortable, then the carbon price will embed that expectation and the market will under-incentivize long-horizon abatement and innovation. This is one reason revenue use and distributional design matter so much: they shape the durability of the political coalition supporting the carbon constraint (Carl & Fedor, 2016). In fiscal terms, carbon pricing can also interact with pre-existing distortions in the tax system, creating either efficiency gains through revenue recycling or losses if revenues are returned in ways that do not reduce distortionary taxes—an issue that ties carbon market performance to broader public finance architecture (Goulder & Schein, 2013). The institutional lens thus reframes "market design" as a commitment technology: rules about cap trajectories, allocation, and revenue recycling are not technical add-ons but core determinants of whether the market can sustain scarcity over decades.

A third perspective treats carbon markets as financial markets whose microstructure influences both prices and the real economy. Once allowances and credits become tradable assets, price formation depends on liquidity, participation, hedging demand, and the availability of derivatives. Microstructure research on the EU ETS, for example, uses high-frequency trading data to characterize market development and informational efficiency in allowance futures (Bredin et al., 2014). Financial economics also highlights that carbon assets can carry risk premia: option-implied and realized volatility can diverge, implying a variance risk premium that reflects compensation for uncertainty and tail risks in carbon pricing—risks that are partly macroeconomic (energy shocks, recessions) and partly political (regime changes, rule revisions) (Chevallier, 2013). This financial perspective matters for policy evaluation because market depth and hedging capacity can reduce compliance-cost volatility and support more ambitious caps; conversely, thin liquidity and unstable expectations can produce politically salient price swings that trigger regulatory backlash. In short, the financialization of carbon markets is neither purely beneficial nor purely harmful; it is a structural feature that must be governed with transparency, surveillance, and stable rulemaking if prices are to remain credible signals for investment.

These three perspectives become especially salient when carbon markets extend beyond compliance allowances into project-based crediting. Voluntary carbon markets highlight the limits of the canonical externality-pricing model because the traded unit is not a right to emit but a claim about an avoided emission or removal relative to a counterfactual baseline. The key economic problem becomes one of information and integrity: additionality, baseline inflation, leakage, and permanence risks can generate adverse selection, weakening demand and undermining the environmental meaning of the unit. Recent empirical synthesis emphasizes that these integrity issues are not peripheral but foundational, arguing for policy frameworks that strengthen governance and transparency across regions and project types (Kochar et al., 2025). This integrity-oriented lens aligns with the broader institutional perspective: credit markets require credible MRV and rule-based accounting to avoid double counting and to ensure that financial flows correspond to real mitigation outcomes rather than paper claims.

Taken together, these theoretical approaches suggest a unified evaluative framework. A carbon market's effectiveness depends on (1) whether it creates an economically meaningful and predictable scarcity signal (welfare and uncertainty), (2) whether that scarcity is politically credible and distributionally sustainable (institutions and public finance), and (3) whether market infrastructure supports robust price discovery and manageable risk (financial economics and microstructure). Carbon market analysis is therefore most informative when it avoids a single-theory diagnosis and instead treats carbon pricing as a governance-embedded financial institution—one that prices an externality, allocates rents, and creates tradable assets whose integrity and risk properties condition the pace and cost of decarbonization (Schmalensee & Stavins, 2017; Goulder & Schein, 2013; Kochar et al., 2025).

Conclusion

Carbon finance has become a central implementation channel for the net-zero transition because it turns emissions and mitigation into priced economic quantities that can discipline corporate behavior, mobilize capital, and generate public revenues. It is argued that carbon markets should be evaluated as governance-embedded financial institutions rather than as "markets" in the abstract. The EU ETS represents the most mature model in terms of policy credibility, market infrastructure, and the integration of carbon pricing into a broader regulatory and fiscal package. China's national ETS illustrates a different pathway: rapid scaling and institutional learning, with an evolving trajectory toward tighter scarcity and broader sectoral coverage. The US case highlights fragmentation: carbon pricing exists through subnational markets and sectoral schemes, complemented by federal incentives and regulation, which can produce meaningful decarbonization pressure but also uneven price signals and higher coordination costs. Across these models, the decisive determinant is not whether a jurisdiction chose "tax" or "trade", but whether the system produces an expected path of scarcity that is credible enough to influence investment and innovation decisions over long horizons.

The governance agenda has also sharpened around integrity and credibility. In compliance markets, the binding constraints are MRV quality, enforcement, and the credibility of tightening trajectories in the face of distributional and competitiveness pressures. Recent EU debates about extending and stabilizing carbon pricing in household-relevant sectors illustrate that political durability increasingly depends on complementary financial mechanisms that cushion adjustment costs, rather than on market design alone. In voluntary carbon markets, the governance constraint is even more fundamental because credit units depend on counterfactual baselines and additionality claims. A global synthesis of empirical evidence argues for policy frameworks that strengthen governance and transparency in VCMs, reflecting the view that private ordering alone is insufficient to resolve quality and legitimacy problems (Kochar et al., 2025).

For investors, carbon finance matters because it increasingly functions as a priced transition-risk factor, with direct and indirect channels into portfolio performance. Direct exposure arises through allowances and carbon credits as tradable assets; indirect exposure arises through the valuation of emissions-intensive firms, the cost of capital for transition projects, and the credibility of corporate net-zero strategies that rely on offsets. The first practical implication is that carbon should be treated as a policy-dependent asset class: expected returns and tail risks are shaped by regulatory credibility, allowance supply rules, and political responses to distributional pressures. The second implication is that "carbon exposure" is not homogeneous. EU allowances, Chinese allowances, US subnational allowances, and high-integrity removals credits embed very different governance risks and price dynamics, so risk management requires jurisdiction- and instrument-specific analysis rather than generic carbon beta assumptions. The third implication concerns due diligence in credit markets. As integrity standards tighten and reputational and legal scrutiny grows, investors should treat additionality, baseline credibility, permanence, and claims integrity as core credit-risk variables, not as ESG add-ons (Ecosystem Marketplace, 2025). Finally, carbon finance interacts with green and transition finance: credible carbon pricing can strengthen project economics for low-carbon investments, while weak or unstable carbon regimes can increase uncertainty premiums and undermine the bankability of transition strategies.

For policymakers, the central lesson is that carbon finance is an institutional project. A carbon market's effectiveness depends on whether it generates a credible scarcity signal and whether that signal survives predictable political stress points—energy-price shocks, competitiveness concerns, and distributional backlash. Durable systems tend to converge on three design principles. First, invest in MRV and enforcement capacity as market infrastructure; without credible measurement and compliance, the price signal becomes informationally weak and politically fragile. Second, treat revenue recycling and distributional policy as first-order design variables. The fiscal scale of carbon pricing is now large enough that how revenues are used can materially affect legitimacy and the speed of technology adoption (World Bank, 2024). Third, recognize that carbon markets increasingly operate in a world of cross-border interaction—through supply chains, competitiveness, and evolving international cooperation under Paris Agreement mechanisms—so governance must address double counting, transparency, and comparability if cross-border carbon finance is to scale credibly.

In sum, carbon finance can accelerate the net-zero transition, but only when it is treated as governance-embedded finance rather than a narrow trading mechanism. Pricing carbon is necessary for aligning private and social costs; making that price credible, investable, and politically durable is the harder task. The next stage of carbon finance development will therefore be defined less by the proliferation of new markets and more by the strengthening of institutional quality—MRV integrity, rule stability, transparent revenue use, and credible claims frameworks—so that carbon prices and credits can serve as reliable signals for long-horizon investment and innovation.

References

Aldy, J. E., & Stavins, R. N. (2012). The promise and problems of pricing carbon: Theory and experience. *The Journal of Environment & Development, 21*(2), 152–180.

Bredin, D., Hyde, S., & Muckley, C. (2014). A microstructure analysis of the carbon finance market. *International Review of Financial Analysis, 34*, 222–234.

California Air Resources Board. (2025). *Auction information: Summary of auction settlement prices and results*. California Air Resources Board.

Carl, J., & Fedor, D. (2016). Tracking global carbon revenues: A survey of carbon taxes versus cap-and-trade in the real world. *Energy Policy, 96*, 50–77.

Chevallier, J. (2013). Variance risk-premia in CO2 markets. *Economic Modelling, 31*, 598–605.

Congressional Research Services. (2024). *California cap-and-trade program: Overview and issues (Report R48314)*. Congressional Research Services.

Ecosystem Marketplace. (2025). *State of the voluntary carbon market 2025*. Ecosystem Marketplace.

Goulder, L., & Schein, A. (2013). Carbon taxes versus cap and trade: A critical review. *Climate Change Economics, 4*(3), 1350010.

Kochar, R., Kalsie, A., & Deka, N. (2025). Voluntary Carbon Markets (VCMs) in a nutshell: A systematic review based on the empirical evidence from across the globe. *Journal of Cleaner Production, 522*, 146261.

Pigou, A. (1920). *The economics of welfare*. Macmillan.

RGGI. (2025). *Annual report on the market for RGGI CO2 allowances: 2024*. Regional Greenhouse Gas Initiative.

RGGI. (2026). *Market monitor reports*. Regional Greenhouse Gas Initiative.

Roshid, M. M., Karim, R., Waaje, A., Islam, S., & Bhowmik, R. C. (2025). Mapping the carbon finance research: A bibliometric exploration of innovation in sustainable finance. *Development and Sustainability in Economics and Finance, 5*, 100048.

Schmalensee, R., & Stavins, R. N. (2017). The design of environmental markets: What have we learned from experience with cap and trade? *Oxford Review of Economic Policy, 33*(4), 572–588.

UN. (1997). *Kyoto protocol to the United Nations framework convention on climate change*. United Nations Framework Convention on Climate Change.

UN. (2015). *Adoption of the Paris Agreement*. United Nations Framework Convention on Climate Change.

Weitzman, M. L. (1974). Prices vs. quantities 12. *The Review of Economic Studies, 41*(4), 477–491.

World Bank. (2024). *State and trends of carbon pricing 2024*. World Bank.

Chapter 9
Carbon Trading

Introduction

Carbon trading has become one of the most consequential market-based carbon finance instruments in global climate governance. At its core, carbon trading seeks to correct a fundamental market failure: greenhouse gas emissions impose substantial social costs, yet these costs are largely external to private decision-making. When emitting carbon is cheap for firms but costly for society, markets systematically overproduce carbon-intensive goods and underinvest in low-carbon alternatives. Carbon trading responds to this problem by creating scarcity over emissions and transforming carbon into a priced, tradable economic asset. In doing so, it embeds climate constraints directly into production, investment, and financial decision-making.

The relevance of carbon trading has expanded sharply alongside the global commitment to net-zero emissions. Achieving net zero by mid-century requires not only technological change but also a sustained reallocation of capital away from carbon-intensive activities and toward low-carbon production systems. Estimates by the International Energy Agency suggest that global clean energy investment alone must rise to over $4 trillion annually by the early 2030s to remain consistent with net-zero pathways. Without an economy-wide price signal that penalizes emissions, such a scale of reallocation is difficult to sustain. Carbon trading therefore occupies a distinctive position within climate finance: unlike green or blue bonds, which channel capital toward specific eligible expenditures, carbon trading operates by pricing the externality itself, reshaping relative prices across the entire economy.

From a policy perspective, carbon trading is not a single market but a family of institutional arrangements. Compliance-based emissions trading systems (ETSs), such as those in the EU, China, and parts of the US, impose legally binding caps on emissions and allow firms to trade allowances. Alongside these systems, voluntary carbon markets facilitate the exchange of offset credits linked to emission

P. Zhou, D. Guo, *Climate Finance in the Net-Zero Transition*, Contributions to Finance and Accounting, https://doi.org/10.1007/978-981-92-0827-2_9

reductions or removals outside compliance obligations. Together, these mechanisms underpin what is often described as the global carbon market. As of the mid-2020s, carbon pricing instruments—including ETSs and carbon taxes—cover roughly one quarter of global greenhouse gas emissions, a share that continues to expand as new jurisdictions adopt pricing mechanisms and existing systems tighten.

The economic appeal of carbon trading rests on several well-established arguments. First, carbon markets are cost-effective: by equalizing marginal abatement costs across firms, they achieve a given emissions reduction at lower total cost than many command-and-control regulations. Second, they provide dynamic incentives for innovation by making low-carbon technologies and processes financially attractive relative to carbon-intensive incumbents. Third, they integrate climate policy into capital markets. Once carbon is priced, emissions exposure becomes a financial risk factor that can be hedged, traded, and priced into asset valuations. This feature links carbon trading directly to investment decisions, portfolio allocation, and corporate finance strategies.

Yet the practical performance of carbon trading has been uneven. Carbon prices have exhibited substantial volatility, and in many systems prices remained too low for extended periods to meaningfully alter investment behavior. Concerns about carbon leakage, distributional impacts, and political acceptability have shaped market design choices, often leading to extensive free allocation of allowances or the use of intensity-based benchmarks rather than absolute caps. Voluntary carbon markets, meanwhile, have faced persistent questions about environmental integrity, additionality, and the credibility of offset claims. These challenges have prompted a shift in both policy and academic discourse away from treating carbon trading as a purely technical pricing exercise and toward understanding it as an institutional and governance problem.

Figure 9.1 illustrates the historical evolution of carbon prices across selected major trading systems, including the EU ETS, California's cap-and-trade program, the Regional Greenhouse Gas Initiative in the northeastern US, and China's national ETS. The figure highlights three stylized facts. First, carbon prices have generally trended upward over time in mature systems, particularly in the EU, reflecting tightening caps and strengthened policy credibility. Second, price levels differ markedly across jurisdictions, indicating heterogeneous policy ambition and institutional capacity. Third, price volatility remains a defining feature of carbon markets, shaped by energy price shocks, macroeconomic cycles, and regulatory expectations. These patterns underscore why carbon trading must be analyzed not only through the lens of welfare economics but also through political economy and financial market theory.

This chapter examines carbon trading as a central component of carbon finance in the net-zero transition. It advances three main objectives. First, it reviews the evolution and current landscape of global carbon trading systems, emphasizing their role in translating climate targets into market incentives. Second, it critically evaluates the academic literature on carbon trading, organizing research findings around key themes such as environmental effectiveness, price dynamics, innovation incentives, and governance challenges. Third, it develops a balanced economic analysis

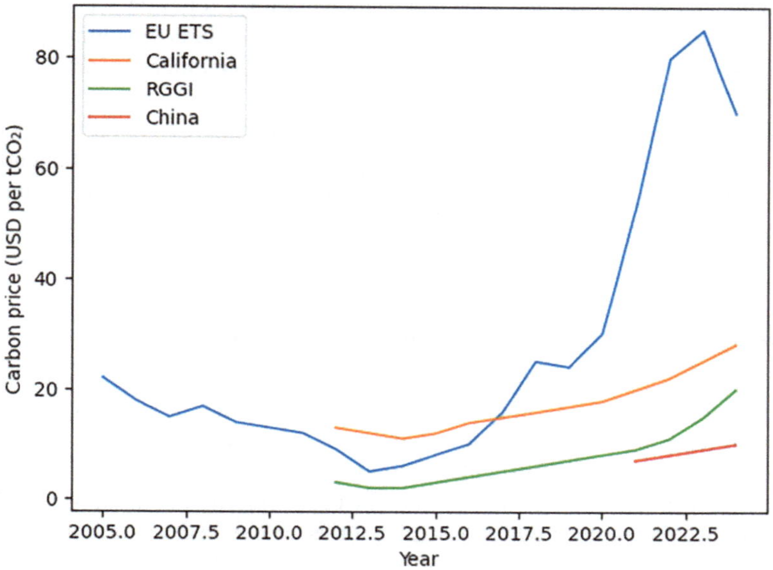

Fig. 9.1 Historical carbon prices in major carbon trading systems. Notes: EU ETS prices are based on European Union Allowance (EUA) market prices from the European Energy Exchange (EEX) emissions market data. California prices are based on the California Air Resources Board (CARB) Cap-and-Trade Program auction settlement prices reported in the official auction notices and results summaries. RGGI prices are based on the Regional Greenhouse Gas Initiative (RGGI) auction clearing prices, reported in the official "Allowance Prices and Volumes" auction results. China national ETS prices are based on official national ETS trading information as summarized by recognized institutional market overviews

that integrates welfare economics, institutional perspectives, and financial market insights to explain why carbon trading systems succeed or fail in practice.

Literature

Academic research on carbon trading has evolved in distinct waves that closely track institutional development. Early studies were largely motivated by the design and initial performance of the EU ETS and the Kyoto-era crediting mechanisms, with an emphasis on how cap-and-trade compared with carbon taxes and command-and-control regulation in terms of efficiency and feasibility (Venmans, 2012). As trading systems matured and carbon prices became economically meaningful, scholarship expanded toward empirical evaluation of environmental effectiveness, price formation and volatility, innovation incentives, and the political economy of allocation (Martin et al., 2016; Sato et al., 2022). More recently, the literature has broadened again, treating carbon markets as hybrid institutions at the intersection of environmental regulation and financial markets, with a renewed focus on governance, integrity, and distributional consequences—particularly in voluntary markets and cross-border transfers under Article 6 of the Paris Agreement (Arora-Jonsson & Gurung, 2023).

This section synthesizes that literature in a thematic way. The objective is not to produce an exhaustive survey, but to identify robust findings, contested claims, and the core mechanisms that explain why carbon trading succeeds in some settings and disappoints in others.

Environmental Effectiveness and Emissions Outcomes

The central empirical question is whether emissions trading systems deliver real emissions reductions beyond what would have occurred in the absence of the policy. Conceptually, a binding cap should ensure reductions by construction. In practice, however, effectiveness hinges on whether the cap is sufficiently tight, whether complementary policies alter emissions trajectories in covered sectors, and whether allowance supply and demand are shaped by macroeconomic shocks that render the cap non-binding.

In the EU ETS, the early evidence is often characterized as mixed, not because the logic of trading was flawed, but because cap stringency and allowance surplus dynamics weakened scarcity in the first decade. The first trading period was marked by overallocation and limited banking, contributing to price collapses and undermining the credibility of the market as a long-run investment signal. The literature generally interprets the EU's subsequent reforms—including tighter caps, expanded auctioning, and market stability mechanisms—as institutional responses to restore scarcity and improve effectiveness (Ellerman et al., 2010; Schmalensee & Stavins, 2017). The policy lesson that dominates this strand is that "launching an ETS" is not the same as "creating an effective carbon price". A well-functioning system requires iterative tightening and credible rulemaking that sustains expected scarcity.

China's ETS evidence base is newer and is shaped by the system's distinctive design: it began with the power sector and relied heavily on benchmarked, intensity-style allocation. In such systems, the short-run relationship between trading and absolute emissions can be muted, especially if benchmarks are generous and compliance incentives are weak. The emerging literature therefore focuses less on "did the ETS reduce emissions immediately?" and more on "did the ETS begin to change managerial attention, reporting quality, investment planning, and the relative economics of generation choices?" (Zhang et al., 2014; Munnings et al., 2016). This reflects an important empirical reality: in an economy undergoing rapid structural change, carbon market effectiveness may initially manifest through governance and information channels rather than immediate, measurable emissions declines.

The US evidence largely comes from subnational systems, which complicates identification because federal and state-level policies interact with carbon markets (Carattini et al., 2018). California's economy-wide cap-and-trade operates alongside renewable portfolio standards, low-carbon fuel standards, and other regulations, making attribution challenging. RGGI's power-sector focus provides cleaner identification in some contexts, but participating states also pursued complementary energy and efficiency programs (Lessmann & Kramer, 2024). A recurring result in the empirical literature is that cap-and-trade effectiveness is easiest to detect when the cap is binding and when complementary policies do not fully dominate the abatement margin. Where complementary regulation delivers most emissions reductions independently, the ETS can drift into a secondary role, influencing allowance prices more than real emissions.

Taken together, the "environmental effectiveness" literature converges on a conditional conclusion. Carbon trading can be effective, but only when scarcity is credible. Over-allocation, weak enforcement, or an overly flexible supply of low-integrity credits can turn an ETS into an accounting exercise rather than an investment driver. The strongest empirical contributions in this area therefore emphasize system design and reforms rather than merely asking whether trading "works" in general.

Cost-Effectiveness and the Equalization of Marginal Abatement Costs

A second research theme assesses whether carbon trading delivers the welfare-theoretic promise of cost-effective abatement. In the canonical model, trading equalizes marginal abatement costs across regulated sources, achieving a given emissions target at minimum cost. Empirical validation is difficult because marginal abatement costs are rarely observed directly. The literature therefore uses indirect approaches: comparing compliance costs across firms, examining permit price behavior relative to fuel switching and technological opportunities, and modeling counterfactual outcomes under alternative regulations.

This strand often emphasizes that cost-effectiveness gains from trading are largest when heterogeneity across sources is substantial and when firms have flexibility to adjust abatement timing through banking and intertemporal optimization. Banking provisions allow firms to smooth abatement costs over time, reducing political resistance to temporary price spikes and encouraging earlier abatement when it is cheaper. Yet this same flexibility can generate controversies: if banking leads to large allowance surpluses, it can weaken near-term prices and delay abatement. In response, the literature increasingly supports hybrid market designs that maintain trading while managing surplus and volatility (Aldy & Stavins, 2012; Goulder & Schein, 2013).

The cost-effectiveness literature is also where the classic "prices versus quantities" debate remains influential. Under uncertainty, taxes and cap-and-trade can differ in welfare performance depending on the slopes of marginal benefits and costs and the nature of uncertainty (Weitzman, 1974). Modern analyses often conclude that real-world policy design tends to converge toward hybrids: caps with stability reserves, price floors, and cost containment mechanisms that dampen extreme price outcomes while preserving an emissions trajectory (Schmalensee & Stavins, 2017). This is an important reframing: empirical debates about whether carbon markets are "too volatile" are not merely about market behavior, but about whether the policy instrument is designed to handle uncertainty consistent with political constraints.

Price Formation, Volatility, and the Financialization of Carbon Markets

As carbon markets mature, allowance prices become economically salient and financial actors enter, prompting a substantial literature on price dynamics, volatility, and market microstructure. This research treats carbon allowances as assets whose prices reflect expected future scarcity, compliance demand, energy prices, macroeconomic conditions, and regulatory credibility. In this view, carbon prices are forward-looking policy variables: they embed expectations about future caps, enforcement, and reform risk.

The EU ETS has received the most attention because of its liquidity and derivatives market depth. Empirical studies document how carbon prices respond to energy prices, particularly natural gas and coal spreads, because fuel switching is a key short-run abatement channel in power markets (Koch et al., 2014). A robust finding is that the carbon price cannot be interpreted in isolation: it is co-determined with energy market fundamentals and macro conditions (Strange et al., 2024). During recessions, emissions fall and allowance demand weakens, depressing prices unless supply is adjusted. This is precisely why institutional reforms such as stability reserves matter: they attempt to prevent macro shocks from permanently eroding scarcity and price signals.

Volatility is another central topic. For policymakers, high volatility can create political backlash and reduce the credibility of carbon pricing as a stable investment signal. For firms and investors, volatility creates hedging demand and motivates the development of futures, options, and risk-management practices. Financial economics research treats carbon markets similarly to other commodity and policy-driven asset markets, emphasizing liquidity, participation, and the risk premium embedded in carbon assets (Chevallier, 2013). This literature often highlights a policy trade-off: financialization can improve liquidity and price discovery, but it also increases the salience of market integrity, surveillance, and regulatory stability.

US subnational markets show a different microstructure due to the centrality of auctions and explicit price containment mechanisms. California and RGGI use auction schedules and reserve mechanisms that shape both the level and distribution of prices. This design can reduce extreme volatility but can also constrain price discovery, since the market is more administratively structured. China's ETS, still in an earlier stage of maturation, has a growing literature emphasizing liquidity constraints, participation structure, and the institutional learning process. Here, research often treats price volatility and low liquidity less as "market failure" and more as transitional features of a system whose coverage and allocation design are still evolving.

Overall, the price formation literature points to a critical interpretive lesson: carbon prices are not merely market outcomes—they are policy expectations expressed in asset prices. This means that stable, credible rulemaking is itself a determinant of market efficiency.

Innovation, Investment, and Dynamic Efficiency

A major promise of carbon trading is dynamic efficiency: by raising the cost of emissions, carbon prices should incentivize innovation and low-carbon investment. The innovation literature spans firm-level evidence on R&D, patenting, and technology adoption, as well as sectoral evidence on capital stock turnover and energy system transitions (Calel & Dechezleprêtre, 2016).

Empirical findings here are more mixed than in the cost-effectiveness literature, largely because carbon prices have often been low or unstable in many systems (Aghion et al., 2016). Where prices are modest and short-run compliance can be achieved through inexpensive operational adjustments, the incentive to undertake costly innovation and capital replacement may be limited. However, when prices rise and, crucially, when firms expect a tightening trajectory, carbon pricing can influence investment planning. This supports a key theoretical point: for innovation incentives, the expected long-run path of carbon prices matters more than short-run price fluctuations (Martin et al., 2016).

Several studies also emphasize complementarities. Carbon trading alone may be insufficient to induce certain innovations due to knowledge spillovers, network externalities, and technology adoption barriers. Hence, carbon pricing is often most effective as part of a policy mix that includes subsidies, standards, and public R&D support. This is not a rejection of carbon trading; rather, it is an application of second-best logic: multiple market failures imply multiple instruments. The literature has increasingly moved away from treating carbon pricing and industrial policy as substitutes, and instead evaluates how they jointly shape dynamic transitions.

Competitiveness, Carbon Leakage, and Border Adjustments

A persistent political and analytical challenge for carbon trading is the risk of carbon leakage: emissions reductions in regulated jurisdictions could be offset by increases elsewhere if production shifts to less regulated regions. The literature distinguishes between short-run leakage through trade and investment adjustments, and longer-run leakage through technology diffusion and capital relocation (Branger & Quirion, 2014).

Empirical evidence suggests leakage risks are sector-specific and most salient for trade-exposed, energy-intensive industries (Dechezleprêtre & Sato, 2017). Policy responses typically involve free allocation to leakage-exposed sectors and, increasingly, border adjustment mechanisms (Fischer & Fox, 2012). The literature debates the effectiveness and distributional consequences of such measures (Martin et al., 2014). Free allocation can reduce competitiveness shocks but may generate windfall profits and weaken price pass-through incentives. Border adjustments aim to preserve competitiveness and maintain incentives but raise complex questions about trade law, administrative feasibility, and the risk of politicizing climate policy through trade conflict.

This theme is now central to global carbon market debates because the net-zero transition is uneven across regions. As carbon constraints tighten in one region, carbon cost differentials become more salient for trade and investment. Academic work increasingly treats leakage not as a peripheral technical issue but as a core political economy challenge that can determine the durability of carbon pricing systems.

Distributional Impacts, Equity, and Political Durability

Another major research stream evaluates distributional impacts. Carbon pricing can be regressive if energy costs rise and lower-income households spend a larger share of income on energy-intensive goods. Firms may also pass carbon costs onto consumers, with heterogeneous impacts across sectors and regions (Fabra & Reguant, 2014).

The literature emphasizes that distributional outcomes are not inherent to carbon trading—they depend on allowance allocation and revenue recycling. Auction revenues can be returned to households, used to reduce distortionary taxes, or invested in public goods such as clean infrastructure. These choices affect both equity and political support. This strand intersects with public finance: under certain conditions, recycling revenues through reductions in distortionary taxes can yield efficiency gains ("double dividend"), though the magnitude and robustness of such effects depend on context (Goulder & Schein, 2013).

The political durability literature frames carbon markets as commitment devices that require stable coalitions. If distributional design is weak, public support may erode when prices rise. Conversely, if revenues are used transparently to fund visible benefits or compensate vulnerable groups, carbon pricing can become more politically resilient. This is particularly relevant to the net-zero transition, which requires sustained carbon constraints over decades.

Governance and Integrity

A final theme—growing rapidly in importance—concerns governance and integrity. Carbon markets rely on measurement, reporting, and verification (MRV) because the traded commodity is an abstract right to emit (allowances) or a claim about avoided emissions/removals (credits). If MRV is weak, the environmental meaning of the market deteriorates (Schneider & La Hoz Theuer, 2019).

In compliance markets, integrity problems typically revolve around cap stringency, enforcement, and the treatment of offsets. In voluntary carbon markets, integrity concerns are more severe because credits are defined relative to counterfactual baselines. The literature highlights risks of non-additional projects, baseline inflation, leakage, impermanence in nature-based solutions, and double counting. These issues can create an adverse selection problem: if buyers cannot distinguish high- from low-quality credits, willingness to pay falls and the market risks unraveling.

The governance agenda has therefore shifted toward standard-setting, transparency, and oversight. Recent reviews emphasize the need for clearer policy frameworks to ensure integrity, particularly as Article 6 cooperation expands and voluntary markets interact with national accounting systems (Kochar et al., 2025). The overarching conclusion is that carbon trading is not merely a market mechanism; it is an institutional system whose credibility depends on governance infrastructure.

Synthesis

Across themes, three synthesis points emerge.

First, the literature strongly supports the view that carbon trading can be cost-effective and can reduce emissions when scarcity is credible. Weak caps, overallocation, or excessive low-integrity credit supply undermine the mechanism.

Second, price dynamics are best understood as policy expectations expressed in asset prices. This means that reforms, credibility, and institutional stability are not background conditions—they are structural determinants of price formation and investment incentives.

Third, carbon markets are embedded in distributional and political constraints. Allocation, revenue use, and competitiveness policies shape not only fairness but also the durability of the system.

At the same time, important debates remain open. The empirical magnitude of innovation effects remains contested and appears sensitive to price levels and expectations. The effectiveness of border measures and the best design for leakage protection remain debated. In voluntary markets, governance solutions are still evolving, and the literature has not fully converged on how to scale crediting without sacrificing integrity.

These findings motivate the next section. A purely welfare-theoretic defense of carbon trading is insufficient; equally, a purely political critique misses the genuine efficiency gains that trading can deliver. The most informative analysis therefore treats carbon trading as a governance-embedded market institution—simultaneously a policy instrument for pricing an externality and a financial market whose microstructure shapes real outcomes. The next section develops this balanced economic analysis.

Theoretical Perspectives

Economic analysis of carbon trading has often been conducted through distinct theoretical lenses—welfare economics, political economy, and financial economics. Each lens captures an important dimension of how carbon markets operate, but none is sufficient on its own to explain real-world outcomes. Carbon trading systems are not abstract markets for a homogeneous commodity; they are governance-embedded institutions that price an externality, allocate rents, and generate tradable assets whose credibility and risk properties condition investment behavior. This section integrates these perspectives to provide a balanced economic analysis of carbon trading in the context of the net-zero transition.

Carbon Trading as Externality Pricing: Welfare Economics Foundations

The welfare-theoretic justification for carbon trading originates in Pigouvian externality theory. Greenhouse gas emissions impose social damages—through climate change impacts—that are not reflected in private production or consumption decisions. In the absence of policy intervention, markets therefore generate excessive emissions relative to the social optimum. A carbon price, whether implemented through a tax or a cap-and-trade system, internalizes this externality by aligning private marginal costs with social marginal damages.

Within this framework, emissions trading is attractive because it delivers cost-effective abatement. If firms face heterogeneous abatement costs, trading allows those with low-cost abatement opportunities to reduce emissions more, while firms with higher costs purchase allowances. In equilibrium, marginal abatement costs are equalized across regulated sources, minimizing the total cost of achieving a given emissions target. This logic underpins the widespread view that carbon trading dominates many command-and-control regulations on efficiency grounds.

However, this first-best result relies on strong assumptions. It presumes perfect information, negligible transaction costs, and a regulator capable of setting a socially optimal cap. In reality, regulators face uncertainty about abatement costs, future damages, and technological change. The cap is therefore necessarily imperfect. This brings uncertainty to the forefront of the economic analysis and explains why carbon trading design has evolved away from rigid quantity constraints toward more flexible, hybrid systems.

The prices-versus-quantities framework provides a canonical way to think about this uncertainty. When marginal abatement costs are highly uncertain and marginal damages rise slowly with emissions, price-based instruments can dominate quantity-based instruments in welfare terms; when damages rise steeply, quantity controls may be preferred. Climate change exhibits features of both cases, which helps explain why real-world carbon trading systems increasingly incorporate price-like elements—such as banking, stability reserves, and soft price floors—into cap-and-trade architectures. These design choices can be understood as attempts to approximate welfare-optimal outcomes under uncertainty rather than as deviations from theoretical purity.

From this welfare perspective, the key efficiency question is not whether carbon trading is conceptually sound, but whether the cap trajectory is sufficiently tight and credible to generate meaningful scarcity. A cap that is non-binding or expected to be relaxed delivers little abatement incentive, regardless of the elegance of the trading mechanism. This insight aligns closely with empirical findings from early trading periods in several jurisdictions, where generous allocation undermined price signals.

Dynamic Efficiency, Investment, and Technological Change

Static cost-effectiveness is only part of the story. The net-zero transition is fundamentally a dynamic problem: it requires large-scale, long-lived investments in low-carbon technologies and infrastructure, alongside the gradual retirement of carbon-intensive capital. Dynamic efficiency therefore becomes central to the economic evaluation of carbon trading.

In theory, a credible and rising carbon price should shift investment incentives by increasing the expected returns to low-carbon technologies and reducing the profitability of carbon-intensive assets. This mechanism operates not only through current prices but, more importantly, through expectations about future policy stringency. Firms planning capital investments with multi-decade lifetimes respond to anticipated carbon costs over those horizons. As a result, the expected long-run price path often matters more than short-run price volatility.

This observation has two implications. First, volatility is not necessarily inefficient if it reflects genuine information about future scarcity or policy changes. Second, volatility becomes problematic when it reflects policy uncertainty or credibility deficits rather than fundamentals. Sudden regulatory reversals, ad hoc interventions, or ambiguous reform signals can undermine investment incentives even if average prices are high. From a dynamic efficiency perspective, the institutional credibility of the carbon market—its perceived durability and rule stability—is therefore a core economic variable.

The literature also emphasizes complementarities between carbon trading and other policy instruments. Knowledge spillovers, network effects, and coordination failures can prevent carbon pricing alone from inducing socially optimal levels of innovation. Subsidies, standards, and public R&D can address these additional market failures. From a second-best perspective, carbon trading should be evaluated as part of a policy mix rather than as a stand-alone solution. This does not weaken the case for trading; rather, it clarifies its role as the backbone incentive that aligns decentralized decisions, while complementary policies address specific barriers to innovation and diffusion.

Political Economy, Rent Allocation, and Commitment

A second analytical lens treats carbon trading as a political economy institution rather than a purely technical policy instrument. Introducing a carbon market creates scarcity rents associated with allowances. How these rents are allocated—through free allocation, auctioning, or hybrid approaches—has profound distributional and political consequences.

From a political economy standpoint, free allocation can be interpreted as a side payment to regulated firms to secure political support and mitigate competitiveness concerns. Auctioning, by contrast, transfers rents to the public sector, creating fiscal resources that can be recycled to households or used to finance public investment. The economic literature highlights a trade-off: free allocation may improve short-run political feasibility but can weaken long-run incentives if it reduces cost pass-through or generates windfall profits; auctioning strengthens transparency and fiscal capacity but can intensify opposition from regulated sectors.

Commitment and time consistency are central issues. A carbon market only delivers efficient outcomes if firms believe that future caps will be enforced and tightened as announced. If policymakers are expected to relax constraints when prices rise, firms will rationally discount future scarcity and underinvest in abatement and innovation. This creates a classic commitment problem. Institutional mechanisms such as legally binding cap trajectories, independent market authorities, and automatic adjustment rules can be interpreted as commitment devices that enhance credibility.

Revenue recycling also plays a role in commitment. When carbon revenues are visibly linked to socially valued uses—such as reducing other taxes, funding green infrastructure, or compensating vulnerable households—political support for carbon pricing can become more durable. This reinforces the view that carbon trading performance cannot be separated from public finance design. The economic efficiency of carbon markets is intertwined with how revenues are used and how distributional concerns are addressed.

Carbon Trading as a Financial Market

A third perspective treats carbon trading systems as financial markets that generate tradable assets—allowances and credits—with distinct risk and return characteristics. From this viewpoint, carbon prices are not merely policy signals; they are asset prices shaped by liquidity, participation, expectations, and risk premia.

Financial market analysis emphasizes that liquidity and market depth affect both price discovery and compliance costs. Liquid markets with active participation allow firms to hedge exposure, smooth compliance costs, and respond flexibly to shocks. Illiquid markets, by contrast, can exhibit price spikes and thin trading that amplify political sensitivity and undermine confidence. The development of futures, options, and clearing infrastructure can therefore improve market functioning, even if it also introduces concerns about speculation and financialization.

Risk is another central concept. Carbon assets embed multiple sources of risk: energy market risk, macroeconomic risk, and regulatory risk. Regulatory risk—uncertainty about future rules, caps, and eligibility—is often dominant, especially in younger markets. Financial economics suggests that investors will demand a risk premium to hold assets exposed to such uncertainty, which can influence price levels and volatility. This insight helps explain why credibility-enhancing reforms can raise carbon prices even without immediate changes in cap stringency: reducing regulatory risk lowers the discount applied to future scarcity.

This financial perspective also clarifies why market integrity matters. If allowances or credits are perceived as low-quality—due to weak enforcement, manipulation, or integrity problems—investors will discount their value. This is particularly salient in voluntary carbon markets, where the traded asset is a claim about emissions reductions or removals rather than a legal compliance instrument. Without credible MRV and governance, such markets can suffer from adverse selection and collapse in demand.

Summary

Taken together, these perspectives suggest that carbon trading should be analyzed as a governance-embedded institution rather than as a simple market mechanism. Welfare economics explains why pricing emissions can reduce costs and align incentives. Political economy explains why allocation rules, revenue use, and commitment devices matter for durability. Financial economics explains how liquidity, risk, and expectations shape price formation and investment responses.

This integrated view helps reconcile apparent contradictions in the empirical literature. For example, periods of low carbon prices do not necessarily imply that carbon trading "failed" in theory; they may reflect weak caps, adverse macro shocks, or credibility deficits. Conversely, rising prices do not guarantee innovation or investment if firms doubt the durability of the policy. The effectiveness of carbon trading therefore depends on institutional design choices that simultaneously address efficiency, equity, credibility, and market integrity.

In the context of the net-zero transition, this analysis carries an important implication. Carbon trading is unlikely to be sufficient on its own to deliver deep decarbonization, but it is difficult to imagine a cost-effective transition without some form of carbon pricing. Trading systems provide the economy-wide signal that aligns private incentives with climate objectives, while complementary policies address technology-specific and distributional challenges. The economic question is therefore not whether to use carbon trading, but how to design and govern it so that it remains credible, investable, and politically sustainable over the long horizon required for net-zero.

This analytical synthesis sets the stage for the concluding section, which draws together the chapter's insights and considers implications for investors and policymakers, as well as the future evolution of carbon trading in an increasingly integrated climate finance landscape.

Conclusion

This chapter has examined carbon trading as a central pillar of carbon finance in the net-zero transition, emphasizing its dual character as both a market-based policy instrument and a governance-embedded financial institution. The analysis has shown that carbon trading is neither a purely technical solution nor a symbolic gesture. When well designed and credibly implemented, it can internalize the carbon externality, guide capital allocation, and support cost-effective decarbonization across heterogeneous sectors and jurisdictions. When poorly designed or weakly governed, however, it risks becoming a low-impact compliance mechanism with limited influence on long-term investment and innovation. Several core conclusions emerge from the discussion.

First, carbon trading works through scarcity and expectations, not merely through the existence of a market. The empirical literature consistently demonstrates that emissions trading systems deliver meaningful abatement incentives only when the cap is binding and expected to tighten over time. Early experiences—most notably in the initial phases of the EU ETS—underscore that over-allocation and policy uncertainty can suppress prices and weaken credibility. Subsequent reforms illustrate an important institutional lesson: carbon markets are iterative policy projects that require adjustment, learning, and political commitment. Static assessments of "success" or "failure" are therefore misleading; what matters is whether the system evolves toward credible long-run scarcity consistent with climate targets.

Second, carbon trading must be understood in dynamic rather than static terms. The net-zero transition is a multi-decade process involving irreversible capital investments, technological change, and structural transformation. In this context, the expected future path of carbon prices is more important than short-term price movements. Stable and credible policy signals—supported by clear cap trajectories, transparent rulemaking, and predictable reform processes—are essential for shaping investment decisions. This insight bridges welfare economics and political economy: efficiency gains from trading depend on institutions that make future scarcity believable.

Third, distributional design and political economy are not peripheral concerns but core determinants of durability. Carbon markets generate rents, and the allocation of those rents shapes both economic outcomes and political support. Free allocation can ease early opposition but risks dampening incentives and generating windfall profits. Auctioning enhances transparency and fiscal capacity but requires careful revenue recycling to address equity and competitiveness concerns. The literature converges on the view that revenue use—whether for household compensation, tax reductions, or green public investment—is a central lever for sustaining carbon pricing over time. Carbon trading systems that ignore distributional impacts risk political backlash that undermines their own effectiveness.

Additionally, carbon trading increasingly operates as a financial market, with all the attendant implications. Allowances and credits are traded assets whose prices reflect expectations, risk premia, and market structure. Liquidity, participation, and risk-management instruments matter for compliance costs and price stability. At the same time, financialization raises governance challenges related to market integrity, transparency, and oversight. These issues are particularly salient in voluntary carbon markets, where asset quality depends on MRV credibility and where integrity failures can trigger adverse selection and loss of confidence. The financial perspective reinforces a broader conclusion: carbon markets require regulatory capacity comparable to that applied to other systemically relevant markets.

From an investor perspective, these findings imply that carbon trading is increasingly material to risk assessment and portfolio strategy. Carbon prices influence cash flows, asset valuations, and transition risk across energy, industry, transport, and finance. Investors cannot treat carbon markets as exogenous policy artifacts; they must be analyzed as evolving institutions whose credibility, design, and reform trajectory shape price dynamics. Sophisticated investment strategies therefore incorporate not only current carbon prices but also expectations about future policy tightening, market stability mechanisms, and interactions with complementary regulation. In voluntary markets, due diligence on credit quality, additionality, and governance has become essential, as integrity risk is now a first-order financial consideration rather than a reputational afterthought.

For policymakers, the chapter points to several priorities. Designing effective carbon trading systems requires balancing efficiency, equity, and credibility. Policymakers must commit to tightening trajectories consistent with net-zero goals, while also investing in the institutional infrastructure—MRV systems, enforcement capacity, and market oversight—that underpins credibility. Complementary policies should be treated as strategic complements rather than substitutes, addressing innovation barriers and distributional concerns that carbon pricing alone cannot resolve. In international contexts, coordination challenges loom large. Divergent carbon prices across jurisdictions raise competitiveness and leakage concerns, motivating border measures and cooperative mechanisms under frameworks such as Article 6.

Here, transparency and accounting integrity are critical to prevent double counting and to ensure that cross-border trading enhances rather than undermines global mitigation efforts.

Looking ahead, the future of carbon trading will be shaped by three interrelated developments. The first is tightening ambition. As net-zero targets move from aspirational commitments to binding policy frameworks, carbon markets will need to deliver stronger and more predictable price signals. This is likely to increase both the economic significance and political salience of carbon pricing. The second is institutional integration. Carbon trading will increasingly interact with sustainable finance instruments, disclosure regimes, and industrial policy. Rather than operating in isolation, carbon markets are becoming part of a broader climate governance architecture that links prices, standards, and capital markets. The third is global coordination. Fragmentation across national and regional systems remains a defining feature of carbon trading. Whether this fragmentation evolves into a loosely connected network of markets or into more integrated arrangements will have major implications for efficiency, equity, and global mitigation outcomes.

In sum, carbon trading should be viewed not as a silver bullet but as a foundational component of climate policy and carbon finance. Its effectiveness depends on institutional design, political commitment, and governance quality as much as on economic theory. For the net-zero transition, the central challenge is not whether carbon trading can work in principle, but whether societies can sustain the credibility, coordination, and equity required for carbon markets to function as long-term drivers of decarbonization.

References

Aghion, P., Dechezleprêtre, A., Hémous, D., Martin, R., & Van Reenen, J. (2016). Carbon taxes, path dependency, and directed technical change: Evidence from the auto industry. *Journal of Political Economy, 124*(1), 1–51.

Aldy, J. E., & Stavins, R. N. (2012). The promise and problems of pricing carbon: Theory and experience. *The Journal of Environment & Development, 21*(2), 152–180.

Arora-Jonsson, S., & Gurung, J. (2023). Changing business as usual in global climate and development action: Making space for social justice in carbon markets. *World Development Perspectives, 29*, 100474.

Branger, F., & Quirion, P. (2014). Would border carbon adjustments prevent carbon leakage and heavy industry competitiveness losses? Insights from a meta-analysis of recent economic studies. *Ecological Economics, 99*, 29–39.

Calel, R., & Dechezleprêtre, A. (2016). Environmental policy and directed technological change: Evidence from the European Carbon Market. *The Review of Economics and Statistics, 98*(1), 173–191.

Carattini, S., Carvalho, M., & Fankhauser, S. (2018). Overcoming public resistance to carbon taxes. *Wiley Interdisciplinary Reviews: Climate Change, 9*(5), e531.

Chevallier, J. (2013). Variance risk-premia in CO2 markets. *Economic Modelling, 31*, 598–605.

Dechezleprêtre, A., & Sato, M. (2017). The impacts of environmental regulations on competitiveness. *Review of Environmental Economics and Policy, 11*(2), 183–206.

Ellerman, A., Convery, F., & de Perthuis, C. (2010). *Pricing carbon: The European Union Emissions Trading Scheme*. Cambridge University Press.

Fabra, N., & Reguant, M. (2014). Pass-through of emissions costs in electricity markets. *American Economic Review, 104*(9), 2872–2899.

Fischer, C., & Fox, A. K. (2012). Comparing policies to combat emissions leakage: Border carbon adjustments versus rebates. *Journal of Environmental Economics and Management, 64*(2), 199–216.

Goulder, L., & Schein, A. (2013). Carbon taxes versus cap and trade: A critical review. *Climate Change Economics, 4*(3), 1350010.

Koch, N., Fuss, S., Grosjean, G., & Edenhofer, O. (2014). Causes of the EU ETS price drop: Recession, CDM, renewable policies or a bit of everything?—New evidence. *Energy Policy, 73*, 676–685.

Kochar, R., Kalsie, A., & Deka, N. (2025). Voluntary Carbon Markets (VCMs) in a nutshell: A systematic review based on the empirical evidence from across the globe. *Journal of Cleaner Production, 522*, 146261.

Lessmann, C., & Kramer, N. (2024). The effect of cap-and-trade on sectoral emissions: Evidence from California. *Energy Policy, 188*, 114066.

Martin, R., Muûls, M., de Preux, L. B., & Wagner, U. J. (2014). Industry compensation under relocation risk: A firm-level analysis of the EU emissions trading scheme. *American Economic Review, 104*(8), 2482–2508.

Martin, R., Muûls, M., & Wagner, U. J. (2016). The impact of the European Union emissions trading scheme on regulated firms: What is the evidence after ten years? *Review of Environmental Economics and Policy, 10*(1), 129–148.

Munnings, C., Morgenstern, R. D., Wang, Z., & Liu, X. (2016). Assessing the design of three carbon trading pilot programs in China. *Energy Policy, 96*, 688–699.

Sato, M., Rafaty, R., Calel, R., & Grubb, M. (2022). Allocation, allocation, allocation! The political economy of the development of the European Union Emissions Trading System. *WIREs Climate Change, 13*(5), e796.

Schmalensee, R., & Stavins, R. N. (2017). The design of environmental markets: What have we learned from experience with cap and trade? *Oxford Review of Economic Policy, 33*(4), 572–588.

Schneider, L., & La Hoz Theuer, S. (2019). Environmental integrity of international carbon market mechanisms under the Paris Agreement. *Climate Policy, 19*(3), 386–400.

Strange, N., Ermgassen, S. z., Marshall, E., Bull, J. W., & Jacobsen, J. B. (2024). Why it matters how biodiversity is measured in environmental valuation studies compared to conservation science. *Biological Conservation, 292*, 110546.

Venmans, F. (2012). A literature-based multi-criteria evaluation of the EU ETS. *Renewable and Sustainable Energy Reviews, 16*(8), 5493–5510.

Weitzman, M. L. (1974). Prices vs. quantities 12. *The Review of Economic Studies, 41*(4), 477–491.

Zhang, D., Karplus, V. J., Cassisa, C., & Zhang, X. (2014). Emissions trading in China: Progress and prospects. *Energy Policy, 75*, 9–16.

Chapter 10
Shaping Sustainable Development

Introduction

Previous chapters explored how innovative financial instruments and market mechanisms are steering public finance toward climate change solutions. Sovereign green bonds showed how governments align debt issuance with climate goals, while blue finance demonstrated the tailoring of investment to ocean sustainability. These debt instruments create climate impact by earmarking capital for green projects, relying on rigorous standards and reporting. Carbon finance, by contrast, operates via prices rather than proceeds: it internalizes the carbon externality into financial markets, creating economy-wide incentives for low-carbon behavior. Carbon pricing schemes like emissions trading systems (ETS) complement green bonds by acting as a "price-of-externality" mechanism, placing a cost on greenhouse gas emissions so that abatement becomes privately profitable. This price signal is increasingly integrated with sustainable finance—for instance, a green bond can fund clean technology deployment while expected carbon credit revenues improve the project's returns. In turn, carbon pricing influences investors' portfolios by altering the risk-return profile of carbon-intensive assets, effectively making climate risks "financially binding". In summary, the prior chapters outlined a landscape where debt instruments and carbon markets together are reshaping public finance and investment behavior under climate constraints.

This chapter focuses on carbon finance, especially carbon trading, and its intersection with the Sustainable Development Goals (SDGs). Carbon trading (cap-and-trade systems) directly targets SDG13 (Climate Action) by capping emissions and creating a market price for carbon. However, climate action does not exist in isolation: the 17 SDGs are deeply interlinked, spanning economic growth, social inclusion, and environmental stewardship. Carbon pricing's ripple effects can thus reach goals like SDG7 (Affordable and Clean Energy), SDG8 (Decent Work and Economic Growth), SDG10 (Reduced Inequalities), and beyond. Importantly, not all impacts

P. Zhou, D. Guo, *Climate Finance in the Net-Zero Transition*, Contributions to Finance and Accounting, https://doi.org/10.1007/978-981-92-0827-2_10

are positive. Prior chapters noted how carbon taxes or trading raise production costs for polluters, which if poorly designed could undermine employment or burden lower-income groups. At the same time, effective carbon markets can drive clean investments, improved air quality, and innovation, supporting multiple SDGs (Lim & Prakash, 2023). This dual nature underscores a central theme: market-based climate policy must be assessed not only on environmental efficiency, but also on its broader sustainable development performance. Accordingly, this chapter builds on the previous discussions of carbon finance architecture and examines whether carbon trading can drive progress across the SDG spectrum. Using a difference-in-differences (DID) approach, we explore quantitatively how carbon trading has shaped development pathways in practice. We begin with the conceptual linkages between carbon pricing and sustainable development goals, then examine the China case study and its findings, before drawing out policy and investment implications for aligning carbon markets with the SDGs.

Theoretical Foundation

Carbon trading is expected to influence sustainable development through multiple channels and feedbacks (Khurshid et al., 2023; Radulescu et al., 2024). At the most direct level, placing a cap on carbon emissions and a price on carbon encourages emitters to cut greenhouse gas output, furthering climate mitigation (SDG13) (Calel & Dechezleprêtre, 2016; Aatola et al., 2013). Firms facing a carbon price are incentivized to invest in energy-efficient processes or switch to cleaner fuels, which can accelerate the transition to affordable and clean energy (SDG7) by making renewables and low-carbon technologies more competitive (Li et al., 2026; Lin & Wang, 2025). By capping pollution and driving cleaner production, an ETS can also yield co-benefits such as improved air quality and public health (supporting SDG3, Good Health and Well-Being) and more sustainable urban environments (SDG11) (Buonocore et al., 2016; Creutzig et al., 2018). In these ways, a well-designed carbon market directly advances several environmental and social objectives.

However, potential trade-offs must be acknowledged. Carbon pricing raises costs for carbon-intensive industries. In the short run, firms may respond by scaling back production or even shutting down high-emission operations rather than investing in upgrades. This contraction can impact employment and economic output, posing a challenge to SDG8 (Decent Work and Economic Growth) if jobs are lost in affected sectors (Martin et al., 2014). Likewise, if the burden of higher energy prices is passed to consumers, there could be regressive effects, potentially exacerbating inequality (contrary to SDG10) if vulnerable populations or regions bear disproportionate costs (Büchs & Schnepf, 2013). The net impact on an economy's sustainable development is therefore a balance of synergies (e.g. climate action and cleaner growth) and trade-offs (e.g. transition costs and distributional effects). Table 10.1 summarizes some expected positive vs. negative impacts of carbon trading (and the underlying energy transition it induces) on four key SDGs, illustrating this balance.

Table 10.1 Potential impacts of carbon trading on selected SDGs

SDG	Potential positive impact	Potential negative impact
SDG7: Affordable & Clean Energy *Ensure access to clean energy*	Clean energy transition accelerated: Carbon pricing increases the share of renewable energy by making fossil fuels more expensive, encouraging investment in sustainable energy sources	Energy cost and access risks: High initial costs for renewables or carbon fees can raise energy prices, potentially affecting affordability and energy access in the short term
SDG8: Decent Work & Economic Growth *Promote inclusive and sustainable economic growth, employment*	Green jobs and industries: ETS-driven demand for low-carbon solutions can spur growth in green industries and create new employment opportunities in clean energy and efficiency sectors	Transitional job losses: Decline of high-carbon industries (e.g. coal power, mining) may result in job losses, especially in regions heavily reliant on those sectors. Without support, workers and communities could face economic hardship during the transition
SDG10: Reduced Inequalities *Reduce inequality within and among countries*	Regional convergence: Climate finance and technology spurred by an ETS can be directed to underdeveloped areas (e.g. investing in renewable projects in poorer regions), helping narrow urban-rural development gaps. In China's case, studies suggest the ETS pilots contributed to reducing income inequality in less-developed, coal-dependent cities	Uneven benefits and burdens: Regions or groups lacking capital and technology may benefit less from low-carbon transitions, even as they bear higher energy costs, potentially exacerbating inequalities if proceeds or investments are not equitably distributed
SDG 13: Climate Action *Take urgent action to combat climate change*	Emissions reduction: By design, a cap-and-trade directly cuts greenhouse gas emissions and incentivizes innovation in carbon abatement, contributing to climate change mitigation targets. This is the primary objective of carbon trading and the area where it unequivocally advances SDGs	Economic adjustments: The initial phase of an ETS or a sudden high carbon price can have short-term negative economic impacts on growth. If not managed, these economic shocks could indirectly affect progress on other goals. However, such effects are typically transient and can be alleviated by reinvesting carbon revenues into the economy

Table 10.1 also highlights the importance of policy context in determining outcomes. Well-designed carbon pricing can unlock synergies: for example, using carbon revenue to subsidize clean energy (making progress on SDG7 affordable for all) or to fund just transition programs for workers (mitigating negative impacts on SDG8 and SDG10). Absent these measures, an ETS might achieve SDG13 at the expense of SDG8 or SDG10, undermining long-term sustainability and public support. Indeed, the literature emphasizes careful design to ensure climate policies "do no harm" to socio-economic development. Overall, the conceptual expectation is that carbon trading, if coupled with supportive policies, can become a strategic tool to simultaneously drive decarbonization and broader sustainable development. The

next sections examine how this plays out in practice, drawing on China's experience with ETS pilots to provide empirical evidence on carbon trading's SDG performance.

Empirical Strategy

China's early experience with carbon trading offers a rich empirical test of these concepts. As part of its climate policy agenda, China launched pilot emissions trading systems in 2013 across seven provinces and cities: Beijing, Shanghai, Tianjin, Chongqing, Hubei, Guangdong, and Shenzhen. These pilots—implemented in economically and geographically diverse regions—created a cap-and-trade mechanism years before the nationwide ETS (which began in 2021). The pilots provide a quasi-experimental setting: only certain cities were directly regulated by an ETS, while others were not, allowing researchers to compare outcomes between "treatment" (pilot) and "control" cities over time. We exploit this natural experiment to assess whether the introduction of carbon trading measurably affected progress on the SDGs at the city level. In essence, this method asks: did cities with an ETS achieve significantly better (or worse) sustainable development outcomes than they would have without the carbon market intervention?

Formally, the baseline DID specification can be written as:

$$SDG_{it} = \alpha + \beta\left(ETS_i \times POST_t\right) + \gamma X_{it} + \mu_i + \lambda_t + \epsilon_{it} \tag{10.1}$$

Where:

- SDG_{it} denotes the composite SDG performance index of city i in year t;
- ETS_i is a binary indicator equal to 1 if city i belongs to an ETS pilot region, and 0 otherwise;
- $POST_t$ is a post-treatment indicator equal to 1 for years after the ETS pilots were launched (2013 onward), and 0 for pre-policy years;
- $ETS_i \times POST_t$ is the DID interaction term of interest;
- X_{it} is a vector of time-varying city-level control variables (e.g., economic development, industrial structure, population characteristics);
- μ_i captures city fixed effects, controlling for time-invariant unobserved heterogeneity across cities;
- λ_t captures year fixed effects, absorbing common macroeconomic shocks and nationwide policy trends;
- ϵ_{it} is the error term.

The coefficient β measures the average treatment effect of carbon trading on SDG performance, i.e., the differential change in SDG outcomes for ETS cities relative to non-ETS cities after the policy was implemented.

The treatment group consists of cities located in the seven ETS pilot regions launched in 2013—Beijing, Shanghai, Tianjin, Chongqing, Guangdong (including Shenzhen), and Hubei. These pilots were selected by the central government based on administrative capacity, emissions profiles, and regional representativeness, rather than short-term SDG performance trends, which strengthens the plausibility of exogeneity.

The control group includes cities that were not covered by any ETS pilot during the sample period. To enhance comparability between treated and untreated cities, we combine DID with propensity score matching (PSM) prior to estimation. Cities are matched on pre-treatment characteristics including wages (lnwa), industrial structure (lnind), foreign direct investment (lnfdi), and pollutant emissions (lnemi). The DID model is then estimated on the matched sample (PSM-DID), reducing bias from observable differences in baseline development trajectories.

Figure 10.1 shows that PSM substantially improves covariate balance between ETS and non-ETS cities. Before matching (solid dots), several covariates exhibit large standardized biases, in some cases exceeding ±30–40%, indicating pronounced systematic differences between treated and control groups. In particular, indicators related to industrial structure and energy or emission intensity display sizable imbalance, suggesting that simple DID without adjustment would risk selection bias. After matching (crosses), standardized biases for all covariates shrink markedly and cluster close to zero, generally within ±10%. This pattern indicates that the matched control group closely resembles the treated group in terms of observed pre-treatment characteristics. No covariate shows residual imbalance of concern.

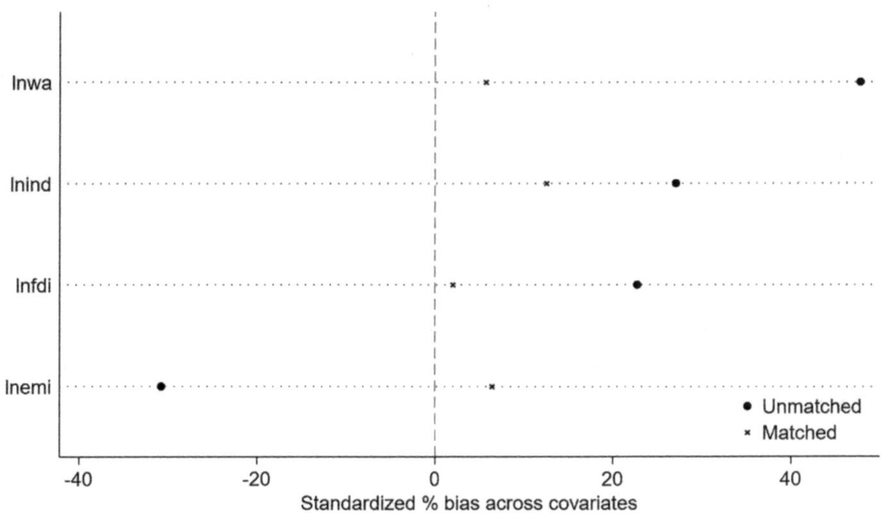

Fig. 10.1 Propensity score matching test

The DID framework is particularly well suited to this research question for several reasons. First, randomized policy implementation is infeasible in the context of large-scale environmental regulation. ETS pilots were implemented through administrative decisions at the regional level, making experimental designs impractical. DID provides a credible alternative by leveraging temporal and cross-sectional variation in policy exposure. Second, the ETS pilots constitute a clearly defined, externally imposed policy shock that directly affects regulated cities but not others. This sharp policy boundary is ideal for DID analysis, especially when combined with city and year fixed effects that absorb confounding heterogeneity. Third, SDG performance is inherently multidimensional and slow-moving. Simple cross-sectional comparisons would confound policy effects with structural differences across cities, while before-after comparisons would conflate ETS impacts with nationwide trends. DID explicitly addresses both issues by focusing on relative changes over time, net of common shocks and time-invariant city characteristics.

Results

The baseline result of estimating Eq. (10.1) is that China's carbon trading pilots significantly improved the overall SDG performance of the cities involved. Quantitatively, the introduction of an ETS is associated with about a $\beta = 5.4\%$ increase in the composite SDG index of pilot cities relative to controls (after a few years of implementation). This estimate is statistically significant at the 1% level, and it emerges robustly across various model specifications. Put simply, the net effect of the ETS policy on sustainable development was positive. This is a noteworthy outcome: despite concerns about potential trade-offs, the data suggest that, on average, the pilot carbon markets helped cities advance their economic, social, and environmental goals in tandem. One interpretation is that the synergies (emissions reductions, cleaner air, energy efficiency gains, green investment flows) outweighed the trade-offs (compliance costs, output losses in polluting industries) in these regions over the study period. The finding aligns with broader evidence that market-based emissions constraints can induce innovation and productivity improvements (e.g. via higher green total factor productivity and energy efficiency gains observed in the pilot cities), which can offset short-term costs and contribute to sustainable growth. It also echoes the result of Fang et al. (2023) that the pilots did not impede—and in some cases even improved—social indicators like income equality in certain areas. Overall, the Chinese pilots demonstrate that carbon trading need not come at the expense of development; on the contrary, it can be a driver of multi-dimensional progress when implemented in a conducive context.

Heterogeneity

While the ETS effect was positive on average, we investigate if it differed between various kinds of cities. They examine heterogeneity along two key dimensions: the city's level of economic development, and its resource endowment (particularly whether the local economy is resource-/coal-intensive or not). Intuitively, we might expect differences—for instance, a carbon cap could bite harder in an industrial, resource-dependent city (but also potentially spur greater improvements there if those industries clean up), whereas a wealthier service-oriented city might find it easier to adapt. The study finds that the ETS's impact was indeed larger in cities with lower per-capita GDP and in those more reliant on resource extraction. In other words, less-developed and resource-dependent locales reaped greater SDG gains from the carbon market than their more developed or diversified counterparts. The estimated treatment effect on the SDG index was roughly 0.07–0.08 (log points) for the low-income and resource-intensive city groups, compared to about 0.04–0.05 for high-income or non-resource-based cities. This pattern is consistent with the idea that high-emission industrial cities had more "low-hanging fruit" to improve: many were burdened by polluting industries that, once constrained by the ETS, either upgraded technologies or scaled back the dirtiest activities, leading to outsized improvements in environmental and health metrics (and even prompting economic upgrading in the longer term). By contrast, wealthier coastal cities with already service-heavy economies had lower baseline emissions and thus saw more modest incremental SDG gains from the carbon cap.

Several insights emerge from these heterogeneous effects (illustrated in Fig. 10.2). First, the fact that poorer cities benefited more suggests carbon pricing

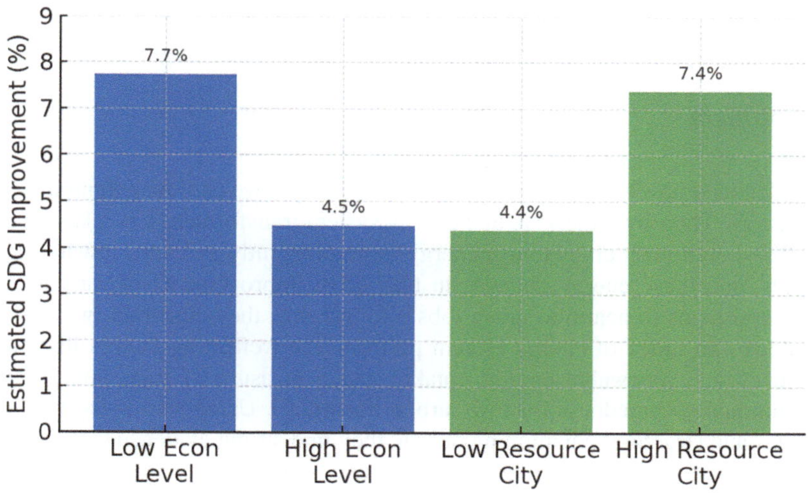

Fig. 10.2 Estimated impact of China's ETS pilots on overall SDG performance

can be a catalyst for sustainable development in less-developed regions, contradicting the fear that climate policy always hurts the poorest. In the Chinese context, many low-income cities also had heavy coal dependence and high pollution; the ETS forced a reckoning with inefficient, high-emission activities, prompting improvements (e.g. in energy efficiency, pollution control) that had immediate local benefits (cleaner air, new investments) and put these cities on a greener trajectory. This aligns with the notion of "high-emissions traps"—regions stuck in polluting development patterns stand to gain the most from breaking out via climate policy. Second, the larger effect in resource-rich industrial cities underscores that emissions trading has teeth where carbon-intensive industries dominate. In these cities, the ETS cap imposed a hard constraint on businesses-as-usual, compelling firms to adapt. Many did so successfully by shifting toward lower-carbon production, which not only cuts emissions (SDG13) but often also reduces co-pollutants (improving health, SDG3) and encourages diversification or technological upgrading (feeding into SDG8 and SDG9). The flip side is that such transitions can be disruptive: as the study notes, curbing energy-intensive industries in resource-dependent cities may pose short-run challenges for employment (SDG8). The authors caution that regions with economies built on fossil fuels could experience job losses and structural adjustment pains—a point echoed by other research on just transitions (Carley & Konisky, 2020; Zhang et al., 2025). Indeed, we find evidence that decent work and economic output took a relative hit in the short term even as broader SDG indicators improved. This reinforces the need for flanking policies in high-impact regions (a topic we return to in the policy implications section). In summary, China's pilot ETS delivered net sustainable development benefits across the board, with especially pronounced gains in the very cities that might have seemed most vulnerable to a carbon cap. The experience suggests that with proper support, carbon markets can be engines of both environmental and social progress, even in coal-dependent economies.

Mechanism

To understand how the ETS improved SDG outcomes, we explore potential mediating factors. Their hypothesis is that energy system transformation is a key conduit: an ETS should push cities to use energy more efficiently and shift toward cleaner sources, and these energy changes in turn drive improvements in various SDGs (from emissions to health to green jobs). To test this, they construct two mediator variables—an index of energy system performance (reflecting factors like energy efficiency and renewable energy uptake) and a measure of transition readiness (institutional preparedness for low-carbon transition). Using a two-step mediation analysis and structural equation modeling, they find strong evidence that the ETS's impact flowed primarily through improvements in the energy system, rather than through abstract transition plans. Concretely, the ETS pilot policy significantly enhanced the energy system performance index in pilot cities (with the policy causing an increase on the order of 0.17 in the log-index, $p < 0.01$). This improved energy performance (e.g. lower energy intensity, more clean energy) then had a positive effect on the overall SDG index of cities (coefficient ~ 0.305, $p < 0.01$). In contrast, the ETS did not have a detectable effect on "transition readiness" metrics, nor did that readiness translate to better SDG outcomes in the short run. In other words, it was the actual changes in energy infrastructure and efficiency brought about by the carbon market—rather than policy announcements or plans—that made the difference. This result makes intuitive sense: requiring firms to stay within carbon caps forced them to adopt tangible changes like upgrading boilers, recovering waste heat, investing in renewables, or improving grid efficiency. These actions directly contribute to multiple SDGs (cheaper and cleaner energy, less pollution, innovation, etc.), validating the notion that energy transition is the lynchpin linking carbon pricing to sustainable development. Meanwhile, mere "transition readiness" (such as having plans or institutions set up) was not enough to move the needle during the study period—highlighting that implementation and outcomes matter more than plans on paper. Therefore, strengthening the operational performance of energy systems (for example, via technical upgrades and increased clean energy capacity) is a critical pathway for carbon markets to deliver SDG co-benefits. This insight underscores the importance of using carbon pricing as part of a broader energy transition strategy: the policy's success should be measured not just in carbon ppm, but in catalyzing real changes in how energy is produced and consumed.

In summary, the China ETS pilot experience offers empirical validation that carbon trading can align with and advance the SDGs, given the right conditions. The pilots achieved meaningful reductions in emissions (helping meet climate targets) while also improving indicators of sustainable development, especially through cleaner energy and environmental improvements. The most carbon-intensive, underdeveloped cities saw the greatest gains—albeit with some transitional pains—suggesting carbon markets can be a force for positive structural change. At the same time, the findings highlight critical policy considerations: outcomes varied by context, and proactive measures (like supporting workers in high-carbon industries, reinvesting in clean energy, and fortifying institutions) are needed to ensure no region is left behind. We now turn to those policy implications.

Discussion

Implications for Policymakers

China's pilot ETS case demonstrates that carbon trading can be harnessed as a tool for sustainable development, but it also flags the importance of policy design in achieving that alignment. Several policy implications emerge for governments and regulators aiming to integrate carbon markets with SDG agendas.

Leverage carbon markets as a strategic SDG tool. Rather than viewing emissions trading narrowly as an environmental policy, policymakers should recognize its cross-cutting development impact. The positive overall effect of the ETS pilots on city-level SDGs suggests that a well-calibrated carbon market can serve as a catalyst for progress on multiple fronts (climate, energy, health, etc.). Incorporating SDG metrics into carbon market design and evaluation could help maximize these co-benefits. For instance, regulators might monitor not only emissions and allowance prices, but also indicators like air quality improvements, green jobs created, or reductions in coal use attributable to the ETS. Framing carbon trading within the SDG context can build broader political support, as it underscores benefits beyond CO_2 reductions.

Expand and strengthen ETS coverage with attention to context. An et al. (2025) advocate for the development and continuous enhancement of a national carbon trading mechanism in China, moving beyond regional pilots. Scaling up to a national ETS (as China has since begun) can amplify the sustainability benefits across the whole economy. However, expansion must heed regional disparities. The heterogeneity results imply that one-size-fits-all may not work: economically underdeveloped and resource-dependent regions warrant special consideration. Policy instruments like differentiated allocation, revenue recycling, or supplementary support should be directed to such areas. For example, an ETS could allocate more free allowances or financial support to industries in poorer regions initially, easing their transition, while using auction revenues to invest in those regions' diversification and worker retraining. Strengthened oversight and capacity-building in underdeveloped localities will ensure they can comply with and benefit from the carbon market. In short, a just and inclusive carbon market design is needed to prevent widening inequalities (SDG10) and to ensure all regions share in the gains.

Use carbon revenues and complementary policies to mitigate trade-offs. Carbon pricing generates economic value—through permit auctions or tax revenues—that can be deployed to offset its own side effects. The policy literature emphasizes recycling carbon revenues in ways that support affected communities and further climate goals. For instance, revenue can finance renewable energy projects (boosting SDG7), energy-efficiency subsidies, or social safety nets and job training programs for displaced workers (supporting SDG8 and SDG10). In China's case, while the pilot markets were relatively small and often provided allowances for free, a national ETS with auctions could mobilize significant funds. Directing those funds to green infrastructure and just transition programs would amplify positive SDG impacts and blunt any negative economic shocks. Moreover, complementary regulations—like labor policies, education and retraining initiatives, and targeted development programs for coal communities—should go hand-in-hand with the carbon market. The goal is to ensure that climate action reinforces inclusive development, aligning carbon policy with the SDGs' leave-no-one-behind principle.

Focus on energy transition outcomes and innovation. The mediation analysis highlighted that tangible improvements in energy systems were the conduit for SDG progress. Policymakers should thus design ETS rules to directly encourage those improvements. This can include stringent caps that tighten over time, forcing continual efficiency gains; support for clean technology deployment (e.g. allowing offsets from verifiable renewable projects or providing tech assistance to firms); and robust MRV (monitoring, reporting, verification) to ensure emission cuts are real. By increasing predictability and stringency gradually, an ETS can drive dynamic innovation—firms invest in R&D for low-carbon solutions when they expect carbon constraints to intensify. The policy implication is to treat the ETS as a living instrument that evolves with greater ambition, using periodic reviews to raise targets in line with both climate and development objectives. Additionally, governments can integrate ETS with other energy policies: for example, phasing out fossil fuel subsidies, updating grid regulations to accommodate renewables, and setting complementary standards (for efficiency or clean energy quotas) that work alongside the carbon price. Such integrated planning ensures the carbon price signal translates into concrete transitions on the ground (new clean energy capacity, modernized industry), thereby maximizing SDG benefits.

Institutional capacity and governance matter. Finally, implementing an ETS that supports sustainable development requires strong institutions. **Chapter 8** argued that carbon markets depend on credible governance: clear property rights, transparent allocation, reliable emissions data, and enforcement against non-compliance. In a developmental context, this governance extends to coordinating across ministries (environment, energy, finance, labor) to align climate and development plans. China's pilots benefited from being embedded in a broader policy push for "high-quality development", where local governments had mandates to improve environmental performance. Going forward, policy alignment is key: climate goals (Paris Agreement targets) and development goals (SDGs) should be pursued in a coordinated framework so that, for instance, a city's economic plan and its ETS implementation plan are mutually reinforcing. Internationally, frameworks like Article 6 of the Paris Agreement and SDG monitoring can be aligned to encourage countries to design carbon markets that explicitly track and report sustainable development impacts. In sum, careful institutional design and cross-sector collaboration will increase the likelihood that carbon trading regimes deliver equitable, sustainable outcomes in practice.

In light of the above, the overarching policy lesson is that carbon markets will not automatically guarantee SDG synergies—they must be intentionally steered to do so. The Chinese ETS pilots show it is feasible: climate policy can be a driver for cleaner energy, innovation, and even social benefits if accompanied by mindful design. Governments aiming to replicate or upscale such systems should embed equity and development objectives from the start, using the levers of revenue use, complementary measures, and differentiated support to ensure that climate finance and SDG finance agendas converge rather than collide. Done right, carbon trading can thus become a cornerstone of sustainable public finance in the climate-constrained era, as part of an integrated strategy alongside green bonds, transition loans, and other instruments highlighted in earlier chapters.

Implications for Investors

The intersection of carbon trading with SDG performance carries important implications for investors, firms, and financial institutions. As carbon pricing reshapes the incentives in the real economy, it likewise influences capital allocation and risk management in financial markets. Several key perspectives emerge:

For carbon market participants (regulated firms and traders): The success of an ETS in driving SDG outcomes implies that companies under the cap face not only compliance obligations but also opportunities for value creation. Firms that innovate early to cut emissions can gain competitive advantage and even generate extra revenue by selling surplus allowances or carbon credits. The ETS essentially puts a price on inefficiency—carbon- and energy-inefficient operations become costly—incentivizing companies to modernize their equipment and energy use. This has investment implications in terms of corporate strategy: businesses are prompted to invest in cleaner technologies, energy management systems, and process improvements, which can yield productivity benefits (as seen in the pilot cities' improved energy efficiency and productivity). From an investor's standpoint, companies that proactively respond to carbon pricing may become more resilient and profitable in the long run, while laggards risk stranded assets or higher costs. Traders and financial intermediaries in carbon markets also play a role—by providing liquidity and price discovery, they help firms hedge carbon risk. With carbon allowances now an asset class, trading firms must incorporate policy risk and SDG trends into their valuation models. If, for example, tightening climate policy is correlated with broader sustainable development efforts, one might see carbon prices rise alongside increased green investment. A sophisticated understanding of the regulatory trajectory and co-benefit measures (like governments potentially intervening to stabilize prices or channel revenues) becomes part of market analysis.

For ESG investors and asset managers: The linkage between ETS policy and SDG performance reinforces the idea that carbon risk is investment risk. Institutional investors integrating Environmental, Social, and Governance (ESG) factors need to account for carbon pricing in their portfolios. Transition risk—the financial risk that high-carbon assets will lose value as the world transitions to a low-carbon economy—is directly tied to carbon market stringency. The China pilot ETS case shows carbon pricing can materially affect economic outcomes at the city/sector level, which means investors should stress-test portfolios for carbon price scenarios. At the same time, the co-benefits to SDGs mean there are upside opportunities: companies or projects that align with the low-carbon transition often contribute to multiple SDGs and may enjoy policy support or reputational gains. ESG investors are thus likely to favor firms with clear decarbonization plans and those in industries enabled by carbon pricing (renewables, efficiency tech, electric mobility, etc.). Moreover, carbon credits and offsets are emerging as investable assets and hedging tools. An investor might purchase carbon allowances as a bet on tightening climate policy, or finance projects that generate tradable SDG-aligned carbon credits (such as forestry or sustainable agriculture projects that sequester carbon while supporting local livelihoods, hitting both climate and inequality goals). The integration of carbon markets into sustainable finance suggests a growing convergence between carbon alpha and ESG alpha—i.e., strategies that reduce carbon footprints often overlap with those that deliver positive social impact and competitive returns. In essence, pricing carbon makes ESG metrics financially salient, strengthening the incentives for investors to allocate capital in ways that are consistent with achieving climate and development targets.

For sovereigns and public investment strategies: Governments and public finance institutions (like development banks) can leverage carbon markets to reinforce their sustainable financing. A notable implication is in fiscal planning: carbon pricing can generate revenues that expand the fiscal space for SDG-oriented spending. For example, auctioning emissions permits can raise significant funds that governments can earmark for green infrastructure, healthcare, or education, directly contributing to SDGs. In the pilots studied, most allowances were freely allocated to ease industries in, but the lesson for a mature system is to gradually introduce auctioning and deploy those proceeds in a "SDG-consistent" manner—effectively turning carbon finance into a form of climate-aligned public finance. Additionally, sovereign issuers that have launched green bonds (as discussed in **Chap. 4**) might find that a robust ETS complements their debt strategy. Carbon pricing bolsters the economics of green projects, making it easier for governments to service green bond-financed projects (since those projects avoid carbon costs or earn carbon credits). It can also improve a sovereign's climate credentials, potentially lowering the cost of capital for sustainable financing. However, sovereigns must also manage the transitional impacts: regions hit by carbon constraints might require fiscal transfers or investments to maintain social cohesion (think of it as a domestic just transition fund). Multilateral development banks and climate funds are increasingly focusing on supporting such transitions, blending carbon finance with concessional finance to address inequality—aligning with SDG10. Another strategic angle is international linkage of carbon markets: as more countries implement ETS (over 40 countries by 2023, covering 18% of global emissions), linking schemes or participating in global carbon trading (Article 6 markets) could attract climate finance flows across borders. Nations with comparative advantage in low-cost abatement could sell credits and use the income for domestic development. This essentially means carbon becomes an export commodity for sustainable development, with proper safeguards to ensure environmental integrity. For sovereign wealth funds and public pension funds, carbon-intensive holdings will be increasingly scrutinized; divestment from high-carbon assets or active ownership to push companies towards SDG alignment will become standard fiduciary practice in a carbon-constrained world.

In summary, the advent of carbon trading as a major climate finance mechanism is altering investment behavior and strategies. It reinforces the financial relevance of sustainability: when carbon has a price, cleaner and more inclusive businesses gain a competitive edge, and unsustainable practices carry tangible costs. Investors—whether private or public—should thus view an ETS not just as an environmental compliance tool, but as a market signal about the future economy. Those signals point toward sectors and business models aligned with the SDGs (renewable energy, circular economy, low-carbon transport, etc.) being the growth drivers, while misaligned activities face secular decline. The China ETS study's message that carbon markets can boost overall development performance provides a degree of confidence that investing in the low-carbon transition can yield broad-based benefits. For market participants, it underscores the importance of engaging in policy dialogues (to advocate for stable, ambitious carbon pricing) and in corporate strategy adjustments (to thrive under such policies). For ESG and impact investors, it offers further evidence that climate action and sustainable development are financially synergistic goals, not opposing ones—reinforcing the case for integrated climate-SDG investment frameworks. Finally, for sovereigns and public finance architects, carbon trading becomes a pillar in the architecture of climate-aligned finance, sitting alongside green bonds and other instruments as a means to fund and foster sustainable development.

Conclusion

Carbon trading has evolved from a niche policy experiment into a central component of climate finance, and this chapter has examined its implications through the lens of sustainable development. Building on prior chapters' insights into green and blue finance, we situated carbon markets as a complementary mechanism that prices the climate externality, thereby influencing a wide array of economic decisions. The empirical evidence from China's ETS pilots provides a hopeful narrative: when designed and executed with care, carbon trading need not be a zero-sum game between climate and development. Instead, it can drive win-win outcomes, cutting emissions (SDG13) while spurring progress in clean energy (SDG7), public health and environment (SDGs 3, 11, 15), and even, under the right conditions, socio-economic well-being (SDGs 8, 10). The key is that those positive outcomes were achieved by actively managing the transition: improvements in energy systems were front and center, and policy support was geared toward helping less-developed regions adapt.

Going forward, the challenge for policymakers and investors is to replicate and scale these successes, ensuring that next-generation carbon markets—whether China's national ETS, expansions in other emerging economies, or linked international systems—are explicitly aligned with the SDGs. This means setting robust caps and price signals to meet climate imperatives, while concurrently deploying the tools of sustainable finance to mitigate risks to jobs, equity, and energy access. The lessons from China's pilots emphasize contextual flexibility, revenue recycling, and complementary measures as ingredients for harmony between carbon pricing and development. For countries newly implementing ETS, these insights are invaluable for avoiding pitfalls and maximizing co-benefits. From a finance perspective, carbon markets are integrating with global capital allocation: climate risk is now investment risk, and climate action is an investment opportunity. Thus, the architecture of climate finance is one where carbon trading, green bonds, and other instruments collectively channel capital toward a low-carbon, sustainable future.

In conclusion, carbon trading should be seen as more than a market mechanism for emissions—it is a lever for sustainable development policy. Its success will ultimately be measured not only in tonnes of CO_2 abated, but in how it contributes to a just and thriving society under the SDGs. The evidence so far suggests that with prudent design and strong governance, an ETS can indeed pull its weight in the grand effort to finance a climate-resilient and inclusive development trajectory. As nations strengthen their climate commitments and gear up investment for the 2030 Agenda, carbon markets are poised to play a pivotal role in shaping public finance and investment behavior—making the cost of carbon a catalyst for innovation, resilience, and shared prosperity in the age of sustainable development.

References

Aatola, P., Ollikainen, M., & Toppinen, A. (2013). Price determination in the EU ETS market: Theory and econometric analysis with market fundamentals. *Energy Economics, 36*, 380–395.

An, Y., Zhai, X., Ding, H., & Zhou, D. (2025). Can carbon trading drive SDG success? Evidence from China's emissions trading pilot schemes. *Energy Economics, 150*, 108877.

Büchs, M., & Schnepf, S. V. (2013). Who emits most? Associations between socio-economic factors and UK households' home energy, transport, indirect and total CO2 emissions. *Ecological Economics, 90*, 114–123.

Buonocore, J. J., Luckow, P., Norris, G., Spengler, J. D., Biewald, B., Fisher, J., & Levy, J. I. (2016). Health and climate benefits of different energy-efficiency and renewable energy choices. *Nature Climate Change, 6*(1), 100–105.

Calel, R., & Dechezleprêtre, A. (2016). Environmental policy and directed technological change: Evidence from the European Carbon Market. *The Review of Economics and Statistics, 98*(1), 173–191.

Carley, S., & Konisky, D. M. (2020). The justice and equity implications of the clean energy transition. *Nature Energy, 5*(8), 569–577.

Creutzig, F., Roy, J., Lamb, W. F., Azevedo, I. M. L., Bruine de Bruin, W., Dalkmann, H., Edelenbosch, O. Y., Geels, F. W., Grubler, A., Hepburn, C., Hertwich, E. G., Khosla, R., Mattauch, L., Minx, J. C., Ramakrishnan, A., Rao, N. D., Steinberger, J. K., Tavoni, M., Ürge-Vorsatz, D., & Weber, E. U. (2018). Towards demand-side solutions for mitigating climate change. *Nature Climate Change, 8*(4), 260–263.

Fang, K., Mao, M., Tian, C., Chen, J., Wang, W., & Tan, R. (2023). Exploring the impact of emissions trading schemes on income inequality between urban and rural areas. *Journal of Environmental Management, 329*, 117067. https://doi.org/10.1016/j.jenvman.2022.117067

Khurshid, A., Rauf, A., Qayyum, S., Calin, A. C., & Duan, W. (2023). Green innovation and carbon emissions: The role of carbon pricing and environmental policies in attaining sustainable development targets of carbon mitigation—Evidence from Central-Eastern Europe. *Environment, Development and Sustainability, 25*(8), 8777–8798.

Li, J., Ding, T., Tan, R., & Liang, L. (2026). Trading characteristics of emissions trading scheme and carbon emission reduction efficiency: Evidence from China. *Energy Economics, 153*, 109072.

Lim, S., & Prakash, A. (2023). Does carbon pricing spur climate innovation? A panel study, 1986–2019. *Journal of Cleaner Production, 395*, 136459.

Lin, W., & Wang, J. (2025). Sustainable finance and carbon Neutrality: The role of green bonds, ESG investments, and carbon pricing. *Journal of Environmental Management, 395*, 127731.

Martin, R., Muûls, M., de Preux, L. B., & Wagner, U. J. (2014). Industry compensation under relocation risk: A firm-level analysis of the EU Emissions Trading Scheme. *American Economic Review, 104*(8), 2482–2508.

Radulescu, M., Hossain, M. R., Alofaysan, H., & Si Mohammed, K. (2024). Do emission trading systems, green technology, and environmental governance matter for environmental quality? Evidence from the European Union. *International Journal of Environmental Research, 19*(1), 6.

Zhang, M., Wood, M. O., Wilson, J., & Wu, T. (2025). The impacts of China's ETS on firm competitiveness: Evidence from the power and heat production sector. *Global Finance Journal, 64*, 101067.

FSC
www.fsc.org
MIX
Papier aus verantwortungsvollen Quellen
Paper from responsible sources
FSC® C105338

If you have any concerns about our products,
you can contact us on
ProductSafety@springernature.com

In case Publisher is established outside the EU,
the EU authorized representative is:
Springer Nature Customer Service Center GmbH
Europaplatz 3, 69115 Heidelberg, Germany

Printed by Libri Plureos GmbH
in Hamburg, Germany